MASKEPETOON

Leader, Warrior, Peacemaker

HUGH A. DEMPSEY

VICTORIA | VANCOUVER | CALGARY

Copyright © 2010 Hugh A. Dempsey

All rights reserved. No part of this publication may be reproduced, stored in a retrieval system or transmitted in any form or by any means—electronic, mechanical, audio recording or otherwise—without the written permission of the publisher or a photocopying licence from Access Copyright, Toronto, Canada.

Heritage House Publishing Company Ltd.
www.heritagehouse.ca

Library and Archives Canada Cataloguing in Publication

Dempsey, Hugh A., 1929–
     Maskepetoon: leader, warrior, peacemaker / Hugh A. Dempsey.

ISBN 978-1-926613-68-0

     1. Maskepetoon, 1807?–1869. 2. Cree Indians—Prairie Provinces—History—19th century. 3. Cree Indians—Kings and rulers—Biography. 4. Cree Indians—Prairie Provinces—Biography. I. Title.

E99.C88D44 2010   971.2004'973230092   C2010-903856-8

Editor: Lesley Reynolds
Proofreader: Karla Decker
Cover and interior designer: Chyla Cardinal
Front-cover photo: Samson, the younger brother of Maskepetoon, photographed in 1886 (Glenbow Archives NA-293-1)

 This book was produced using FSC-certified, acid-free paper, processed chlorine free and printed with vegetable-based inks.

Heritage House acknowledges the financial support for its publishing program from the Government of Canada through the Canada Book Fund (CBF), Canada Council for the Arts and the province of British Columbia through the British Columbia Arts Council and the Book Publishing Tax Credit.

Printed in Canada

CONTENTS

Introduction 5
Chapter One: The Rocky Mountain Crees 9
Chapter Two: Maskepetoon's Early Years 19
Chapter Three: Leadership 37
Chapter Four: Edging onto the Plains 45
Chapter Five: The Other Maskepetoon 59
Chapter Six: The Methodists 66
Chapter Seven: The Wanderers 74
Chapter Eight: Battle for Souls 96
Chapter Nine: Visitors 107
Chapter Ten: The Life of a Chief 113
Chapter Eleven: Out to the Plains 131
Chapter Twelve: The Buffalo 147
Chapter Thirteen: War Again 161
Chapter Fourteen: The McDougalls 174
Chapter Fifteen: A Christian Leader 187
Chapter Sixteen: Death on the Plains 218
Epilogue 228
Notes 233
Bibliography 246
Index 250

INTRODUCTION

The history of the Canadian West has been greatly enriched by the deeds and achievements of Native leaders who, through wise leadership in peace and defiance in war, have had an impact on how the West was settled. Among them were Peguis, who played a major role in the Red River Settlement; Piapot, who campaigned for a better deal for his followers; Crowfoot, who brought the Blackfoot and the West safely through the early years of settlement; Big Bear, who was a great leader but failed to achieve a proper deal for his people; Poundmaker, who learned that a high price can be paid for standing up against the government; and Red Crow, who was able to retain pride and a warrior spirit even in the face of government dominance.

These men had one thing in common—their first responsibility was to their own people, not to missionaries, fur traders or government officials. If they co-operated with incoming whites, it was in their interest to do so. If they tried to alter or stop the incoming invasion, it too was for their people. The government used the term "loyal" in describing some Native leaders, implying loyalty to the Crown; in fact, their loyalty lay elsewhere—to their own lodges where a woman might have been boiling buffalo meat for supper, to a nearby hillside where an old man was singing his evening prayers, to the young dandy who was combing his long black hair in view of some giggling girls, and to the little boys playing games of war. These leaders were loyal to them.

Another such man was Maskepetoon—Broken Arm—chief of the Rocky Mountain Crees, whose descendants settled on the four reserves at Hobbema, in central Alberta. For many years after his death in 1869, white people lionized Maskepetoon for his support of the Methodist Church and his aid to their missionaries. But this is not the true reason why he was a great man. Like other chiefs before and after him, his achievements were within his camp and on the plains, where leadership was essential for survival. When Maskepetoon first met missionary Robert Rundle in 1841, the two became friends—not because the chief wanted to become a Christian, but because they shared ideals of peace, honour and leadership. Rundle taught him to read and baptized his children. Maskepetoon saw the need for education and was among the chiefs who wanted a school. "We are as if our eyes were covered, and cannot see as white men see," he said.

For most of his years, Maskepetoon followed his own religion. Only during the latter part of his life did he agree to be converted to Christianity. In all those intervening years, his conduct gave white people who admired him a reason to use him as an example of the correct path of life. But it was his own path, not theirs. He simply followed his own inclinations for peace, wise leadership and friendship. Yet, if necessary, he could kill with impunity, rule with an iron hand and show no mercy where he believed none should be shown.

Maskepetoon's role as peacemaker was legendary, but it was a role fraught with danger that in the end killed him. The establishment of peace was the only way he could guarantee that his followers had the opportunity to hunt buffalo on the Blackfoot-dominated plains and stave off starvation in the dying days of the buffalo hunt. And so he risked his life, time after time, to bring peace to the land.

Research for this book started in 1976, when I was asked to prepare a biography of Maskepetoon for the *Dictionary of Canadian Biography*. All that existed at that time was one book, *The Great Chief*, by Kerry Wood, and a few tracts by United Church followers. *The Great Chief* turned out to be almost all fiction. Kerry Wood drew from the records of Rev. Robert

Rundle and Rev. John McDougall for a few facts and, as he says, used "some of the methods of fiction to make the story more appealing for young readers." Names of people, events from Maskepetoon's childhood and most of his adventures came from the author's fertile imagination. The result is a well-written and exciting work of fiction.

Over the years, it seems that no one has thought to ask the Crees themselves about their great leader. When I went to do research, I found a real treasure trove on the Samson and Ermineskin reserves, where descendants of Maskepetoon still live. After all these years, their information was fragmentary, but their insights were invaluable. In addition, I was able to draw together a quarter century of my own research and to venture into untapped fields. Rich sources were found in the Hudson's Bay Company records at the Provincial Archives of Manitoba, in the Provincial Archives of British Columbia and at the Glenbow Archives in Calgary.

Thanks go to Beverley L. Crier of the Samson Archives, who assisted in some interviews, and also to Brian Lightning of the Samson Archives. Roy and Judy Louis, Wayne Roan, Henry Nepoose, Philomene Samson, Pearl Crier, Marjory Memnook, George Littlechild, Billy Morin and others are thanked for sharing their knowledge with me, while Bruce Cutknife showed why he is an expert on Maskepetoon. Finally, Joe Deschamps acted as my guide and interpreter and also provided information of his own.

Farther afield, I wish to thank the staff of the Glenbow Library and Archives; Frederike Verspoor of the Provincial Archives of British Columbia; the staff of the Provincial Archives of Manitoba, Winnipeg; Rick Martinez of the US National Archives, Washington, DC; Nicholas Vrooman, executive director of the Helena Indian Alliance, Montana, for sharing with me his knowledge of the American Maskepetoon; Dr. Juliette Champagne, Edmonton, for translating some early Catholic missionary reports; Dr. Donald B. Smith, University of Calgary, for guidance on missionary records; and the staff of the Provincial Archives of Alberta, Edmonton. I also wish to thank the Alberta Foundation for the Arts for providing a grant in aid of research.

Throughout his life, Maskepetoon fought like a lion in times of war, sought peace when the opportunity arose and took his people from the woodlands out to the open plains to seek the declining herds of buffalo. In this book, we tell the story of the chief and his people.

Hugh A. Dempsey

CHAPTER ONE

The Rocky Mountain Crees

The Crees had just moved their camp to a site where the grazing was good for their horses. It was 1807, the weather was mild and the spring hunt had been successful. Although the scouts were out, no one was worried, as the truce had been made with the Blackfoot just weeks before. Everyone knew it wouldn't last, but while it was in place, people could move freely and not worry about the loss of horses or human lives.

A week earlier, before they shifted camp, they had enjoyed an exciting horse race on the open prairie. The choice of track had been a good one, following a straight, clear pathway through the clumps of bushes and buffalo wallows that dotted the landscape. Two of the best runners in the band had been pitted against each other, racing a mile across the prairie to a post, swinging about, then galloping back amid the cheers and cries of the people. The winner was a favourite, so the gamblers who had believed in the superior prowess of its opponent now grudgingly handed over blankets, moccasins, bullets and other goods that they had bet.

Now everyone was busy in the new camp. Dogs barked and howled, sometimes for no reason at all. An old man was singing his holy song in a quavering, faltering voice. A woman wailed for the death of her infant child. And a small crowd gathered as two boys wrestled on the grass. While this was going on, a couple of men went back to the old racetrack looking for a lost whip.

As they rode along, they heard the pitiful sound of a baby crying. Looking around for the child or its mother, they saw no one. Then the baby wailed again, and this time the men traced the sound to one of the buffalo wallows. There, in the deep depression, lay a tiny baby, its legs thrashing as it cried in its misery.

One rider scooped the infant up in his arms and said to his companion, "Go tell the others that we found this child. I will wait here."[1]

As he waited, the man noticed that the baby, a boy, had a broken arm. Perhaps that is why he had been abandoned. But in the protective arms of the stranger, he settled down and was soon asleep.

When the man's companion reached the new camp, he told the leader that a baby had been discovered in a buffalo wallow. Instead of dashing off to the place, the chief said, "We will move, but first we will make a lodge."[2] Under his instructions, the women put up poles and covered them with new buffalo-skin covers, installed the liners and mats and made the lodge ready for use for a council meeting. A procession of leaders and warriors then rode to the racetrack, and in procession they escorted the man and child back to the lodge. Once inside, the chief summoned the pipe holders, who went through a ceremony to purify the baby and to sanctify the lodge. Formalities completed, they now were ready to talk about the foundling and what to do with him.

They discussed what a strange place it was to find a baby and how the mother must have cast him aside for a good reason— perhaps because of the broken arm. But now the child needed a new mother, one who would love him and care for him. One pipe holder recalled that a young woman had just suffered the loss of her own child. All had heard her crying in her grief. Perhaps the baby might be given to her. After some discussion, all agreed this was a good idea, and so the grieving couple was summoned.

"We have constructed this lodge for a council," said the chief (handing the baby to the young woman), "and now we want you to take this as your new home and your new child."[3]

They both were thrilled. The mother took the baby in her arms, hugged it and kissed it. Her husband smiled, obviously pleased with this unexpected addition to their lonely lodge. They noticed the arm and asked a holy man, known for his spiritual powers, to give the baby a name, so a feast was held in the new lodge with the holy man as an honoured guest. When everyone was settled, the new father rose and invited the holy man to name the child, at the same time presenting him with a filled pipe and a piece of cloth to be set out as an offering. The holy man intoned a long prayer in which he told of his exploits and the reason he had the power to name this child. He sang his personal holy song, then asked for the child to be placed in his arms. He looked at the baby, prayed again, and then announced that henceforth the child would be called Maskepetoon, Broken Arm.[4] The baby was passed from person to person in the lodge, each addressing him as Maskepetoon and praying for his future happiness. The boy was given to his new mother, and everyone had a feast in commemoration of the happy event.

In a matter of weeks, Maskepetoon's arm healed, and the only reminder of the fracture was his name. While not certain, it is possible that the new parents were named Sekacheen and Papas, for these were the parents of Kanatakasu, or Samson, Maskepetoon's younger brother.[5] Samson, too, was probably adopted by this couple, as he once explained that "his early life was that of an orphan. He never saw his father, and his mother was blind."[6]

By the time Maskepetoon was born, the Rocky Mountain Crees had lived in the foothills for two or three generations. They had been part of a great Cree migration that had taken the people from the eastern woodlands westward along the great North Saskatchewan River. They had been encouraged by the fur-trading companies to trap for beaver and bring their annual catches all the way to the shores of Hudson Bay. As they moved west, the harvest of furs was richer, but the distance from the trading posts grew farther and farther. Then, in order to counter the aggressive efforts of French traders from Montreal, the English company, the Hudson's Bay Company, was forced to move into the interior. In 1774, Cumberland House was built on the lower waters of the Saskatchewan River and, two years later, Hudson's House, farther upstream, followed by Manchester House in 1786 on the edge of the Great Plains. Those bands farther west were satisfied to trade their furs to middlemen and then continue on their westward trek of discovery. The middlemen were the ones who made the journeys to the forts and brought back knives, axes, guns, tobacco, kettles and the other European objects that had become part of Cree life.

The westward migration finally came to a halt when it washed against the base of the rugged Rocky Mountains. Here remained the vanguards, the resolute ones who had been willing to seek new lands and new enemies in pursuit of fresh hunting and trapping areas. They became known as the Rocky Mountain Crees. Their territory extended from the Rockies to the edge of the woods, and from the North Saskatchewan south beyond the Bow, skirting the edge of the plains. To the east of them were the Plains Crees, who exulted in the buffalo hunt, the endless prairies and the freedom offered by the land.

The Plains Crees and Rocky Mountain Crees maintained friendly relations with the Blackfoot[7] until 1787, when Crees attacked a camp of Bloods and killed women and children near Manchester House. This did not elevate into full-scale warfare, as some Peigans came to the fort on a peace mission "to make it up between the Blood Indians and Crees."[8] Yet the die had been cast, and for the next ninety years, warfare interspersed with periods of peace became the way of life for the western Crees.

By 1794, the trading companies had extended their chain of forts ever closer to the Rocky Mountains in their insatiable pursuit of furs, particularly the rich beaver pelts. In that year, they built Buckingham House and Fort George, not far from the present town of Elk Point. From there, they served the Plains Crees, mixed with a few Rocky Mountain people. The trading process at the fort was described by Duncan McGillivray:

> When a Band of Indians approach near the Fort it is customary for the Cheifs [sic] to send a few young men before them to announce their arrival, and to procure a few articles which they are accustomed to receive on these occasions—such as Powder, a piece of Tobacco and a little paint to besmear their faces, an operation which they seldom fail to perform previous to their presenting themselves before the White People.[9]

After the young men returned to their band, they all marched in procession to the fort, firing their guns in the air. The traders responded by hoisting their flag and firing a few rounds of their own. The chiefs and men then entered the fort, where they were disarmed and treated to free rum and tobacco. Later, the women also received presents of rum, and the whole band drank for the rest of the day. The next day, when they were more or less sober, they began to trade. Everything was based upon the value of one prime beaver skin, or Made Beaver (MB). It cost the Crees the value of thirty MB for a keg of rum, fourteen MB for a long gun, six MB for a three-point blanket, two MB for an axe and three MB for a twist of tobacco.[10]

A major change in the lives of the Rocky Mountain Crees occurred in 1795, when the twin posts of Fort Edmonton of the Hudson's Bay Company and Fort Augustus of the North West Company were built within easy reach of their hunting grounds. A trader noted that the forts would be in "a rich and plentiful Country, abounding with all kinds of animals especially Beavers & Otters, which are said to be so numerous that the Women & children kill them with Sticks and hatchets."[11] It was a land of plenty, with an abundance of fur-bearing animals, buffalo close at hand and woodlands for shelter. This would become Maskepetoon's homeland.

When the Crees had reached the edge of the Rockies in the 18th century, there were small bands of Kootenais called the *Tunaxa*, or "open country attackers," who lived there. At first, there was antagonism between the tribes as the Kootenais fought to retain their hunting grounds.[12] But peace finally came to the two tribes and is remembered in a traditional Kootenai tale.

A young Kootenai named Sistianwi had a vision in which he received spiritual powers from a hawk, a rabbit and a red ant. When he first went to war with these protectors, he proved to be an exceptional fighter, striking down the Crees with a war club made from a buffalo horn filled with stones. His brother wanted to turn his chieftainship over to him, but Sistianwi refused. Instead, he became a war chief and, according to a Kootenai elder, "From then on, the Cree Indians had a difficult time holding off attacks by Sistianwi and the Kootenai."

After some months of warfare, the Crees finally decided to sue for peace, so a chief sent his beautiful daughter with gifts to the enemy camp. When she entered Sistianwi's lodge, she said in sign language, "My father has sent me to give you this." She opened a small bundle and took out a red stone pipe, which she filled with tobacco and red willow bark. "My father offers you this smoke," she continued. "He wishes to be friends with you. He has also sent you these gifts for your people. He also sent me to become your wife."

According to a Kootenai elder, Sistianwi looked around in embarrassment, not knowing what to do. His brother laughed and said, "What can you do? The Cree chief has given you his daughter and these gifts. We have to smoke this pipe."

The pipe was lit and handed to Sistianwi and then to the Cree girl, each of whom took three puffs. A plate of meat was handed to them, and they ate, and vessels of water from which they drank. After this ceremony, they sat side by side and were married. "Thereafter peace was maintained between the two tribes," recalled an elder.[13]

Over the next few years, the Kootenais gradually withdrew across the mountains to be with their relatives, and the foothills were left to the Crees. There were no trading posts on the west side of the Rockies, so the Crees became middlemen, providing trade goods, tobacco and rum to the Kootenais in exchange for their furs. Ethnologist Claude Schaeffer was told by Kootenai elders about trade relations between the two tribes:

> Traditions have come down among the Kutenai of their initial contacts with the Cree Indians and the latter's introduction of European trade goods. Thus the first firearms ever seen by the Kutenai were carried to them by Cree traders. They made a present of a gun to one of the Kutenai and told him it was for the purpose of killing game. Thereafter the Kutenai bartered for as many guns as they could get, giving furs of various kinds in return. The Cree also introduced commercial tobacco to the Kutenai.[14]

However, the Kootenais wanted to deal directly with the traders and cut out the middlemen. When explorer Peter Fidler met a few Kootenais near Crowsnest Pass in 1792, they complained: "They was never near any of the Trading Settlements altho they much wish it But the Muddy River [Peigan], Blood, Black Feet & Southern [Cree] Indians always prevents them, they wishing to monopolize all their skins to themselves, which they do giving the Poor Indians only a mere trifle for, they scarce give them as much for 10 Skins as they can get for one at the Trading Settlements."[15]

Finally, in 1798, two Kootenais faced the wrath of the eastern-slope tribes and travelled to Fort Edmonton. The chief factor commented that, "Those have not brought any furs of any kind but by their account their country abounds with all kinds, but far off."[16] After hearing their stories, both the

Hudson's Bay Company and North West Company decided to build forts closer to the mountains so that the Kootenais would not have to travel through hostile territory to trade. When the Rocky Mountain Crees learned of this in the spring of 1799, they demonstrated their opposition by halting a crew of men loaded with building supplies headed upstream to find a good location for a fort. An angry chief factor sent the crew out again with orders not to come back until the fort was finished. He knew that the Rocky Mountain Crees were generally a peaceful people and the likelihood of violence was remote.

By the summer of 1799, Rocky Mountain House and Acton House had been built at the confluence of the North Saskatchewan and Clearwater rivers, right in the heart of Cree hunting grounds. To reach there, the Kootenais could safely travel the mountain passes with their beaver pelts and other furs. Soon afterwards, traders crossed the mountains themselves and built forts in Kootenai country.

Rocky Mountain House, besides serving the Kootenai and local Crees, also offered a good trading place for the Blackfoot tribes, as the prairies extended almost to the fort. This provided a safer and easier access than Fort Edmonton and so became the trading centre of choice for the plains tribes.

The Rocky Mountain Crees became accustomed to using metal goods, and with an insatiable desire for tobacco, cloth, rum and other trade goods, they patterned their annual movements around the needs of the trading posts. In the fall, small groups came with a few furs, dried meat and other supplies that they used to pay off their debts from the previous spring. While they were trading, they met with friends, gambled, sang and generally enjoyed themselves. If a newly arrived party was treated to a free supply of rum, they willingly shared it with their neighbours until the first rays of dawn sent them back to their lodges. Meanwhile, young boys guarded the horses and the women tended the dogs that were tied up near their owners' lodges. The beasts snapped and snarled at each other and always were on the lookout for anything edible, including moccasins and saddles. It was the women's task to make sure they ate only what they were supposed to eat. A whack with a handy stick sent any potential thief scurrying for cover.

When they were ready to trade, the men went to the fort's Indian room, where long counters were used to examine their furs. Shelves in the next room held piles of blankets, rolls of tobacco, barrels of powder and shot, trays of mirrors, packets of vermilion paint, bunches of beads and rolls of brass wire, all within easy reach of the trader but out of the hands of their customers. Carefully, the men made their selections, usually taking care not to forget their wives. They also traded for a quantity of rum or brandy and consumed it in a wild and sometimes violent binge one or two days before leaving.

At the end of the trading session, the men received on credit the goods they needed for the winter—mostly ammunition and tobacco. They then moved to their trapping areas close to the mountains, where they would stay for the winter months, subsisting on deer, moose and other creatures that inhabited the area. If the weather was good, they might also skirt the edge of the plains looking for buffalo. In the spring, they brought their catches of beaver, otter, foxes, martens, lynx and wolverines, paid off their debts and bought whatever they needed for the summer.

In the summer months, they seldom ventured very far onto the plains. They were a woodland people, and even in times of peace, they were more at home among the tamaracks and willows that flanked the plains. There were buffalo in the area, although perhaps not as many as on the open plains, but enough to give them fresh meat and buffalo robes. Excess meat could be dried and sold to the traders. There also were fish to be caught or trapped in the many lakes and streams within their hunting grounds.

As the eighteenth century came to an end, the Rocky Mountain Crees were secure in their new homeland. A nephew of Maskepetoon recalled those days and gave credit to the Great Spirit for providing them with this bountiful land. He wrote:

> These things were given to us on this earth by the One Who Owns All, the Great Spirit. If he did not give us these things, then no one would be alive amongst us people. Everything that is alive on this earth, all that we see in the sky when we look up, the clouds that are drifting by, this is where the rain that falls on the land comes from. Our land will be wet when it rains. When there is sunshine, the sun warms the land everywhere, this is where we get our good health, also our good life on earth. When it is winter, it can get very cold. All that grows on this earth are frozen solid. The trees, the grasses, everything. But the sun has travelled and shined on this earth since the land has existed. The One Who Owns All, the Great Spirit, made the sun for all of us on earth. He has so much wisdom.[17]

CHAPTER TWO

Maskepetoon's Early Years

Maskepetoon's infancy was described in a florid Victorian style by a missionary who knew him:

> Maskepetoon was born; his birthright the common heritage of natural man, his birthplace the Rocky Mountains, his cradle lullaby the crash of tumbling avalanches and the roarings of mighty "chinooks." The shrill cry of the mountain lion, the deep bass note of the buffalo, the ripplings of limpid streams and the ragings of mountain torrents in their wild race to a common level—these with the pagan's death wail, the rattle of the conjurer's drum, and the warrior's shout of triumph were sounds familiar to his baby ears.[1]

Maskepetoon was born as his people wavered between peace and war. There had been amity between the Crees and Blackfoot for a number of years, but in the summer of 1806 a bloody quarrel erupted when some four hundred Peigans, Siksikas and Bloods faced in battle an equal number of Crees and Plains Assiniboines.[2] Twenty-eight Peigans[3] and three Crees were slain. Then, just when it seemed that the Crees might win the day, hundreds more Blackfoot warriors surged into the battleground, sweeping their enemies before them. The Crees were forced to retreat, abandoning their horses and baggage as they fled for their lives. Even after the battle was over, the Crees—who had been the aggressors—feared the wrath of the plains tribes and, according to a trader, were "fleeing in all Quarters to conceal themselves in the woods, and that the Blackfeet threaten indiscriminate vengeance."[4] This, according to a trader, left the Blackfoot "masters of the plains from South Branch to Acton House."[5]

Less than a month later, four lodges of Crees, unaware of the outbreak of hostilities, were about a hundred miles from Edmonton near the Red Deer River when they were attacked by two or three hundred Blackfoot. "Two men made their escape," said the trader, "but the rest, men, women and children, were either butchered or taken Slaves."[6]

All this happened in 1806, a year before Maskepetoon was born.

Realizing that the Crees would be in a state of unrest and do very little trapping, the traders at Edmonton decided "to prevail on the Indians of this place to pass next Season in the Rocky Mountains where some Beaver have been lately discovered."[7] The territory in question was on the upper waters of the many streams that flowed into the North Saskatchewan, Red Deer and Bow rivers. It included the mountain passes, the Kootenay Plains and the shores of Lake Minnewanka. In places, this territory was shared with the Stoneys, who were arm's-length allies.

This was a long distance from the vast plains and the large buffalo herds, but also far away from the warlike Blackfoot. To the Rocky Mountain Crees, it was part of their homeland, but for Plains Crees who came there seeking refuge, the woodlands were a safe haven during that season of war.

Perhaps symbolic of Maskepetoon's future role of peacemaker, 1807—the year of his birth—was a good time to negotiate peace. In the spring, a peace party, led by the great Siksika chief The Feather, arrived at Fort Edmonton to see if there was a way to end the hostilities. The traders were supportive, for as long as there was war, the Crees would not venture onto the plains to procure meat for the fort, and the Blackfoot would not come to trade. No one wanted that, particularly the Blackfoot. Referring to The Feather, the trader reported:

> This Man tells us that his country Men all wish sincerely for Peace, that having long accustomed to be supplied with Brandy, Tobacco, &c., these articles are become objects of primary necessity to them and nothing but absolute Danger can prevent their coming to procure them as usual. Conceiving himself to be beloved by the Crees, he says, he has come therefore to ascertain their sentiments towards his Country Men.[8]

The Feather went on to say that if the Crees agreed, the Blackfoot would come early in May to make peace and to trade. A survey of local Crees indicated that there was a general desire for peace, although there was always the danger that a few young men might "take this opportunity of revenging the Death of their relations who were so cruelly butchered last fall."[9] True to their word, bands of Siksikas and Bloods arrived on May 10, and James Bird, chief factor at Edmonton House, was able to report, "Peace is reestablished among the natives."[10] Some weeks later, Maskepetoon was discovered thrashing about at the bottom of a buffalo wallow.

The Rocky Mountain Crees passed a pleasant summer fishing at Wabamun and Gull lakes, hunting buffalo on the edge of the plains and travelling deep into the foothills. Families came together in large camps where they visited, performed their ceremonies, raced their horses and enjoyed a season free from fear. Women tanned hides for moccasins and clothing; if a woman's lodge was worn out, she sent a message to others in the camp seeking help. Soon several women were at work, tanning hides, cutting them to size and sewing them securely with sinew thread to make a new lodge.

In the fall, the camps broke up into small family groups and, as the local trader explained in 1807, "moved off to make their winter Hunts."[11] Maskepetoon would have been snug in a tiny moss bag carried on his mother's back as his parents moved deep into the woods and prepared their camp for winter.

The Rocky Mountain Crees could not stay together during the winter in a single band, as there were few buffalo in the woods, and smaller animals such as deer and moose, as well as fish, did not provide enough food for a multitude. Rather, single families drifted into winter quarters, where they would remain if the hunting and trapping were good, or they would move from place to place in search of better prospects. The few who owned horses often camped beside a pond or slough where the grass was sufficient to keep their stock alive all winter and where water was readily available.

Soon the days became shorter and the nights longer as snow drifted around their leather tipis; the wind whistled through the branches of the leafless trees, and the aurora borealis shimmered and whispered in the night sky. Quietness ruled the forest, broken only by the lonely howl of a timber wolf, the cluck-cluck of a grouse, or the querying hoot of the great horned owl. Blending in with these sounds of nature were the gurgling, happy sounds from Maskepetoon, the fussing of his mother, the snapping noises as she broke branches for firewood, the neighing of horses as they pawed through the snow for a mouthful of grass, and the voice of Maskepetoon's father as he quieted the dogs while hitching them to the toboggan for a tour of his trapline.

In 1807, steel traps were unknown to the tribe. Instead, Maskepetoon's father used deadfalls and snares to gather his furs. Deadfalls usually were efficient wooden traps open at one end and baited with something appealing to the prey, such as castoreum mixed with aspen buds. A heavy log was fastened above the trap, and when an animal, such as a marten or fisher, entered to check the bait, the log fell across its neck and killed it instantly. Snares made of rawhide or strong cord could be used in a number of ways. To trap larger animals, such as lynx, a noose was placed at the entrance of a boxlike wooden trap. When the animal was lured inside by bait and its head was in the noose, the trap was tripped and the animal was swung aloft and died. For rabbits, a noose was placed in a narrow space between bushes that the animal used as a pathway. When it jumped through the space, its head caught in the noose and, as with the lynx, the trap was sprung and the rabbit carried aloft.

Maskepetoon's father made his rounds with a dog team and sled, picking up frozen animals and resetting his traps. Back in camp, the carcasses were thawed, skinned, and prepared for market. Rabbits were caught primarily for food, as their pelts were of little interest to the trading posts. However, Maskepetoon's mother could cut the skins into strips and weave them to make a warm and comfortable blanket for the baby. The robes soon wore out but served their purpose during the winter months.

The winter of 1807–8 was a mild one with little snow, which was both a blessing and a curse. People were not caught in blinding blizzards or hampered from travelling in search of game, but animals left no tracks to be followed on the frozen ground, and there were no trails to determine where traps should be set. For Crees still out on the plains, it was difficult to chase buffalo on frozen ground or kill wolves, which could easily elude a hunter on horseback. But in the bush, Maskepetoon's father and the other trappers did well enough to avoid starvation that winter, and reasonable catches of beaver, foxes and lynx were taken to Edmonton or Rocky Mountain House.

The weather and nature were not always so kind. In 1810, fires ripped through the Rocky Mountain Crees' hunting grounds and virtually wiped out the marten population, which had been a mainstay of the trappers. The same fire swept across the prairies, driving the buffalo herds far to the south, cutting off an essential food supply. In January 1811, a Cree came to Fort Edmonton to say that all he had trapped during the winter were seven otters and one beaver. He told the trader, "They could find no Martens and that, owing to the great Depth of snow,

Starvation Drove them from the woods."¹² Their diet consisted of whatever they could find. If game was scarce, if rabbits were not to be found, and if the lake ice was too thick to be fished, they starved. Such a situation was not unusual. A mild winter caused the buffalo to graze far out on the plains, away from Cree hunters, while cold weather and heavy snows could bring starvation to all who wintered in the woods. The Rocky Mountain Crees accepted both famine and plenty as natural parts of their lives.

For the next couple of years, the terrible weather continued. By the spring of 1813, starvation was general on the plains, with no buffalo being found north of the Bow River. Prairie fires raged all summer, and in the fall, when a few Sarcees visited Edmonton House, they reported "that the plains are already burnt between the Red Deer River and this [North Saskatchewan] River, from the Beaver Lake to the Rocky Mountains."¹³ They had not seen a buffalo for a month.

The Rocky Mountain Crees had fared no better, and after a lean summer, they prayed for a better winter with enough snow to track the deer and cold enough temperatures for the pelts to be prime. Maskepetoon's father and the others received advances from the fur traders and went into the burned-out land looking for good winter quarters. But it was another bad winter for trapping. In the spring of 1814, two Rocky Mountain Crees who had spent the winter near the abandoned Rocky Mountain House came out almost empty-handed.¹⁴

Maskepetoon's family went through all the good times and bad with the rest of their people. The baby graduated from a moss bag to a place near his mother in their lodge. Only when he was older would he be given over to his father or another male relative to learn the responsibilities of being a man. The people remembered that, even as a child, Maskepetoon showed leadership. "He was smart and had extraordinary talent," said a member of his band.¹⁵ His intelligence, boldness and determination seemed to distinguish him from the other boys.

As a child, he played games that were popular with his people. In winter, they spun wooden tops on the ice, with the winner taking the other's top. "They had another game that they played on a snowbank," recalled an elder. "They set up a dummy rabbit way off on a hill and the boys had long sticks, called snow snakes. They threw these and they slid along the snow for a long way. The trick was to hit the rabbit with your snow snake."[16] In a second snow-snake game, the winner was the one who could hurl his stick the farthest.

Another activity was to select an icy slope about five feet long. A row of twelve holes were dug at the bottom, some larger than others. The boys then cut the ends of buffalo horns and rounded them into marbles. Each was decorated in a different way. Sixteen marbles were used, eight to a side. The game consisted of rolling the marbles down the slope to try to get them in the holes—the smaller the hole, the higher the score. Considerable skill was required to win, so the game often was a slow one, but fun.[17]

In the spring, a game of "war" was played. Two teams were selected, each member cutting a green willow stick, scooping up gobs of mud and fastening it to the ends of his stick. "You throw it at your opponents," said an elder. "Sometimes they would put little rocks in them."[18] The result was mayhem, a few bruises and one team finally causing the other to retreat. In summer, a favourite game was called *itachikan*, or arrow-shooting game. A boy shot the first "target" arrow as far as he could. The challenge was for the others to get as close to the arrow as possible, the closest being the winner.[19]

These were just a few of the enjoyable games that also had the purpose of preparing the boys for manhood. They learned the use of the bow and arrow, strengthened their bodies with physical exertion and imitated war as a prelude to the real thing.

Because of their location, the Rocky Mountain Crees followed a woodland culture, more at home trapping in the bush than hunting on the open plains. Generally they were peaceful, although they took to arms to defend their camps or respond to an insult, and their young people were not averse to raiding an enemy in order to gain the prestige that came with being a warrior. The bands to the east of them, the Beaver Hills Crees, were much different. They sometimes retreated into the bush, but their life was on the plains, hunting buffalo for food and fighting with the Blackfoot. The Beaver Hills people travelled in large bands during the summer, camping together for protection. They followed a plains culture made up of secret societies, public rituals and the proclamation of war honours. Their hunting grounds were vast, extending all the way into the present province of Saskatchewan and south as far as Blackfoot territory. They were divided into a number of bands, some trading at Edmonton and others at Fort Carlton. At Edmonton, the Beaver Hills people often mixed with the Rocky Mountain Crees, while those downstream made contact with plains-oriented River People, Middle Crees and Calling River people, as well as with the warlike Plains Assiniboine.

The activities of the Crees trading out of Fort Edmonton and those downriver at Fort Carlton contrasted sharply. While those near Edmonton tried to maintain relatively peaceful relations with the Blackfoot, the downriver Middle Crees and the eastern branch of the Beaver Hills Crees joined with the Plains Assiniboines in an apparent attempt to wipe out the whole Blackfoot nation. In the period after 1808, a relatively small number of incidents of horse stealing and murder occurred near Edmonton. In 1809, the Rocky Mountain Crees killed a Peigan on the Blind Man River, south of Edmonton, and a year later the Peigans responded by killing a number of Crees on Pipestone Creek in retaliation.[20] However, these were not enough to set off a full-scale war.

But young Rocky Mountain Crees still aspired to be warriors, and if they could not fight the Blackfoot, they were determined to seek other enemies. One choice was the Snare Indians, who were an offshoot of the Shuswaps from the west side of the Rockies. The Snares inhabited the area now encompassing Jasper National Park, where they eked out a precarious existence. Unlike the plains tribes, their homes were pits dug into the ground, and they lived off bighorn sheep, moose and deer. Alexander Henry described them as "defenceless Indians, who know not the use of firearms, have only bows and arrows, and are scattered in small camps of three and four tents—an easy prey to the Crees."[21]

A raid occurred in May 1811, after Crees had assembled west of Fort Edmonton and smoked their pipes before setting off. There is no record of their success or failure, but trader Henry observed that Snare territory "is so nearly destitute of animals that the Crees suffer from famine when they go to war upon those people, and are frequently obliged to return before they can fall upon them."[22] Not so with the raid that took place a year later. A number of Crees, made up mostly from the Rocky Mountain group and perhaps including Maskepetoon's relatives, gathered near the mouth of Wabamun Creek to plan for war. Much to the consternation of the fur traders, they had no intention of working their traplines, but would attempt a late-winter raid on the western tribe. If the weather was cold, the muskegs would be frozen and animals more easily tracked to provide food on the journey. John Park, who was in charge of a trading post on Wabamun Creek, confirmed that "all the Indians of his place, except two, are gone to war on the Snare Indians who inhabit the Rocky Mountains."[23] Later, he offered the news that "the War Party, in which were twenty of our Traders, has returned to that place with twelve Slaves, the sole survivors of five Tents of Snare Indians that they discovered in the Mountains."[24]

The death in 1814 of the great Siksika peacemaker The Feather was a blow to peace in the region. Through his leadership and respect, he had been able to hold the Crees and Blackfoot at bay. Wrote a trader at Edmonton:

> A band of Blackfeet Indians arrived, all in mourning for the Death of their Chief called the Feather, who was shot a few days since by a man of their own Nation, but of another Tribe. This Chief was always eminently instrumental in preserving peace between the Southward [Cree] Indians and Stone Indians, and those of his own Nation and their Allies; he was also the firm friend of white men and as he possessed much influence his Death may be of more than ordinary consequence on this River. His Sons and other relatives have already killed his murderer and vow revenge on the whole tribe to which he belonged.[25]

Just as Maskepetoon would later become a peacemaker, influencing both ally and enemy, so did The Feather's steadying hand prevent minor skirmishes from developing into full-scale wars. Such peacemakers were common among the plains tribes. With kindly men like The Feather, it was often in a sincere effort to stem the needless flow of blood between nations. In other instances, a man might have been a peacemaker simply to demonstrate his bravery. He would go into an enemy camp with only a pipe in his hands, literally risking his life to make a pact that everyone knew would be temporary. Yet taking this bold action was tantamount to a man going to war and was an honour he could recite at a Sun Dance or warriors' dance.

As he grew older, Maskepetoon graduated from his mother's care to become a student in the arts of hunting and trapping. Like other children, he had already learned how to use a bow and arrow and was able to kill small animals. He knew that the best bows were sinew-backed and made of willow or birch wood; the arrows were tipped with iron from the traders. While some men had guns, all still relied on the bow as a silent killer that needed no ammunition. In winter, prairie chickens could be plucked off trees one by one with well-placed arrows without frightening the flock. A deer could be brought down with a single arrow and a beaver shot in the head so as not to spoil its hide. As he grew up, Maskepetoon learned to walk silently in the woods and be keenly aware of everything that was going on around him. He could sense a change in the weather, particularly in winter. He had to, for his life depended upon it. A sudden blizzard could catch a man far from camp and the warmth of his campfire. A crackling of bushes might signify a bear making her way to a berry patch, her cubs not far behind. Meeting her, or getting between her and her offspring, could result in a painful death. To survive in the woods, there were lessons to be learned and remembered.

Maskepetoon's boyhood friends became his comrades who would accompany him when he was old enough to go to war. He probably went on his first foray about 1821, when the Crees were at war. He would have gone as a servant and to get an education in the art of raiding for horses. As a beginner, he would be under the direction and tutelage of a seasoned veteran; he learned how to travel into enemy territory, keeping a sharp lookout for enemies and watching the horizon for smoke that indicated a Blackfoot camp. He learned that the best horses were kept near their owners' tipis and could be taken at night if a warrior was brave enough to creep into an enemy camp. He would receive no booty from his first raids, not until he could go as a full-fledged warrior. This probably didn't happen until about 1823, when he was sixteen.

War was a way to gain prestige. No one would ever become a chief unless he had an impressive war record, and girls would despise him if he stayed at home. A war expedition was organized by the tribe's leaders for the specific purpose of attacking and killing the enemy. Most often, such raids occurred after the tribe had suffered a loss of life at the hand of the enemy. Perhaps a peaceful trading party had been waylaid and exterminated, or some young horse thieves discovered and slain. When a decision was made to launch such an attack, pipes were sent to other bands, asking them to join the expedition. Smoking the pipe indicated their agreement. The raiders assembled at a predetermined location while scouts were out looking for a likely prey. When it was found, a savage attack occurred in an effort to kill as many men, women and children as possible. Of course, attackers did not miss the opportunity of taking horses, shields and other gear, but that was not the primary reason for the raid. A retaliatory attack by the decimated tribe would likely occur, and the tribes again would be at war.

On the other hand, the goal of a simple horse raid was to gain personal wealth and prestige. The whole idea was to avoid conflict and to get in and out of enemy territory without being seen. It was the road to fame and riches for aspiring warriors—and the road to death for others. When leaving camp to go on a horse raid, members of a party danced and sang their war songs. Their families gave them a stock of moccasins for the long walk ahead, while others in the camp gave them food, tobacco or other gifts. As they reached enemy territory, they travelled at night, the more seasoned warriors being scouts who were constantly on the alert. When the raid itself took place, the young boys sometimes stayed back and only watched, as part of their education. After the raid, the party gathered at a prearranged spot where those who had been unlucky may have been given horses. However, if they had been discovered during the raid, each made his own way home, sometimes meeting along the trail. Back in camp, captured horses often were given away to parents, respected elders or sweethearts, the warriors keeping none for themselves. For them, the goal had been fame and recognition more than material wealth.

During the years of Maskepetoon's youth, the Rocky Mountain Crees continued to use the area east of the Rockies as their main hunting grounds. One of their favourite camping areas was near the mouth of Wabamun Creek, west of Edmonton. This was on the edge of the plains but far from marauding parties of Blackfoot. Another preferred area was near Pigeon Lake. Sometimes they went to Rocky Mountain House, but that trading post, built primarily to serve the Blackfoot tribes, opened and closed depending upon the success of the Plains Indian trade. When the Beaver Hills Crees moved farther east to hunt, the Rocky Mountain group sometimes penetrated the plains as far east as Buffalo Lake. However, the Sarcees claimed this territory, and although the two tribes generally got along, there was always the threat of violence.

Starvation continued to plague the Rocky Mountain Crees during the early 1820s, and at one point a trader at Edmonton learned that his best trappers were abandoning the bush in the middle of winter during the peak of the trapping season. He was told that "the Strong wood Cris are leaving the Woods and going to the Plains, starvation driving them out of the strong wood, animals being scarce and they not overstocked with ammunition."[26] A trader anxiously went in pursuit to convince them to return to the woods. When he caught up with them, he offered them tobacco and enough ammunition to last them the rest of the winter. A few disagreed, but most returned to their traplines.[27] In fact, the threat to leave may have been a ploy to force the traders to supply them with ammunition.

On their way back, the Crees caught a Sarcee stealing their horses and killed him. About the same time, two Crees were killed by a Blackfoot, an act which a trader said "very likely will be the cause of war being declared between these 2 Tribes."[28] In an attempt to maintain the peace, the Blackfoot took their trade to Rocky Mountain House, instead of Edmonton, and the Beaver Hills Crees went to Fort Carlton, both sides wishing to avoid a confrontation. The Rocky Mountain group kept to the woods for the rest of the winter.

During these years, the locations of the various bands began to shift, often because of the location of Hudson's Bay and North West Company trading posts along the North Saskatchewan. The opening of a trading post in 1817 at Dog Rump Creek, downstream from Edmonton, had caused many Beaver Hills Crees to split from the Edmonton band and frequent that place. When it closed a couple of years later, they spread out, some moving farther east to trade at Fort Carlton while a lesser number remained in the district. Soon the Beaver Hills Crees could be found all the way from Edmonton to Carlton. During these years, war continued to rage between the downriver Crees and the Blackfoot tribes.

In the winter of 1823–24, an attempt was made to resolve the dispute that instead escalated it. A mixed party of Beaver Hills Crees and Assiniboines from Carlton went to the Blackfoot camps, where they were well received. They smoked their pipes and promised everlasting friendship, but when they left, they stole about thirty Blackfoot horses, then set the plains afire so they could not be followed. In spite of the fire, the angry Blackfoot pursued them and caught them on Vermilion Creek, where they killed one Cree and recovered half of their horses.[29]

With this news of escalating violence, many Beaver Hills Crees took to the woods for safety, hoping to live off buffalo at the edge of the plains. But as a trader explained, "they have fallen in with no Buffalo since they came to the border of the Plains and do not feel disposed to proceed any further through them for fear of the Plain tribes."[30] Later in the fall, the situation worsened when a large war party of Blackfoot surrounded Fort Carlton, forcing Three Bulls and a few of his Beaver Hills Cree followers to find refuge inside its walls. The Blackfoot stole most of their horses, killed an old woman and set the plains on fire to drive off the buffalo.

And so the cycle of killing and retaliation continued. In October 1824, the conflict reached new heights when the eastern Beaver Hills Crees attacked thirty-five lodges of Blackfoot while the men were away hunting. Said a fur-trade report, "The women and children to the amount it is supposed of four Hundred were all massacred, excepting about twenty whom they received as Slaves."[31] With this calamitous news, Fort Carlton was inundated with Beaver Hills Crees seeking supplies to "enable them to pass the winter in the Strong Woods, being too much afraid to return to the plains after having massacred so many helpless women and children."[32] The Crees tried hiding in the woods during the winter, but starvation drove them out to the Eagle Hills, near the present town of Battleford, where they built an impoundment for trapping buffalo. There they were attacked by a Blackfoot war party and lost several horses. By February of 1825, the Crees and Assiniboines were camped upstream from Carlton on the north side of the North Saskatchewan, where they again were attacked by the Blackfoot, who killed two Assiniboines and took thirty Cree horses.[33]

Come spring, the Crees retaliated. In May 1825, they discovered a Blackfoot camp on the Battle River. "The result," said a trader, "was that they killed nine Blackfeet men and about a score of women and children, captured about a hundred and forty Horses and brought forty-seven women and Children as prisoners to their camp. Three of the women they afterwards killed and sent one back with Tobacco and a message to her friends. The message some say was an offer of peace."[34]

These battles were taking place far out on the plains and beyond the hunting grounds of the Rocky Mountain Crees, but they left the foothills people in a constant state of watchfulness. As an eighteen-year-old, Maskepetoon would have been one of those who acted as a guard or scout protecting the people from sunrise attacks. As a guard, he would patrol the hunting camp throughout the night, listening for sounds such as the hoot of an owl or the yapping of a kit fox, which could be the enemy signalling each other. The guard had to check the horse herd, aware of every whinny or restless movement of the animals. They might simply be nervous, sensing a nearby wolf, or they could be unsettled because there was a stranger creeping among them.

If acting as a scout, Maskepetoon would ride out during the day, circling the camp and wandering farther afield if something suspicious appeared on the horizon. When moving camp, some scouts rode ahead of the procession while others guarded the flanks and the rear. These precautions were not an everyday occurrence but were prudent when warfare was at its height and there were rumours that the enemy was near.

In the spring of 1825, traders at Edmonton outfitted a number of Crees to hunt and trap near the mountains and on the upper waters of the Bow River. However, while en route, their horses were stolen by a Blackfoot war party, and the Crees went in pursuit. "The Consequence," said a trader, "was that it ended in Blood Shed and the Crees had to fly from those Lands and passed the rest of the Summer eating & singing their war songs."[35] Later in the season, the Peigans attacked sixteen tents of Beaver Hills Crees, killing them all and losing seven of their own men. These had been a disastrous few years. According to a trader:

> The word with them is still war & war, a thing so Common now that it is not worth mentioning. The consequences of this last mentioned Business between the Crees & Blackfeet will again be the cause we will collect no great quantity of Dried Provisions. Both tribes will keep at a respectable distance from the Establishment, that should the Buffalos be numerous about their Camps they will destroy all they can make themselves.[36]

And the carnage was not over. In 1826, Plains Assiniboine war parties came in large numbers to the Edmonton area to waylay any Blackfoot who might be coming to trade. When those Indians could not be found, they decided to raid Fort Edmonton itself and help themselves to the company's horses and those of a few Crees. They took a dozen horses but were hotly pursued by Crees and men from the fort. When overtaken, the Assiniboines abandoned the herd and fled on two of the best horses. However, a Metis named Francois Lucier (later painted by Paul Kane), had a better horse and caught up with one of the raiders and shot him. When the injured Assiniboine tried to fight, Lucier stabbed him to death with his dagger.

A day later, four more horses were stolen from the fort, and on the following day, October 9, their raids turned into a major confrontation. Wrote trader John Rowand:

> Early in the morning the alarm was again given that more Stone Indians had attempted to steal the horses while the men, Half Breeds and Indians, were guarding them and a few minutes afterwards one Stone Indian was taken and brought into the Fort by Baptiste Pumois' son and a Cree, while the rest of the men accompanied by the Indians (Crees) and Half Breeds, who as I said before were altogether guarding the horses at the same place, all went off in a band in search of the Thieves, which they found, when collected together to consist of about 30 armed men.[37]

The raiders had been hiding in haystacks almost within sight of the fort and opened fire when discovered. In the brief skirmish, three Assiniboines were killed, while the fort's interpreter was seriously wounded in the chest and arm. As he stumbled back to the fort, he saw the Assiniboine prisoner supposedly in the act of escaping, so he stabbed him to death with his bayonet. According to Rowand:

> The Stone Indians during this time continued to fly across the Point of the Fort to the edge of the River, where it is supposed they had previously made holes in the ground as the last resource in case of being pursued where they kept firing for some time & we had the mortification to see 2 of our men and 2 Indians brought home wounded. One of the men, Breban, got an arrow in the Breast which I fear will kill him, Pepin our Blacksmith, a ball in the haunch, Sinam the Cree, one of our hunters, got

a Ball through the left shoulder, the Little Assiniboine a Ball through his Neck and one arm broken . . . Had I taken or sent the Cannon across the River opposite where they were, not one would have escaped, but No, they were allowed to make their escape, and they did take advantage of the night for that purpose.[38]

The situation was now so serious that Rowand even considered abandoning Fort Edmonton and letting the Indians kill each other. Three more years were to pass before another peace treaty could be made.

The 1820s might have been a disastrous decade for all the tribes involved, but they were good years for Maskepetoon. It was an ideal time for the teenager to build a war record for himself. He could go with warriors from his home camp or search out the Beaver Hills people and join in the raiding, killing and fighting to demonstrate the kind of bravery and leadership that would mark him as a possible future chief.

There was no reason for him to show restraint or compassion. Crees were being killed all around him, and the resounding call was for revenge. With a pile of moccasins made by his mother and a scalping knife in his hand, he joined the others in travelling the plains to proclaim the superiority of the Crees. Whether participating in a horse raid or a revenge party, he was ready to use all his skills to capture or kill. Whatever needed to be done, he would do it, for he was a Cree warrior.

CHAPTER THREE

Leadership

During the savage years of the 1820s, the Rocky Mountain Crees remained close to their traditional lands, while many Beaver Hills Crees went east to trade at Fort Carlton. At this time, a name appeared in the fur-trade records that would have great significance to the Rocky Mountain Crees. He was Louis Piche, a prominent member of the Beaver Hills Crees who was born about 1790. Piche's father was a white man from Quebec and his mother a Cree. In his youth, he had worked for the North West Company, and in 1810, while a hunter at Upper Terre Blanche Fort, he came to the attention of trader Alexander Henry. "Piche and other lads came in from my hunter's tent on a visit," he wrote. "Piche had made the wife of one of my hunters desert, and she is lurking in the woods near the fort."[1] Shortly afterwards, he left the traders and was "off with his fair deserter."[2]

This is probably when Piche joined the Beaver Hills Crees, although he continued to work from time to time for the North West Company. About 1820, he married a Cree woman named Wanakew, and they had a daughter named Catherine.[3] During the troubles of the 1820s, Piche took another wife, Eamowishk, and while they were near Fort Carlton, they had a son named Big Thunder, or Louis.[4] In 1825, when many Crees were retreating northward into the woods in fear of the Blackfoot, the factor at Carlton wrote that "the little Governor and Piche a half breed were with a large party of other Crees and their families gone to Green Lake on a trading expedition."⁵ Green Lake is in north-central Saskatchewan and was far from the turmoil of war.

During these years, Piche gained a war record, and although details of it are not remembered, he had the reputation of being an aggressive fighter. There is one story, although not about war, that reflects his uncompromising character:

> A medicine man, having dunned Peechee [Piche] in vain for a present of a fine horse, told him that henceforward all his stud would have large feet; and when Peechee, suspecting foul play, found the knave hammering away at the hoofs of his horses with a stone, he very quietly sent a bullet through his head.⁶

Piche's chief was Crow Shoes, a Beaver Hills Cree, who was described as "a great villain but can nevertheless do good when he pleases."⁷ Crow Shoes' father was a Peigan chief, and during times of peace, he sometimes stayed with that tribe.⁸ In the spring of 1826, Crow Shoes led his followers from Carlton back to the Edmonton region, perhaps to get away from the violence or, as the traders suspected, "to steal horses from the Slave [Blackfoot] Indians."⁹ After the chief and another group arrived, the trader noted, "Three young Crees arrived from the Crow Shoes Tent. They are come for Tobacco. They say the Crow Shoes has a few [musk]Rats but not many." Two days later he wrote, "Piche, a half breed who was one of the thirteen arrived on Sunday went off this morning in company with 2 Crees. He solicited very much to take goods upon Debt to a certain amount but could not prevail. I advanced him what I thought."¹⁰

At Fort Edmonton, the new arrivals met eleven lodges of Rocky Mountain Crees from Whitemud Creek. The trader said, "Two Indians, one named the Entering Bear, arrived from their Tents in White Mud Lake [Wabamun] where they are encamped and starving, in the Place of killing fur and living well, but there is no good animal hunting with them as is evident from the number of Moose in that direction. A piece of Tobc. with a few balls and powder is the purpose of their visit."[11]

The Rocky Mountain and those Beaver Hills Crees who stayed near Edmonton had a relatively quiet summer, even if they were uneasy about the violence farther east. But not to be denied their chances for raiding an enemy, a mixed party of Rocky Mountain and Beaver Hills Crees under Crow Shoes set off west across the mountains to attack the Kootenais. They were successful, and on their triumphant return, they announced they had killed four men and two women.[12] Said the trader at Edmonton, "The Crowshoes once more made his appearance . . . The Crees who are now here pass the day in feasting, dancing, and rejoicing at the success of those who had lately returned from War upon those poor Indians in the Mountains."[13]

Piche came to the fort in the fall of 1826 and brought in a few furs, then left with others to go east to Moose Hills, Red Deer Hills and Whitefish Lake. The winter was a bitter one, with no buffalo in the area. A visitor to the fort reported that "the Beaver Hill Crees are encamped near the Red Deer Hill and that their number is reduced to thirty Tents only. They say that Buffaloe are very scarce along the banks of the river and indeed wherever they have been."[14] In spite of this, Piche had a successful winter trapping, and in the spring of 1827, he brought in furs valued at a hundred beaver skins. This was one of the biggest catches of the season. The others with him had little or nothing, perhaps reflecting Piche's industriousness, as well as his leadership. In gratitude, the traders gave Piche "the present of a little Rum."[15]

Piche was at Fort Edmonton when the first steps were taken to establish a general peace treaty between the Blackfoot tribes on one side and the Crees and Assiniboines on the other. In March 1827, Blood chief Bull Back Fat arrived at Edmonton and approached Crow Shoes, Piche and companions, saying he "invited the Crees to smoke a pipe with him and his companions as a token of peace, which he solicits on behalf of himself and his country men and has left Tobacco and a little weed and a piece of Buffalos backfat tied together and to be sent to the Stone Indians and Crees of Carlton."[16]

The "weed" was sweetgrass, and the token was a common way to offer peace to an enemy. If the Crees purified themselves in the smoke of the sweetgrass, painted themselves with ochre mixed with the backfat and smoked the tobacco, this would be an indication of their acceptance of the offer. A similar token might be sent to the Blackfoot tribes preparatory to holding a peace council. At this time, Bull Back Fat was the leading chief of the Bloods, while The Feather (the son of The Feather who was killed in 1814) was chief of the Siksika.

The peace efforts had no immediate results, yet violent confrontations became noticeably fewer. Several weeks later, Bull Back Fat made another attempt at peace when he and a Blood delegation went to Fort Carlton to meet with the Crees and Plains Assiniboines from the lower country. They captured a Cree woman, gave her presents and sent her to the fort to inform them of their coming. However, the peacemakers were discovered by Cree warriors, who opened fire on them and killed one of their party. At that point, the Bloods gave up any idea of making peace and retreated south, where they stacked all the presents and furs they had brought with them and burned them.[17]

A month later, Bull Back Fat joined Siksika chief The Feather and Sarcee chief Cut Nose to try again. When they found no Crees at Carlton, some young men wanted to search for them and attack them, but the leaders prevailed and they left peacefully after trading. As a mark of disdain, they burned the prairies behind them as they left. After these failures, nothing more happened until the following summer, when The Feather finally succeeded in making peace.

In the period that followed, many Beaver Hills Crees near Edmonton returned downriver, taking their trade back to

Carlton. Others, including Piche and his chief, Crow Shoes, decided to stay farther west. Late in 1829, traders en route from Edmonton to Rocky Mountain House (again open for business) met Piche on the trail, and he accompanied them to their fort.[18] About the same time, Crow Shoes, who was probably from the same camp, brought in furs to trade.

Crow Shoes and his companions then moved to the edge of the prairies, where they made an impoundment for trapping buffalo. A Cree elder described the construction and use of such pounds. He said they were built near wooded areas at the edge of the prairies, where the Crees had access to the necessary timber. The pound consisted of a large circular fence at least seven feet high, with one end open, and a four-foot-high gallery around the outside where the hunters could stand while they were shooting the buffalo. A V-shaped fence was erected from the mouth of the pound and extended back a considerable distance. The trap was built at the bottom of a small hill and a cut made so that once the buffalo fell inside, they could not get out. At the ends of the V, brush was piled up to provide a hiding place for those who would stampede the buffalo into the pound. Said the elder, "All the time that the work of building was going on, the poundmaker was in a state of prayer. He sang and beat on a drum for some time every night, beseeching the Father of All to assist him in enticing the buffalo to enter his pound willingly."[19]

When all was in readiness, the poundmaker went out on the prairie to round up a small herd. By running, whistling and praying, he moved them along slowly to the entrance of the gates. "It is strange but true," continued the elder, "that a poundmaker could always drive the herd he wanted safely into the enclosure without much assistance."[20]

As the buffalo were herded towards the gates, the men and women hiding near the opening of the fence suddenly jumped up, waved their blankets and stampeded the herd towards certain death. Snorting and bellowing, the old bulls saw the danger ahead, but they could not control the frightened herd behind them as they were pushed into the corral. Once they tumbled inside, they were met with a hail of arrows from men and boys and fell in lifeless heaps. When the run was over, men and women entered the pound and began to butcher the kill. Hides were peeled off, delicious parts like the kidney were eaten raw, prized cuts like backfat were set aside and the carcass carefully taken apart with the skill of a surgeon. The people were soon up to their elbows in blood as the corral became a butchering ground. By this time, most women had double-bladed metal knives that were shaped like beaver tails. These could be sharpened and resharpened as the butchering progressed.

Meanwhile, the master of the pound divided the meat so that all got a fair share. Whatever was left behind was greedily devoured by the wolflike dogs that had waited impatiently outside the fence. A visitor to such a Cree pound commented, "On arriving at the Camp our noses were assailed by an offensive smell which would have proved fatal to more delicate organs: It proceeded from the Carcasses in the Pound and the mangled limbs of Buffaloes scattered among the Lodges."[21] The meat that could not be eaten fresh was dried and stored away, made into pemmican or sold to the traders.

In later years, Maskepetoon commonly used such impoundments to make sure that his people were fed. However, on this occasion in the winter of 1829–30, it was Crow Shoes, Piche and other plains-oriented people who made use of the pound. When Crow Shoes and his followers were successful, hunters from Rocky Mountain House came out from their fort and used it as well. In January 1830, they killed twenty-two buffalo in that pound, four men with dogsleds being needed to bring in the meat. In February, another twenty-eight animals were taken in the same pound.[22] How many buffalo were slaughtered by the Crees was not recorded.

When spring came, Piche abandoned the pound and set off with his family to trap. He was away all summer, but heavy rains and flooded rivers ruined his season. In the fall, the trader at Rocky Mountain House reported, "Piche a half Breed & four Men arrived. He Passed the Summer along the River La Biche [Red Deer River]. He killed nothing but twenty Beavers. He says that the River has been so high all summer which prevented him from setting his traps."[23] When his trade was finished, Piche announced that he planned "to go and make his winter hunt somewhere about the Red Deers River."[24] This time he had more success. When he came back in April 1831, he brought in 530 muskrats, 13 beaver and 6 dressed moose hides—again one of the best catches of those trading at Rocky Mountain House.[25]

Meanwhile, as more and more Beaver Hills Crees wintered downriver near Moose Hills and Whitefish Lake, the Hudson's Bay Company decided to open a trading post in the area to better serve them. In 1829, Fort Pitt was established halfway between Carlton and Edmonton, built "for the accommodation of the Middle & Beaver Hill Crees, who would Otherwise idle away their time in the Plains . . . and altho it has yet barely time to be known, its returns were this past Spring very respectable."[26] The result was that almost all the Beaver Hills Crees, including Crow Shoes, moved eastward to the new fort.

Over the next few years, the Beaver Hills Crees moved back and forth, but the final separation between them and the Rocky Mountain Crees occurred in the spring of 1834. "Our Strong Wood Crees," wrote a trader, "have divided from Crow Shoes & the Little Chief's Party and are determined to stick to the strong woods."[27] Piche did not go with them. Whether he liked the trapping, the land or the more peacefully inclined people, he severed his association with the Beaver Hills group and adopted the Rocky Mountain Crees as his own. His war reputation, his leadership and his success as a trapper were all attributes that the Crees could appreciate, and people gravitated to him. About forty years old, he was accepted as one of the leaders whose opinions and direction came to be appreciated. A few of the Beaver Hills Crees may have remained with him, but most, including his wife's father, returned east.[28] During these years, Piche's second son, Bob Tail, was born "along the Saskatchewan River," followed by a third son, Ermine Skin.[29]

The fact that Piche was a successful hunter placed him in good stead with the Hudson's Bay Company. He may have spoken French, but if so, he made no effort to mix with other Metis at the forts. While some fur-trade records referred to him as a half-breed, he was sometimes considered to be a Cree in such entries as, "Piche and five other Crees arrived."[30]

During the 1830s, Piche's position became entrenched, and while he was only one of the leaders of the Rocky Mountain Crees, he was probably the most prominent. His good relations with the traders were decidedly an asset, as he was more likely to get gifts from them such as rum, ammunition and tobacco. He was something of a wanderer and had an aggressive and warlike spirit gained from his Beaver Hills experiences. Yet he became friends with the Siksika, Peigan and Sarcee during times of peace when they traded at Rocky Mountain House. It was not uncommon for Piche to camp with them when at the fort and to learn their language.

As he grew older, war did not seem to play such an important part in Piche's life. Rather, he was a worker—a hunter and trapper—who seemed to prefer the seclusion of the foothills and mountains to life on the war-ravaged plains.

CHAPTER FOUR

Edging onto the Plains

By the early 1830s, Maskepetoon of the Rocky Mountain Crees was in his mid-twenties. He had at least three brothers, and the youngest, Samson, later recalled, "My brother [Maskepetoon] was killed by the Blackfeet, another by the Stonies, and another by the Crees; thus you will see we were not only at war with other tribes, but fought among ourselves."[1]

Sources say that Maskepetoon was a great warrior, but few specific examples of his fighting prowess are recorded or remembered in oral history. Missionary George McDougall, who knew Maskepetoon personally, said the man "was peerless among Crees. In early life, war was his pastime; he was a prince among horse-thieves, and many were his hairbreadth escapes. Once attacked by three Blackfeet . . . he rushed upon them with his knife and despatched the whole."[2] The Rev. John McDougall described Maskepetoon as "the perfect horseman, the successful hunter, and the brave and victorious warrior."[3]

Informants among the Crees agree with this assessment. One elder stated, "Maskepetoon was a warrior himself. That's why he was a leader. All warriors were leaders. The chiefs earned their leadership."[4] The informant added, "There is one story of how they were attacked and won the battle."[5] The qualities required for future leadership often were recognized during raids on enemy camps or horse herds. Like Maskepetoon, such men were wise, strong-willed and fearless in the face of danger.

They displayed the qualities needed both in times of war and in peace.

Maskepetoon, while still a young man, was said to have turned from war to peace. While he was revelling in his victories, his father told him he was making a mistake in following the war trail. He said:

> The glory you are now seeking will be short-lived. Delighting in war, taking pleasure in the spilling of man's blood, is all wrong. If you want to be a great man, if you want to be remembered long, turn about and work for peace. This is the only thing that will give you true fame.[6]

Six times his father spoke to him, and six times the young warrior rejected the idea of peace. But his father's comments bothered him, so he sought the advice of a holy man. The old man said, "Your father is more capable of advising you than I am," but when Maskepetoon persisted, the holy man told the young warrior to gather eight sticks of different lengths. These he placed on the ground in two rows. He said:

> Now these sticks represent two lines of life. I will give them names. These four are falsehood, dishonesty, hatred of fellow men, war; those are truth, honesty, love of fellow men, peace. I will speak of each one; and now since you have come to me, my son, I want you to open your ears and treasure in your heart what I have to say.[7]

The holy man then gave his interpretation of the meaning of the sticks, and when he was finished, he gathered together the four sticks relating to war. "Shall we keep these, or shall I burn them?" he asked. "Burn them," said Maskepetoon. The holy man then took the other four sticks, bound them together and handed them to the young warrior. In this way, Maskepetoon chose peace over war.

This account, if true, would indicate that Maskepetoon had declared himself a peacemaker at an early age. However, the story is probably more apocryphal than real, told by Methodist missionaries while on fundraising tours of eastern Canada. In it, Maskepetoon seems to be depicted as an ideal Christian accepting the "good" sticks and rejecting the "bad." In reality, warfare was necessary for the protection of one's hunting grounds, and bravery in war was extolled.

Maskepetoon was married about 1826 to Sussewisk, or Sarcee Land. She was either a Sarcee or a Siksika woman. They had a daughter about a year later.[8] The couple had at least four boys and a number of girls. In later years, Maskepetoon had three other wives: Onahtah-me-nahoose, or Good Hunter; Susihiskayo, or Fierce Woman; and Maton-now-a-cap, or Crying Eyes.[9] His first wife, Sussewisk, outlived him by twenty years, dying on the Samson Reserve about 1890.

Because their marriage took place during a period of peace, it is likely Maskepetoon met Sussewisk when two tribes were visiting each other. Marriages were not always based upon love, but it did happen. For her to be chosen—or offered—she must have proven herself to be industrious and skilful in beading, quillworking, sewing and the other abilities expected of a wife. And, as a Cree elder stated, "A man had to be a good hunter and had to have a war record in order to have a good standing in marriage. As long as he had a good name it didn't matter if he had few relatives."[10]

As soon as he took his bride, Maskepetoon moved out of his father's lodge and into his own tipi. If he was lucky and Sussewisk's family was in the camp, they would have provided the lodge. If not, he had to rely on his own relatives. The fact that their marriage lasted so long is an indication that Sussewisk fitted well into the band and was accepted by his family and friends. She was not the only outsider in the Cree camp. Cree men were known to have married women from Siksika, Sarcee, Stoney, Kootenai and other tribes, drawn perhaps by the mystique of a "foreign" woman, or because she was presented to him during a visit to another tribe. Some men even married captive women.

But there was danger in such inter-tribal alliances, for when war broke out again, the woman might be killed simply for being from the enemy tribe. In one instance, after a war party was wiped out, the father of one of the dead boys went to a captive wife and shot her. No one tried to stop him. Some years later, when war erupted, a missionary noted, "A half Cree, the wife of a Blackfoot, arrived at the fort, her husband having threatened to kill her in consequence of the recent affray. She had travelled for five days and had carried her little child, without any subsistence except wild roots, &c." [11] If Sussewisk ever faced such danger, there is no record of it. Rather, she became the mother of Maskepetoon's children, travelled with him and supported him as he rose to fame and power.

Meanwhile, during the 1830s, events were taking place far south on the Missouri River that ultimately had a profound effect on the future of the Rocky Mountain Crees. Ever since members of Lewis and Clark's expedition of 1804–6 had killed a Peigan, any Americans coming up the Missouri were considered to be enemies. Not only that, but their method of gathering furs became the focus of Blackfoot hostility. Whereas British traders encouraged Natives to trap and sell their furs to the trading posts, the Americans did their own trapping. Small parties of "mountain men" penetrated the rich beaver country in the mountains and foothills, trapped the beaver and then sold their furs to buyers from St. Louis. As a result, the Blackfoot considered the Americans to be interlopers who were stealing their furs, and they treated them accordingly.

In 1808, a trading party of Bloods at Fort Edmonton reported that they had "discovered in their Summer War excursions, on a southern branch of the Mississoury, two small settlements which they plundered of goods to a considerable amount, besides about 300 Beaver skins. One of the Men belonging to these Settlements was killed and the rest (ten in number) after being stripped were permitted to escape." Then, just two weeks later, some Sarcees arrived with beaver skins which "have been taken from the Settlements above mentioned," and a day later a few Gros Ventres appeared who had "likewise plundered a small American settlement on the Mississoury, and as they confess themselves, killed two of the Men belonging to it."[12]

Faced with deadly hostility from the Blackfoot, the American trappers withdrew from the region until 1821, when the Missouri Fur Company built a fort on the Yellowstone River. But the trappers they sent out fared no better than their earlier counterparts, and most of them were slaughtered. A year later, the Rocky Mountain Fur Company tried to enter the region, but its men were attacked near Great Falls and four of them killed. As historian John Ewers noted:

> Through the remaining years of the twenties and in the thirties war parties of Blackfeet and Gros Ventres ranged far and wide on both sides of the Rockies south of the Three Forks. Repeatedly, they attacked the mountain men in their isolated camps or on the trail . . . Alfred Jacob Miller reckoned the beaver trappers' losses averaged forty or fifty men in a season.[13]

The breakthrough in relations between the Blackfoot tribes and Americans occurred in 1831, the year Maskepetoon turned twenty-four. After delicate negotiations, the American Fur Company was permitted to build Fort Piegan for the purpose of trading, but not as a centre for trapping. Offering goods at much lower prices than the Hudson's Bay Company and accepting buffalo robes that the British refused as being too cumbersome to ship, they soon had the Peigans flocking to their post. Besides trade goods, they also sold whisky in competition with British rum and brandy. The fort had a successful winter, receiving 6,450 pounds of beaver skins that would otherwise have gone to the British.[14] The following year, a more permanent structure,

Fort McKenzie, was built. The trader, Kenneth McKenzie, who had once worked for the Hudson's Bay Company, followed that company's methods of buying furs from the Indians, rather than sending trappers out on their own. This approach resulted in a large trade in furs and buffalo robes.

Convinced that they could lure the Peigans back to Edmonton and Rocky Mountain House, a Hudson's Bay Company expedition under Chief Factor John Rowand set out for the Missouri River in 1832, "for the purpose of ascertaining the cause of the Peigans having left off trading with us as usual, and in order to get them back to their old Station."[15] Rowand met with the leading Peigan chiefs, heard their complaints and, in order to provide them with easier access, built Peagan Post on the Bow River, near the present village of Morley. At the same time, they closed Rocky Mountain House, which had been a favourite post for the Rocky Mountain Crees. The problem now was that only the Peigans would be permitted to trade at Peagan Post; everyone else would have to go to Fort Edmonton. This was a decided disadvantage for those Crees who trapped deep within the foothills and into the passes of the Rocky Mountains.

The British effort to regain the Peigan trade was a failure. The Bloods, angry that they would not be permitted to trade at the Bow River post, prevented the Peigans from going there. This resulted in a fight that left several dead on both sides. Some Peigans who did choose to go north were intercepted by couriers from the American forts who offered high prices for their robes and furs. In the end, the Hudson's Bay men garnered only 645 beaver pelts, 290 half pelts, 350 buffalo robes and a few other pelts from Peagan Post and Rocky Mountain House for the season. Although not acquired in large quantities, buffalo robes were needed for clothing, especially for their northern posts.

At this time, most of the Peigans—the largest of the three tribes making up the Blackfoot nation—were located in the present state of Montana and north to the Medicine Hat region. The Bloods were immediately north of them up to the Bow River, and the Siksika were on the Red Deer and Battle rivers. The North Peigans, an offshoot of the main body, were in the foothills south of the Bow River and the Sarcees in the Buffalo Lake region.

The competition between the British and Americans had a major effect on the Rocky Mountain Crees, for it marked the beginning of a major shift in their tribal hunting grounds. With the Peigans now gravitating to the south, the Siksika and Bloods soon followed. The Siksika extended their range southward to the Bow River, often leaving the northern part of their hunting grounds underpopulated for much of the year. During the summer, many Blackfoot were far east on the open plains. In 1832, for example, "seventy tents of Blackfeet [Siksika] are pitched about the Nose [north of the present town of Coronation], further that the remainder of that tribe with the Blood Indians & Piegans are encamped somewhere about the Sweet Grass Hills."[16]

The result was that the Rocky Mountain Crees began to move into the Pigeon Lake and upper Battle River areas. This meant more interaction with the Beaver Hills Crees and other bands downriver, as well as with Metis hunters. By July of 1832, there already were signs that the Rocky Mountain Crees were on the move. Stated a trader, "In the course of the day four young men of that tribe came in. They come from Gull Lake."[17] And in the following year, Edmonton was visited by "two men (Crees) from the Southward near the Buffalo Lake informing us that their tribe have had a battle with the Surcees in which no lives were lost."[18] Buffalo Lake was well out on the plains and formerly had been the exclusive territory of the Sarcees.

Maskepetoon, with his wife and family, could join others in making an impoundment during the autumn so that they would have an assured supply of dried meat when they retreated into the bush for the winter. As long as peace prevailed and the Sarcees were far out on the plains, the open areas adjacent to the woods were now theirs.

For a number of years there had been relative peace between the Crees and Blackfoot trading at Fort Edmonton, even though horse stealing and bloody confrontations were still occurring downstream at forts Pitt and Carlton. But the more warlike Cree bands had a habit of coming west, hoping to catch the Blackfoot on their way to trade at Edmonton. Although the Rocky Mountain Crees tried to stay neutral, it wasn't always possible. On one occasion, some of their people were coming back from a trading expedition to the Kootenais when they met a large band of Peigans under Chief Big Lake on the Bow River. They had a friendly trade, the Blackfoot giving horses and the Crees offering guns and leather lodges. The Peigan chief said that "the Main Tribes are keeping far to the southward to avoid an encounter with the Crees and Assiniboines."[19]

Shortly after this friendly meeting, the Peigans met a number of Plains Crees under the leadership of Iron Mouth's son. They professed peace, smoked the pipe and were feasting when the Crees opened fire and killed three of them on the spot. Some of the Peigans had been suspicious and had ridden off just before the killing began. Afterwards, one of the Crees claimed as his war honour that he had killed two of the Peigans with a single shot. The Crees lost one man in the melee.[20] With this incident, the Crees and Blackfoot in the area were effectively back at war.

In the summer of 1833, some Blackfoot came to trade at Edmonton, and a number of Cree leaders under Walking Wolf and his son Old Squirrel decided to approach them about a peace treaty. However, as the Cree party approached them, an angry young Blackfoot opened fire, causing them to retreat. Not wishing to lose the chance of a treaty with the southern tribes, Chief Factor Patrick Small went across the river and brought the Blackfoot over. He wrote:

> When seated amongst their enemies, Old Squirrel got up and in the Peagan language declared that it was the Crees inhabiting the lower part of the country who always

began war and that nothing could be more desirable to those of the upper country, of which he was one, than a long continuance of peace. A Blackfoot Chief in his turn replied that the Indians of the Peagan, Siksika, Sarcee and Blood Indian tribes were always anxious to treat a Cree well, but that they were such ungrateful dogs that kindness, instead of making them better, made them only worse. They were constantly making peace and at the same time doing everything in their power to break it.[21]

Needless to say, no treaty was made.

A couple of months later, a mixed war party of Beaver Hills and Middle Crees arrived at Edmonton. They said they were "in search of the Slave [Blackfoot] Indians in order to steal their horses and, if in their power, take the scalps of the owners."[22] In the face of these possible dangers, the Rocky Mountain Crees, including Maskepetoon, simply retreated into the bush to pursue their work of trapping and surviving. In November 1833, a number of them brought in 1,100 muskrats and said that they had "a good hunt."[23]

Over the next couple of years, warfare and violence surged around them, seriously endangering the more-or-less friendly relations they had maintained with the Sarcees, who were part of the Blackfoot Confederacy. Usually they simply avoided each other, but if this was impossible, both sides kept their young men in check while the elders smoked their pipes and spoke of peace. If relations were good, they camped side by side, either on the edge of the plains or at the trading posts, where they gambled, arranged marriages or just visited.

In August 1834, the peaceful relations suffered a severe setback when a Plains Cree war party from the Fort Carlton area, some forty strong, set out to search for any Indians of the Blackfoot Confederacy—Siksikas, Bloods, Peigans or Sarcees. This was undoubtedly a revenge party out to seek scalps, not horses. After more than a month of searching the seemingly vacant prairies, the Cree scouts found a Sarcee camp southwest of the Sweet Grass Hills. According to a trader, "they fell in with about 25 Circees near the Rocky Mountains of which they killed 5 men, and had one killed of their own Party."[24]

Some Rocky Mountain Crees, particularly the young men, did not back down from a fight or a chance to humble their prairie foes if the opportunity arose. A year later, these young Crees and their prairie allies set out to raid the Blackfoot and did not hesitate to act when they found some Sarcees on the trail. According to a trader:

> A month or two ago a war party consisting of 200 Strong-wood [Rocky Mountain] and Beaver Hill Crees made a hostile incursion into the Blackfoot country, and accidentally fell in with a straggling party of 20 Circus warriors who on perceiving the enemy threw themselves into a thicket of trees, and after hastily constructing a temporary barricade, boldly opened a spirited fire on the Crees who not relishing the idea of a rapid advance on their determined enemy contented themselves with maintaining a weak and desultory fire during the day.[25]

That night, the Sarcees took advantage of darkness and slipped away from their fortification, leaving eleven dead. The Crees suffered three killed and ten wounded. Said the trader:

> The Circus who escaped reached their main camp and a strong party of their friends gave pursuit to the Crees, who took up a strong position in the woods where they could not be attacked but at a manifest disadvantage. The two parties finally separated, without any further attempt on either side.[26]

While this incident did not deteriorate into protracted open warfare, the Sarcees were still viewed as an integral part of the

Blackfoot Confederacy, rather than arm's-length neighbours. A peace treaty made at Fort Pitt a year later lasted for only a year. The war continued, but mostly on the eastern plains. In April of 1837, a revenge party of Plains Assiniboines fell upon a Blackfoot camp, killing two women and two children. To add to the confusion of plains warfare, two Crees living with the Blackfoot also were killed by their supposed allies. "This Affair will create War again among the Plain Tribes," wrote the Fort Carlton factor.[27]

But before any retaliatory raids could be launched, a much more dangerous threat appeared on the horizon: smallpox. One of the first reports of the contagion in Cree and Blackfoot territory came from Fort Edmonton in a letter to Governor George Simpson dated Christmas Day, 1837. Chief Factor John Rowand reported on the "different accounts which have reached me from the Plains and that by some of our principal Chiefs belonging to the Slave [Blackfoot] tribes who visited this place this season who... informed me that more than half of all the Plains tribes were no more."[28] He added, "It was on the 11th November when I first heard of the raging Sickness from a party of Circees who I had to supply with what Medicine I had; at that time they told me they might be one Hundred Tents of them, who I am sorry to say, are already reduced to only Thirty."[29]

The epidemic had its beginning on the Missouri River, the disease breaking out among some white and Native passengers on the steamboat *St. Peters* while it delivered goods to the various trading posts along the river.[30] The captain knew he had smallpox on board but still made his scheduled stops at Fort Pierre and Fort Clark. There the plague was transmitted to the Arikara, Sioux and Mandan, virtually wiping out the latter tribe.[31]

When the boat arrived at Fort Union on June 24, 1837, there were no Indians camped nearby, but a short time later, a Plains Assiniboine chief came to trade. He contracted the disease and took it back to his tribe, whose villages extended from northern Montana into south and central Saskatchewan.

The Assiniboines were struck hard by the smallpox, with an estimated 80 percent of its victims, or three thousand people, dying of the disease.[32]

Meanwhile, the American fur traders had done nothing to control the spread of the disease. In early June, a keel boat loaded with goods for the Blackfoot trade was going upstream towards Fort McKenzie when smallpox broke out among the passengers and crew. The boat arrived at the fort with its deadly load at the end of June.[33] Because of their beliefs, the Blackfoot ignored the threat of an epidemic. A historian wrote, "Their theory of most diseases was that an evil spirit had entered into the body of the sufferer and that a cure could only be effected by its expulsion. For this purpose the charms of the medicine men were believed to have peculiar potency, which procured their almost invariable employment."[34]

Within a short time, smallpox had broken out among the employees of the trading post and twenty-nine died. The epidemic quickly reached the Blackfoot tribes and hundreds perished. At the confluence of the St. Mary and Oldman rivers, near the present city of Lethbridge, so many Bloods died that the region forever became known as "Many Died."[35] From the tribes on the Missouri, the contagion quickly spread to the other members of the Blackfoot Confederacy, including the hapless Sarcees.

The epidemic reached the Crees near Fort Edmonton from two directions—the Sarcees and Siksikas from the south, and fellow Crees and Plains Assiniboine from the east. According to Chief Factor Rowand, the sickness began with a dreadful pain in the head, back and neck, followed by bleeding from the nose; once a person contracted the disease, they usually died within two or three days.

George Simpson learned of the epidemic while he was in Montreal and shipped vaccine to York Factory and Moose Factory and from there to the various inland posts. At the same time, circulars were sent out, urging the chief factors to immunize everyone within reach, "by force if necessary," to stem the spread of the contagion.[36] The disease reached Fort Carlton in November, where the officer in charge had vaccinated his men, but the vaccine proved ineffective. Historian Arthur Ray noted, "The situation was equally desperate at Edmonton House. Rowand, who was in charge of the district, does not appear to have had any vaccine on hand when smallpox reached the area, nor any familiarity with vaccination procedures."[37]

The disease did not reach the Rocky Mountain Crees until the winter of 1837–38, when most of them were out on their traplines. One of the solutions—perhaps the only solution—to the epidemic was to avoid contact with those who were afflicted. This was difficult for those living on the plains; their life was communal, and their interaction with others was frequent. However, seclusion in the bush was a way of life with the Rocky Mountain group, and this saved many lives. They probably had no real understanding of the disease, but circumstances were in their favour. From their winter camps, Maskepetoon and others heard of deaths taking place on the plains, but stayed in the protective isolation of the woods and followed their traplines. They came out alive and well the following spring, when most of the danger had passed.

In August 1838, Fort Carlton was able to report that "two Saulteaux Indians & one woman arrived from the North Side of the River on a trade. They inform that there is no more Indians who are attacked of the Small Pock & are all well."[38]

One poignant story about the epidemic among the Rocky Mountain Crees was told by a man named Buffalo Child. During the contagion, the disease struck a camp, killing most of its inhabitants. One man crawled feebly from his lodge, the only one still alive. According to the story, "Staggering from the death-camp, he was arrested by a whimper, to see a tiny babe at the cold breast of its dead mother. The man took the child with him to another camp, and the babe, after a battle with death, finally survived."[39]

Five years later, the boy wandered away from the camp in the autumn and could not be found. The next spring, a Cree hunter saw a small brown object run between the legs of an old buffalo cow. Continued the storyteller, "Amazed, they rode close, to find that the object was none other than the five-year-old boy whom they had lost from the camp the previous fall. The boy, fleet as a deer, evaded capture for some time, while the old buffalo put up a determined battle for her strange ward."[40] The young boy had wintered with the buffalo and was believed to have possessed certain powers because of his survival of the 1837 epidemic. After his rescue, he was said to have grown to manhood and became a prominent member of the Cree people.

One of the results of the epidemic was that the Siksika tribe, which had suffered more grievously than the Crees, found it expedient to withdraw from the Battle River and permanently move to the Bow River. According to an 1838 Siksika winter count, the Blackfoot "moved to the Blackfoot Crossing in the month of June."[41] Farther east, many of the devastated Assiniboines migrated southward into Montana, abandoning much of the southwestern Saskatchewan plains. These movements offered the Rocky Mountain Crees another opportunity to spread their wings and venture onto the plains. Most still preferred the woodlands in winter, but more and more they flirted with a prairie life dominated by the buffalo. Also, it was an opportune time for thirty-year-old Maskepetoon to rise to power, bringing together individuals and leaderless families who needed someone wise and strong to guide and protect them.

CHAPTER FIVE

The Other Maskepetoon

When Maskepetoon was twenty-four years old, another man with the same name was demonstrating his leadership among the Crees of North Dakota. The American Maskepetoon—usually called Broken Arm by American authorities—was born around 1799, so was about eight years older than his northern namesake. During the many years he was chief, his band hunted near Turtle Mountain and the Missouri River in North Dakota. According to Indian Agent Joshua Pilcher, these Crees "have been drawn over to the Missouri, and trade at Fort Union near the Mouth of the Yellowstone."[1] They were closely allied to the Assiniboines and often travelled with them.

In 1831, the Secretary of War in Washington directed that representative chiefs from the Upper Missouri should be invited to the nation's capital so that they could see the kindness and the power of the government. Indian Agent F.A. Sanford was directed to select the nine chiefs from his sub-agency, representing those along the Missouri River, but because of fear of a smallpox epidemic in the East and concerns about travelling to a strange land, only four men were willing to go. These were an Assiniboine named The Light (also known as Pigeon's Egg Head), Broken Arm or Maskepetoon (also known as Eyes on Both Sides), and two unnamed men, an Ojibwa and a Sioux. They arrived in St. Louis in December 1831, where their health was checked and they were vaccinated against smallpox. While in the city, Broken Arm and The Light were painted by the famous artist George Catlin. The artist described the Cree chief as follows: "Amongst the foremost and most renowned of their warriors, is Bro-cas-sie [Bras Casse], the broken arm, in a handsome dress; and by the side of him, his wife, a simple and comely looking woman."[2]

As stated by historian John Ewers, "Catlin portrayed 'Broken Arm' as a good looking young man of dignified bearing. The entire upper half of his face was painted vermilion. In addition to his decorated skin shirt he wore an elaborate choker covered with blue and white glass trade beads, ear drops of silver and a frontlet composed of large necklace beads and tubular white shell ornaments known to Indians and traders as 'hair pipes.'"[3]

From St. Louis, the delegation travelled by stagecoach to Kentucky, down the Ohio Valley and on to Maryland. From Baltimore, they went by train to Washington. The Light was the star of the delegation, with his good looks, powerful physique, beautiful clothing and colourful oratory. He made a particular hit with President Andrew Jackson by giving him an Assiniboine name.[4] After touring the nation's capital, the chiefs were taken to Philadelphia and New York, viewing sights that no Upper Missouri Indian had ever seen before. To give the visitors some idea of the country's military strength, they were shown fortresses, armouries, large cannon, ocean-going ships, railroads and even hot-air balloons.

The four chiefs were back in St. Louis by the spring of 1832 and boarded the American Fur Company's steamboat *Yellowstone* on their return journey. It is obvious that The Light was quite impressed with his new-found knowledge. When leaving the steamboat at Fort Union, he was dressed in a military uniform and strutted around with two small kegs of whisky in his pockets. Soon he was regaling his fellow Assiniboines about what he had seen, but his fanciful stories of tall buildings, railroad trains and thousands of white people were beyond their comprehension. Broken Arm was wiser. Without speaking of events that his people would consider strange, he simply resumed his role of Cree chief. Agent Sanford summed up the government's viewpoint by saying, "The Indians I got back safe to their country and highly gratified with their trip and that it will be attended with great advantages to our traders."[5]

A year later, Prince Maximilian met Broken Arm and The Light when he visited Fort Union. Of Broken Arm he said, "The chief of the Crees was Maschkepiton (the broken arm), who had a medal with the effigy of the President hung round his neck, which he had received on a visit to Washington."[6] When the prince met The Light a few days later, he commented, "The first chief of this new band [to visit the fort] was Ayanyan, generally called General Jackson, because he had made a journey to Washington. He was a handsome man, in a fine dress; he wore a beautifully embroidered black leather shirt, a new scarlet blanket, and the great medal around his neck."[7]

The Light lived for just over a year after his return. As trader Edwin Denig explained, "Day after day and night after night this man described the wonders of machinery, the fine horses and carriages, furniture, dress and all the display of eastern cities. In all this the Indian told the truth, and less than the truth, for their simple minds could not grasp the truth of what he recounted."[8] The Light was branded a liar because of his stories, and after one heated exchange, he killed a fellow Assiniboine and in turn was killed by the dead man's brother. Broken Arm, who had shown restraint and wisdom in telling of his trip, suffered no such indignity.

Broken Arm continued to trade at Fort Union. In 1835 a trader commented, "About ten oclock the Bras Casé a Cree indian chief who was at Washington . . . arrived with a few of his young men with the expectation to see Mr McKenzie and the agent but was disappointed."[9]

At this time, the American government estimated the Cree population at 3,000 and the allied Assiniboines at 20,000.[10] When the great smallpox epidemic of 1837–38 struck,

Assiniboines were said to have lost 3,840 people, with no estimate being made for Cree losses.[11] After that date, it appeared convenient for the American authorities to lump the Crees in with the Assiniboines for official purposes. Accordingly, they virtually lost their identity to the Assiniboines in government records.

The Indian agents thought the trip to Washington would have beneficial effects, particularly for the traders who had to deal with the people of the Upper Missouri on a day-to-day basis. This was not the case with all delegates. Rather than coming under the traders' influence, or that of the Indian agent, one chief had no hesitation in berating them when he believed the Assiniboine/Cree people were being deceived and exploited. Five years after the trip to Washington, Sub-Agent Fulkerson noted the following speech in which the chief complained of broken promises:

> They say that their Great Father sent for some of their tribe to go to Washington, for what reason or purpose they know not, that they left their families exposed to hunger & to enemies, were a long time gone, [and] suffered much from the fatigues of the trip, that the Great White Chief had declared to them that so long as they continued friendly to the whites, they should every Year receive presents of powder, balls, tobacco and other articles, but since their return they have not received even a pipe full of tobacco. They say that the goods must certainly been sent, and purloined by the traders on the way, for so Great a Chief cannot tell so great a falsehood. They declare that all the talk at Washington was very fine and fair, but that it is now forgotten entirely, that those promises cannot be denied for nearly all the Chiefs and Interpreters who heard them still live, and they ask what crime have they committed to forfeit their claims under these fine promises."[12]

Broken Arm must have shared this attitude, so it is not surprising that trader Edwin Denig had no love for the recalcitrant Cree chief. "He is a scheming, mean beggerly Indian," Denig wrote, "and on his return proved himself unworthy the attention bestowed upon him."[13]

In January 1844, Charles Larpenteur met Broken Arm during a trading expedition from Fort Union.[14] Travelling several days through blizzards and bitterly cold weather, the trading party finally came in view of the Cree camp, located in a deep valley. At this point, Larpenteur sent his guide on ahead, saying "that I wished him to go on into camp and tell Broken Arm, the chief of the Crees, that I wished him to prepare me a large lodge, and make ready for a big spree to-night." When Larpenteur arrived, he immediately started trading robes for whisky. Recalled the trader, "The liquor trade commenced with a rush, and it was not long before the whole camp was in a fearful uproar; but they were good Indians, and there was no more trouble than is usual on such occasions."[15] When it was over, Larpenteur had managed to garner 180 prime dressed buffalo robes for a mere five gallons of diluted liquor. Next morning, the trader said that "breakfast was served by the wife of Mr. Broken Arm, the great chief of the Crees, who had been to Washington."[16]

In 1851, Broken Arm was a tribal delegate to the Fort Laramie Treaty Council to map and set the boundaries of northern plains tribes.[17] And two years later, despite Denig's low opinion of the chief, he finally admitted that Broken Arm "had some influence among his own people."[18]

Broken Arm remained chief of the Turtle Mountain Crees until about 1869, when he and his son Young Man were killed near the confluence of the Missouri and Yellowstone rivers.[19] The tradition of Broken Arm's travel to Washington is well known today to his descendants, who live on or near the Turtle Mountain Reservation and have taken the surname of Cree. Sylvia Cree, whose married name is Morin, commented, "We have always heard that Broken Arm had gone to Washington. He was my relative."[20]

Her son, Bill Morin, recalled the following story about the famous 1831–32 trip:

> When Broken Arm went to Washington he was with another guy who was his enemy. They started to talk and the other chief said, "We had many wars with you and killed many of your people." Then Broken Arm turned around and told him, "Yes," Broken Arm says, "but when you killed one of us we killed five of yours because we got guns from the Hudson's Bay. You guys didn't have guns." They started to argue and then this guy from Washington says, "Okay you guys. We didn't bring you up here to do this. We didn't bring you up here to fight."[21]

Local genealogical lists, likely from Catholic Church records at St. Ann's Mission on the Turtle Mountain Reservation, confirm that Broken Arm (or Cripple Arm) was the father of Young Man. The son married a woman named Cochan, and they had Little Boy. He, in turn, had a son in 1873 who took the name of Charlie Cree Sr. and married Light Moon Walker and later Selina Henry. His son, Charlie Jr., was born in 1895, married Rose St. Claire in 1922 and had several children.[22]

It is a remarkable coincidence that two men with the same name, both showing great leadership, were born eight years apart within the Cree nation.[23] The confusion between the two men by Native people and historians is understandable. Broken Arm's descendants at Turtle Mountain attribute some of the Canadian Maskepetoon's deeds to their ancestor, while people on the Samson Reserve in central Alberta insist that their man was the one who went to Washington. Many historians, including this writer,[24] at one time believed they were one and the same person. Allen Ronaghan came closer than any other historian to questioning whether there might have been two Maskepetoons. He stated in 1976, "One cannot conclusively prove, on the basis of existing evidence, either that there were two Maskipitons—one known to the Americans and the other to the British—or that they were one and the same man."[25] Since then, fieldwork conducted on the Samson Reserve and Turtle Mountain Reservation has provided that missing information. In summary, baptismal and genealogical records show that there were two Maskepetoons, not one. One man traded at Fort Edmonton on the Saskatchewan River, and the other at Fort Union, six hundred miles away on the Missouri. The Maskepetoon near Fort Union was regularly identified as the man who had been to Washington and wore the president's medal. On the other hand, during his lifetime, the Rocky Mountain Cree Maskepetoon wore no medal nor made any mention of making a Washington trip—not to his good friends Robert Rundle, Thomas Woolsey, George or John McDougall, nor any Hudson's Bay Company fur trader. Had the northern Maskepetoon made such a trip, the occasion of meeting the president of the United States would have been too important to have been ignored. Not only that, but the Indian agent was directed to select delegates from the Upper Missouri, where the Americans held sway, and was unlikely to choose a "British" Indian from the far north who traded with the rival Hudson's Bay Company.

CHAPTER SIX

The Methodists

The year 1840 was a pivotal one for Maskepetoon, for it saw the arrival of the first Christian missionaries on the western plains. These men were to have a great effect upon his future influence and prestige. Since 1832, the Methodist Church had expressed an interest in sending missionaries to the Far West, but there had been reluctance on the part of George Simpson and others to permit any changes in the status quo that might affect the Hudson's Bay Company's fur-trading activities. Finally, the Wesleyan Missionary Society in England appealed directly to the company's headquarters in London. As a result, an agreement was made on January 22, 1840, to permit the Wesleyan Methodists to send three missionaries into a region that previously had been closed to any religious endeavours. This decision was transmitted to the Northern Council of the Hudson's Bay Company, and on June 18, it passed the following resolution:

> That three Missions be established in the Northern Department this season—say one at Norway House under the charge of the Revd. Mr. Evans, one at Lac la Pluie under the charge of Revd. Mr. Mason, and one at Edmonton under the charge of the Revd. Mr. Rundle; that every facility be afforded them for successfully conducting their spiritual labours.[1]

The decision was welcomed with little enthusiasm in the field, some traders presumably deciding to merely acknowledge the existence of the missionaries and little else. As a result, a later directive was sent, which stated:

> In order to remove any misapprehension that may exist as to the footing on which the Gentlemen connected with the Wesleyan Missionary Society are intended to be placed at the Company's Establishments, it is Resolved That Board and Lodging be afforded to the different Missionaries at the Establishments at which they are stationed in like manner as is provided for Commissioned Gentlemen in the Honble. Company's Service.[2]

The resolution went on to say that missionaries would eat at the "Gentlemen's" table, be provided with allowances, have use of Company interpreters and be provided transportation when needed.

The Edmonton-bound missionary, Rev. Robert Terrill Rundle, was born in Cornwall, England, and was attending a Methodist training school when the call came for recruits. He volunteered and was dispatched to Bristol, where he took the first packet to New York. Born in 1811, he was four years younger than Maskepetoon. He knew Fort Edmonton would be his station, and by the time he reached Hudson's Bay territory, he also knew that ministering to the Rocky Mountain Crees would become his primary goal. It is likely he heard about them en route from John Edward Harriott, a fellow Methodist and a trader at Rocky Mountain House. When Rundle first met the Rocky Mountain Crees, he commented that these were the Indians "whom I came especially to see."[3]

Rundle reached Fort Edmonton in mid-October at a time when the Rocky Mountain Crees had already left for their winter trapping grounds. He was disappointed at having missed them, and even more so at the beginning of November when Harriott arrived from Rocky Mountain House to say that "a party of Cree Indians in that quarter have heard of my arrival & are very desirous of seeing me."[4]

The only Natives around Fort Edmonton were Metis, mostly French-speaking, and Beaver Hills Crees. The majority of the latter band had permanently moved to the Fort Pitt and Fort Carlton regions, but a few families had remained in the Edmonton area. Their leader was a man named Lapotac (a corruption of the French *La Patat*, or The Potato). He was a wise and influential leader and the primary hunter for the fort. When Rundle arrived, Lapotac and his followers had built a pound about seventy-five miles southeast of the fort and were supplying Edmonton with fresh meat. Rundle noted, "The pound was strewn with half-devoured carcasses of the animals, the spoils of previous captures. These fragments afforded a fine feast for the wolves which came during the night seasons & gorged themselves at their pleasures."[5] Rundle became good friends with Lapotac over the winter, and he became one of the missionary's early converts.

Early in February, Rundle set out for Rocky Mountain House to greet any Blackfoot coming to trade and to finally meet the Rocky Mountain Crees. On arrival, he learned that the Blackfoot and Crees were at war, so that any Crees who were at their traplines would not come to the fort as long as their enemies were there. Then, late in the month, someone brought tobacco from the Crees and offered it to the Blackfoot as a peace offering. This was smoked by the Blackfoot chiefs and, as Rundle said, "Peace was restored between them."[6]

The first member of the band to contact Rundle was not Maskepetoon or one of his followers, but Catherine, the daughter of Louis Piche. On March 14, she and her husband, Augustin Lambert, brought their baby daughter, Marie, to be baptized.[7] It is quite possible that Piche himself was there, as Rundle noted: "The two Indians whom I addressed on Sunday

& the half breeds have left the Fort. One half breed intends bringing his children for baptism in the course of a week or so."[8] This would appear to be Piche, for two weeks later, on April 9, he did indeed bring his children in for baptism: Margaret, Leleet, Marie, Louis and Catherine.

The first meeting between the missionary and Maskepetoon took place at Rocky Mountain House on March 24, 1841. Rundle did not mention the chief by name, but his presence was later confirmed by the Rev. George McDougall. Rundle wrote:

> The long expected band of Ry. Mt. Crees (those whom I came especially to see) arrived today & were accompanied by a party of Strong Wood Assiniboines. One of the party came on ahead to inquire if they must make a different kind of approach to the Fort as I was there. Soon after their arrival I addressed them on the Creation & Fall. After the service one of them remarked that now they resembled young birds in a nest when visited by the old ones; like the young birds they stood hungry with their mouths open waiting to be fed."[9]

The allegory offered at that time is similar to some of Maskepetoon's pronouncements in later years.

Rundle now had two great leaders of the Rocky Mountain Crees with him—Maskepetoon and Piche. They were together in the same camp and for a little while listened to the teachings of the same church. One was the elder veteran of many wars and respected by the traders for his hard work. The other, much younger, was gaining his own reputation and was being favourably received by the traders at Edmonton and Rocky Mountain House. But their future paths would be starkly different as each went his own way.

Did the Crees really understand who Rundle was and what he represented? Probably not. Harriott had been providing some religious instruction prior to the missionary's arrival, but they all knew him as a man who traded furs for knives, tobacco and rum. When Rundle arrived, the Blackfoot believed he was going to open a shop for them. "When told by Mr. Harriott that he had nothing to give them but good words, they were quite disappointed, and said they expected better things of him."[10] Rundle himself was told of a mythical version of his arrival. "Heard that Indians say I came down from heaven in a bit of paper which was opened by one of the Co.'s gentlemen at the Forts, & Lo I came out."[11]

Rundle was unlike any man they had ever seen before, so they found him difficult to categorize. Primarily, they perceived him as the white man's version of their own medicine men, someone with God-given powers that he was willing to share with them. Baptism would protect their children, prayers would give them good luck and the strange tales of Philip and the Ethiopian Eunuch, Naaman the Syrian leper and the raising of Lazarus were undoubtedly stories from his own supernatural world. They could see that the traders treated him with respect, and as these men were the most powerful the Crees had ever seen, then Rundle must be even greater than them. They accepted Rundle's Christianity into their lives as another protective force to be added to the ones they already had, rather than accepting the concept of one God. Later, of course, many began to gain a more accurate idea of what Christianity was all about.

While Rundle was at Rocky Mountain House, he established a strong relationship with trader Harriott, whom he called "my kind friend."[12] As a fellow Methodist, Harriott openly supported the Wesleyan cause, unlike his superior, John Rowand, who was Catholic.

When Rundle left Rocky Mountain House in the spring of 1841, he travelled southeast and after three days found the main Cree camp on the Red Deer River. This was where Louis Piche's children were baptized. As the missionary approached the camp, Piche and others came to meet him. Rundle stated:

I met with a very warm reception. Nearly the whole of the Camp, men, women & children, I believe, came out to meet me on my approach. It was a very interesting & cheering sight to behold. They all walked in procession with their Chief at their head. The ceremony of shaking hands then, which I performed on horseback.[13]

Maskepetoon was among the group but was not yet recognized by the missionary as a future ally. Rather, Louis Piche appeared to be the one in whom Rundle could place his trust. Piche arranged for a large tent to be made available and fully supported the missionary's endeavours. A few days later, when the entire camp moved south, Piche, Maskepetoon and Rundle were with them. Easter Sunday was spent speaking to the parents of children scheduled for baptism. "I devoted some time in the morning service," Rundle said, "explaining the subj. to them. I tried to show them what was required of the parents in bringing children to have it performed."[14] Maskepetoon, and perhaps his two wives, sat with the missionary and accepted his words, and on the following day he presented two children for baptism. These were one-year-old Joseph, son of Maskepetoon and his first wife, Sussewisk, and Peter, also one year old, with Maskepetoon's second wife, Maton-now-a-cap. They were among the fifty baptisms and five marriages performed that day. Among the parents were three half-breeds who likely were part of Piche's clan. They were Pierre Cadien, Edward Burlow and Baptiste Brenow.[15]

Rundle's diary shows that the Rocky Mountain Crees in the spring of 1841 were a unified group with Piche as their leader and Maskepetoon perhaps a minor chief. Within the group were a number of family clans, but all looked to Piche as their chief. In winter, they split into family groups to follow their traplines. If several families did come together, one man was recognized as the leader and took charge. The other family heads formed his council and met on a regular basis to discuss matters of hunting, protection, disputes and other activities that could affect the group as a whole.

Rundle was pleased with his success, finding both the Crees and Blackfoot very friendly and open to his teachings. Yet he felt that more missionaries were needed while the field was still theirs. "No time should be lost," he told the Wesleyan Missionary Society, "for . . . the Roman Catholics are I think casting a jealous eye over the plains of the Saskatchewan."[16]

How right he was. For a number of years, Bishop Joseph-Norbert Provencher at Red River had been refused permission to send a priest with the boats going to Fort Edmonton. Therefore, he was surprised when Rundle and his companions were not only given transportation but also accommodation at the company forts and the use of their interpreters.

A solution to the bishop's problem came in an unexpected way. George Simpson, who was making a voyage around the world, needed a guide to take him to the foot of the Rocky Mountains. Factor John Rowand suggested Louis Piche, and in order to have him on hand when needed, Rowand invited the chief to accompany him on a trip to Red River. Once there, Piche saw the great cathedral at St. Boniface, and the memories of his father's faith came tumbling back to him. So the recent supporter of the Methodist cause in the West promptly changed his allegiance to the Catholics. On July 23, 1841, Bishop Provencher wrote to a fellow bishop in Quebec, saying:

> A Métis, bearing the name of Picher (or Pichet) and living with Indians close to the mountains, has come this year to see priests and have me promise to send one among the numerous Crees living out there. Mr. Thibault, knowledgeable in their language, instructed him as best he could with the use of Mr. Blanchet's pictorial catechism, a copy of which the man carried back with him so that he could tell his people what the Catholic priests teach, ere they accept the teachings of the Protestant

minister living in a fort not too distant from these people. I promised to send Mr. Thibault to them next Spring, on condition that this Métis would meet him half way.[17]

Piche remained in the employ of Simpson for the next three months, so he had no opportunity to introduce his new-found religion to his fellow Crees. This meant that Rundle could still carry on with his labours, unaware of what lay just over the horizon. Whenever he was at Fort Edmonton, Rundle conducted services and instructed children for baptism. Some were Metis, but most were Beaver Hills Crees under their chief Lapotac. In June, he went to Fort Pitt, and on his return he found a Rocky Mountain Cree family waiting for him, wanting to know when he would come to visit their camps again. The missionary was "much cheered by hearing such good accounts of them"[18] and promised to meet them at Gull Lake. On his way there, he met a number of Indians who accompanied him to the main camp. There were some 170 in attendance at the Sunday service, so he took the occasion to reprimand them for permitting conjuring to take place. He then turned his attention to catechizing the children and spent the next ten days teaching, singing hymns and holding services. Piche was away, but Maskepetoon likely was among the group; the missionary seldom made any mention of individuals by name in his journal, and as yet the two had not formed a friendship. Before returning to Edmonton, Rundle promised to see them again in October at Rocky Mountain House, just before they went into their winter camps.

CHAPTER SEVEN

The Wanderers

Maskepetoon and Louis Piche each set out on memorable journeys in 1841 as guides for two separate expeditions. Piche's task was to guide Sir George Simpson, governor of the Hudson's Bay Company, to the entrance to the Rockies as part of his trip around the world, while Maskepetoon was to lead a party of Red River settlers to new farming lands near the Pacific coast. Neither was known to have guided before, but their rising positions within the Rocky Mountain Crees made both of them logical people to lead such expeditions. Both knew the mountains well, having crossed them while hunting or going to war.

A month before leaving London on his epic journey, Simpson had been knighted by Queen Victoria. With a secretary at his side, his plan was to circumnavigate the globe and leave a published record befitting his new title. Arriving at Montreal in March, he and his party followed the fur-trade canoe route to Red River, where Piche and Rowand were waiting for him. Simpson commented:

> In the Spring of the year, Mr. Rowand had secured the services as guide of a man of the name of Peechee, a half breed native of the Kootonais country, and a chief of the Mountain Crees, who would be useful to us as guide. To make sure of this man's being at hand when required, Mr. Rowand took him to Red River from whence he

had returned with us; he undertook to guide us as far as the Bow River Traverse. I may here observe that this Peechee was a quiet, well conducted man, who although a half breed, had been brought up as an Indian and as he possessed some influence among the Indians in & near the Mountains, we considered it desirable to keep him with us.[1]

Instead of travelling the usual canoe route across Lake Winnipeg and up the Saskatchewan River, Simpson opted for a faster overland trip. Rowand had brought thirty horses from Edmonton for the occasion, so Piche was kept busy as a wrangler both coming and going. En route from Red River, they met a traveller who told them that they would be riding into a war zone because of new fighting between the Crees and Blackfoot. The traveller explained, "Peace having been made between the two tribes, the Crees paid a visit to the Blackfeet, who were encamped at a place called the Nose, a little to the south of Fort Pitt, for the purpose of buying horses, in payment for which they gave all they possessed, even their guns & ammunition."[2]

When the trading was finished, a horse race was held in which the Blackfoot were victorious. However, when they went to collect their winnings, one Cree refused to give up an old, worn capote that he had wagered. The Blackfoot took this as a sign of hostility and fled to their lodges. On their way, they met Piche's former leader, Crow Shoes, and killed him and two companions. The traveller said, "This was the commencement of hostilities & war parties were already ranging over the country."[3]

Although Simpson's party, carrying the Hudson's Bay Company flag, was unlikely to be mistaken for Crees, the danger always existed that some Blackfoot would view the Crees and Metis cart drivers in the party, including Piche, as fair game. A couple of days later, the party reached Fort Pitt, where they found eleven lodges of Crees camped nearby. Simpson noted, "These Crees, like all those we have previously met, were flying from the Blackfeet in consequence of the recent war which had broken out between them at the Battle of the Racecourse."[4]

Simpson visited one of the wounded Crees. A ball had struck him in the right shoulder, passed across his spine and lodged in the joint of his left shoulder. Simpson wrote, "This man had killed one Blackfoot in the fight & when he was overpowered by numbers & his party fled from the field, he lay down on his horse's back to escape being shot & was in that position that the ball struck him & took the extraordinary path in his body."[5]

Just as Simpson's party was preparing to leave, there was excitement when the fort hunters came back unexpectedly. They claimed that they had encountered a war party, presumably Blackfoot, and fired on them before retreating. "As we were about to pass through the same country," said Simpson, "this news was by no means agreeable; it did not derange our plans however, as these wars & alarms are constantly occurring in the Plains."[6]

In spite of the danger, Simpson decided to travel on the south side of the North Saskatchewan River, which he considered to be Blackfoot territory. "We should lessen the distance to Edmonton by one whole day's march," he observed.[7] The trip was made without incident until they were close to Edmonton and observed an Indian watching them from a hill. They pursued him and, instead of an enemy, found a hunter for the fort. He had just succeeded in killing a buffalo bull, a moose and an elk for the governor's dinner table.

The man proved to be Lapotac, a friend of Piche and leader of the Edmonton section of the Beaver Hills Crees. "This hunter rejoiced in the name of 'Potato,'" said Simpson. "His brother was equally blessed with the title of 'Turnip.'"[8] The Edmonton traders considered Lapotac to be a greater chief than either Piche or Maskepetoon, but the fact that he had close ties with the fort may have influenced their opinion.

Simpson described Fort Edmonton as having a martial appearance, due to its warlike customers. But what were most impressive were the paintings. "This fort, both inside and outside," he said, "is decorated with paintings and devices to suit the tastes of the savages that frequent it. Over the gateway are a most fanciful variety of vanes; but the hall, of which both the ceiling and the walls present the grandest colors and the most fantastic sculptures, absolutely rivets the astonished natives to the spot with wonder and admiration."[9]

While they were resting at Edmonton, some 350 lodges of Siksika, Blood, Peigan and Sarcee Indians came to trade. Some of their chiefs met Simpson and were given presents of tobacco and ammunition. Simpson found them to be very friendly, but he knew the situation might be different if he encountered them away from the fortified trading post. "Though we resolved to make a start to-day," he wrote, "yet we could not safely resume our journey while these Indians were hanging about the place, inasmuch as they would have given information to the approaching bands and then we should have been annoyed, and perhaps plundered, by the fellows for whole days in succession."[10] His solution was to load the party's luggage into a boat in the evening and have it taken about six miles upstream, where it was hidden. Early the next morning, July 28, the travellers slipped away from the fort, leaving their carts behind. Knowing the Blackfoot were camped south of the river, they stayed on the north side as they rode west through the woods to find the boat. There they crossed the river and rode south, keeping to the woods and away from the trails used by the plains tribes. Simpson's party included his secretary Edward Hopkins, trader John Rowand, a Mr. McIntyre, Piche and a number of servants.

Simpson had crossed the mountains before, but always up the Athabasca River and over a well-used fur-trading route west of Jasper House. On this occasion, to save time, he decided to go south to the Bow River and find a place there to cross the mountains. This is where Piche was so important to his plans.

Out on the plains, the route was clear and free of obstructions, but along their chosen path they encountered muskegs, windfalls, burned-over areas and a good deal of difficulty. In spite of these conditions, they made sixty miles the first day, right through Piche's hunting grounds. Along the way, they met Rev. Rundle, and Piche obligingly drew him a map to show the location of various lakes and streams. If there was any animosity on the part of the now-Catholic Piche, it certainly was not evident.

After two days, they reached Battle River, where Simpson commented, "The scenery, as we approached the mountains, was becoming bolder every hour. The plains were replaced by ranges of lofty hills; and we were straining our eyes to catch the first glimpse of the perpetual snows of the mighty barrier that lay in our path."[11]

The next night, they camped at Gull Lake, where they heard the sound of a musket shot echoing across the water. When the party fired an answering shot, they were soon joined by fifteen Rocky Mountain Crees (who Simpson called "Mr. Rundle's Crees"), with Piche's relatives among them. They were almost starving and had only scraps of elk meat to share. The encounter gave Simpson the opportunity to see for himself the position that Piche held within his Cree community:

> They remained with us two or three hours, smoking and chatting; and our guide, Peechee, being a great man among them, they formed a circle around him, whistling and talking and listening for, notwithstanding the taciturnity of savages among whites, they are, when by themselves, the most loquacious of mortals, apparently regarding idle gossip as one of the grand objects of life.[12]

The next day, Simpson crossed the Blindman River, passed Sylvan Lake and proceeded onto the prairies, which proved to be much more inviting than the muskegs and fire-burned areas they had experienced since leaving Edmonton. As they rode through bushes after crossing the Red Deer River, the caravan scattered when they suddenly encountered a war party of Sarcees. Simpson wrote:

> The savages appeared to be taken as much by surprise as ourselves and, in a moment, the guns were uncovered on both sides; a halt, of course, was made, and a parley ensued, the subject of discussion being the present war between the Crees and Blackfeet ... With the aid of a little tobacco and ammunition, we prolonged the conversation for a sufficient length of time to allow all our people to get fairly out of sight; and we parted from our fickle customers on the most friendly terms.[13]

Fearing a possible raid on their horse herd, Simpson took his men southwest and crossed the steep banks of a stream in order to put as much room as possible between them and the Sarcees. They travelled quickly for the rest of the day and camped that night on high ground, where they had good visibility. The next morning, although they saw tracks, no enemy Indians appeared. To be safe, the party pushed on, entering the pine forests of the foothills. Piche led them down a trail which, "besides being obstructed by fallen timber, was so narrow as seriously to impede the pack-horses."[14] They hoped to find game near Grease Creek, a tributary of the Little Red Deer, but had no luck and were forced to rely on their scanty supplies of pemmican and dried meat.

At Grease Creek, Simpson gained his first view of the snow-capped Rockies, which to him looked like clouds on the edge of the horizon. This also was the place where the topography changed dramatically. Piche took them along an old Stoney trail that led them straight through swamps where horses sank up to their bellies and sometimes dislodged their packs as they fought to free themselves. When they did strike dry ground, the pine forests were thick and almost impassable in places. Near the end of the day, they finally broke out of the tangled forest and came upon a long open valley. Simpson liked what he saw:

> We obtained one of those majestic views found only midst mountain fastness. As far as the eye could reach, mountain rose above mountain, while at our feet lay a valley surrounded by an amphitheatre of cold, bare, rugged peaks. In these crags, which were almost perpendicular, neither could tree plant its roots nor goat find a resting-place.[15]

Piche knew exactly where he was going on the first leg of the journey; he was bound for his own camp to see how his family was faring. The next day, they reached Lake Minnewanka, which was described as the "guide's usual home,"[16] but Piche was doomed to disappointment, for his wife and children were gone, likely driven away by a shortage of food. Simpson named the lake in Piche's honour, but somehow the name became lost in the sands of time. In 1888, the federal government named it Minnewanka. To partially rectify the omission, Tombstone Mountain, about fourteen kilometres northeast of Banff, was renamed Mount Peechee.[17]

While camped, Piche told a story about an incident that had occurred on the approach to the lake. A Cree who the party had seen near Gull Lake the previous day had been hunting in the area with his family when they were surrounded by five young warriors from an enemy tribe. The Cree feared they all would be killed and urged his women to surrender. His wife, however, responded that she would defend herself to the end. To make the point, she took her husband's gun and shot the leading attacker. The husband, shamed by his wife's bravery, killed two more enemies with arrows. A fourth dashed towards the woman with a raised tomahawk, but he stumbled and fell and the woman stabbed him to death. The fifth warrior, seeing the carnage, shot the man in the arm and then fled the scene.

The next day, the Simpson party reached the Bow River, where they saw the impressive Cascade Falls, which Simpson said were known as The Spout. When they reached a site near the present town of Banff, Piche's work was supposed to be finished. According to Simpson:

> In expectation of our adopting that [southern] route, horses were to have been sent from Colvile to meet us at what are called the Kootonais Lakes [Windermere], & a guide was to be despatched to await us at the Bow River Transverse, who would thence conduct us across the Mountains to Fort Colvile. All therefore that was necessary to be done on our part, was to take horses & a guide to Bow River, where Berland (the Colvile guide) was to await our arrival.[18]

But Berland was nowhere in sight. After Simpson's men had searched the region without any luck, it was left to Piche to lead them over the Rockies. Fortunately, they had chosen a man who knew the country well.

They crossed the Bow River on rafts and camped for the night. The next morning, with still no sign of Berland, they travelled about six miles west until they reached Healy Creek. This route, Piche told them, would lead them directly to the height of land. By riding when they could and walking when they couldn't, they reached the summit after seven hours of hard travel. This point was later called Simpson Pass, as he was the first white man known to have traversed it. At the summit on August 4, Simpson wrote:

> We breakfasted on the level isthmus, which did not exceed fourteen paces in width, filling our kettles for this our lonely meal at once from the crystal sources of the Columbia and the Saskatchewan, while these welling feeders of two opposite oceans, murmuring over their beds of mossy stones as if to bid each other a long farewell, could hardly fail to attune our minds to the sublimity of the scene.[19]

Piche led the party down the slope to innumerable streams that had to be forded. They crossed one rivulet twenty-three times before lunch, the stream gaining in strength and size until it finally exulted in the name of Simpson River. Piche advised them to spend the night at a small lake, but they found it was dry, and men had to be sent back for water. "We were obliged to hoard up every morsel of food we had with us," Simpson wrote, "as in the absence of a guide it was impossible to say how long we might be finding our way to Fort Colvile by this new and unknown route."[20] That whole day the party went only twenty miles, much slower than Simpson's usual rapid rate of travel.

The following day was even worse. The terrain was rugged, the rock-strewn path leading through bogs, tangled forests and fallen trees. Four hours into the day, they had gone only two miles, but later in the afternoon they broke into a clearing and had a meal at the confluence of the Simpson and Vermilion rivers. From there they proceeded southwest to the Columbia, passing Radium Hot Springs, which Simpson called Red Rock, and arrived at the head of Lake Windermere, where they found a pictographic note from the long-lost Edward Berland. Simpson wrote:

> We speedily interpreted this welcome letter to mean that Edward Berland was awaiting us with a band of twenty-seven horses at the point where our river received a tributary before expanding itself into two consecutive lakes. As the spot in question was supposed to be within a few miles of us, Peechee was dispatched to secure our phantom guide.[21]

From all indications, Piche knew this country well, for it was the hunting grounds of the Flatbow and Kootenai Indians with whom he had fought and traded. Although Berland was now the guide, Piche continued to travel with the Simpson party. They passed a Flatbow lodge, visited Fairmont Hot Springs and came to a camp of Kootenais near the end of the day.

Simpson was not impressed with them. "They were a miserable set of beings," he said, "small, decrepit and dirty."[22] Their chief, Grande Queue, had no particular love for the traders. Many years earlier, they had taken his son, Kootonais Pelly, to school in Red River, where he had died.

After a couple of days, the party met Archibald McDonald, the trader at Fort Colvile, and a new guide, William Pion, who was to replace the ailing Berland. Piche continued to travel with them, although his role of guide was now over. A few days later, they met a chief named Charlo, who had come from Fort Colvile with supplies, and as they travelled southward, they encountered bands of Kootenais and Pend d'Oreilles. At last, on August 18, they reached the Colvile valley, which held the Hudson's Bay fort and cultivated fields of wheat and corn. Simpson described the fort as large and "enclosed with pickets and bastions. The houses are of cedar, neatly built and well finished, and the whole place bears a cleaner and more comfortable aspect than any establishment between itself and Red River."[23]

Piche had led the party through some seemingly impassable country, and Simpson was happy they came through it without injury. "We had great cause to be thankful that no serious accident had occurred to man or beast," he said, "more particularly as we had traversed every kind of ground, rocks and swamps, rugged mountains and rapid rivers, tangled brush and burning forests."[24] In spite of the challenging terrain, Simpson was quite satisfied with the selection of Piche's route. In gratitude, he presented the Cree with a telescope and paid him handsomely for his services.

On August 21, the day after Simpson continued down the Columbia on his round-the-world voyage, Archibald McDonald wrote the following letter to John Harriott at Fort Edmonton:

> The man called Piché is about leaving us to day for your quarter via the Kootanais & the R[ocky] Mountain House.

THE WANDERERS ◆ 83

The Memorandum left me by Mr. Rowand, of the old man's wants, has been attended to the letter. He would not however encumber himself with the goods he was offered as part payment for his trip. What he did take are as per enclosed note. He has a very excellent horse for himself & two others to be made over to the Establishment.²⁵

Piche was back in his home territory by September and ready to begin his proselytizing on behalf of the Catholic Church.²⁶

Now it was Maskepetoon's turn. Earlier, when Simpson and his party were crossing the plains in July, they had caught up with a slow-moving train of settlers, carts and horses. Simpson noted, "Each family had two or three carts, together with bands of horses, cattle and dogs ... As they marched in single file their cavalcade extended above a mile long."²⁷ This caravan was an ambitious project, supported by the Hudson's Bay Company, to send settlers to the Oregon country on the west coast. Its leader, James Sinclair, was an English half-breed who had been educated in Scotland and later became a free trader at Red River. He soon became the unofficial leader of the Metis there and took a seat on the Council of Assiniboia. However, he also gained the ill will of the local Hudson's Bay Company governor, who opposed any independent trading that was not controlled by the company. Some of the unrest among the Metis at the settlement was also laid at Sinclair's door. This led to a showdown about free trade, and when Sinclair petitioned the Hudson's Bay Company on behalf of the Metis, he was rebuffed by the governor. He also was threatened with the withdrawal of company services, such as the use of ships to transport his goods to and from Britain.

About this time, Simpson came up with the idea of sending Metis settlers to the west coast to counteract the impact of American immigration on Hudson's Bay territory. Simpson said that settlers dispatched from Red River would be given assistance in settling in the Cowlitz, Willamette and Nisqually areas to establish a British presence. Another benefit of the expedition would be to clear Red River of some of its Metis dissidents, including Sinclair. The leadership of the expedition was offered to Sinclair, and he accepted. Some twenty-three families[28] agreed to make the trek; all were Metis except for three Englishmen.[29] To assist them in their journey, the Hudson's Bay Company provided each family with £10, adequate supplies and the promise of more provisions at each fort they visited on their way. At the end of the journey, they would be given houses, barns, ploughed fields and other amenities.

When they set out on June 3, 1841, the caravan consisted of eighty people,[30] as well as Red River carts, oxen, horses, cows and innumerable dogs. Although routes across the prairies to the various Hudson's Bay Company forts were well known, Sinclair decided he needed a guide, particularly when travelling through Blackfoot territory. His choice was his brother-in-law, Jimmy Jock Bird, a man well known to both the Crees and the Blackfoot. Bird agreed to take the party as far as the Bow River Traverse, near the present site of Banff, where another guide would take them across the mountains.

Bird was a controversial character. The son of a Hudson's Bay Company officer, he became an interpreter and was sent to live with the Blackfoot Indians. However, he broke with the Hudson's Bay Company in 1830 and joined the Americans at their new posts on the Missouri River, where he wielded great influence over the Peigan tribe. He was with the Peigans a year later when they killed a prominent American trader, so he returned to the British. Thereafter he was distrusted by both sides. He also interpreted for Rundle and for Father Pierre-Jean De Smet, but his relationship with both ended in disagreement. Bird caught up with Sinclair east of Fort Carlton and remained with them for the rest of their prairie journey.

The party reached Carlton on June 23, where they remained for two days while they traded horses and stocked up on provisions. Near the fort, they came across a battleground where a fight had recently taken place between the Blackfoot and Crees. One of the travellers commented, "We kept men on guard, night and day. War parties were on every side. We now began to believe what others had told us, that we should never get through. Still, we forced our way on, and, on the 10th of July, crossed the Saskatchewan river to Fort Pitt."[31]

Like Simpson, the Sinclair party saw the wounded Crees who had fled to the fort for protection after their ill-fated fight with the Blackfoot.

Travelling on the north side of the North Saskatchewan River to avoid the plains tribes, they arrived at Fort Edmonton on July 20 and, after a brief stop, proceeded south with Bird guiding them safely near the edge of the plains. They reached the Bow River near the site of Old Bow Fort, where they camped for a few days waiting for two of the Flett brothers, members of the party who had gone missing and were feared killed by Blackfoot. When he rejoined the group, John Flett told what had happened:

> While out hunting we were surrounded by hostile Indians. We concealed ourselves until dark, and in the twilight swam the cold, swift river. Having stripped off our outer clothing, we fastened it on to our horses and plunged in. The water was cold, icy cold, the river was very swift and about 200 yards wide. Twice we swam the river, and after wandering about for two days, we at last reached camp in safety.[32]

Bird told Sinclair that they could not take their carts through the mountains, so they abandoned them and packed everything on their horses and oxen. The horses took to the trail readily enough, but the oxen, unaccustomed to this mode of travel, were frightened and stampeded. "Then what a sight," said Flett, "oxen bellowing, kicking, running, horses neighing, rearing, plunging, children squalling, women crying, men swearing, shouting and laughing; while the air seemed full of blankets, kettles, sacks of pots, pans and jerked buffalo."[33] At last, the oxen settled down and passively entered the wooded foothills as Bird led them westward along an old Indian trail. Unlike the route past Lake Minnewanka chosen by Piche, Bird went straight up the Bow River, past Ghost River. After two days, they reached the Bow River Traverse, where they were met by Maskepetoon.

Most likely Bird chose Maskepetoon as their guide. As an interpreter, Bird knew all the local leaders and would have selected the man who was most qualified to make the mountain journey. Bird now left, "bidding adieu to his friends and relatives."[34]

With Maskepetoon in charge, the party took only nine days to cross the Rockies. Wrote John Flett:

> On the 5th of August we reached the summit, and found ourselves on a small plateau. Here we saw a huge snowdrift whose melted waters formed three little rills; one running east through a deep canyon, and finding its way through the Saskatchewan into Hudson's Bay; another running southeast into the Missouri, and at last in the gulf, while the third one sent its waters through those 'continuous woods where rolls the Oregon.'[35]

Geographers have identified the summit as White Man's Pass, perhaps named for the three white men who were part of the Sinclair group. To reach this location, Maskepetoon may have led them up the Spray River to the pass and down the other side via Cross River to the Kootenay River. The fact that men, women, children, horses and oxen were able to make the trip in a little more than a week is a clear indication that the route was not as difficult as Simpson's. In fact, Simpson commented that Maskepetoon "carried them through a little to the southward [of our route] by a pass infinitely superior to ours."[36]

From the Kootenay River, on the west side of the Rockies, Maskepetoon led the Sinclair party along the valley until they struck a westward-flowing stream that took them over a height of land and into an impressive cut through the mountains called Red Rock Gorge. It was later named Sinclair Canyon in honour of the party's indefatigable leader. Travelling through this shadowy, narrow canyon, Maskepetoon took the travellers to Radium Hot Springs and to the open valley of the Columbia River. South past Lake Windermere, the expedition reached Canal Flats, following approximately the same route used by Simpson a few weeks earlier. According to Flett:

> To avoid some marshy land which lay in our course, we climbed the projecting point of a high mountain . . . Then our route lay through a flat, marshy country until we came to a deep, sluggish river, called by the Indians Paddling river. Then our course lay to the southwest, through a rich country with plenty of grass, until we came to Lake Pend d'Oreille.[37]

By this time, the expedition was running low on food, so one of the party, Joseph Cline, was sent ahead with a local Indian guide to Fort Colvile for supplies. He returned with some mouldy flour, bran and dried peas—enough to take them to the fort. When they reached Colvile, Sinclair was greeted by Archibald McDonald, chief trader, who had been a friend of his father. The fort itself was the first sign of civilization he had seen since leaving Edmonton. The stockade held nineteen buildings and boasted a flour mill, sawmill, dairy, blacksmith and carpentry shops, and men's quarters. It also had one hundred and thirty acres of land under cultivation. McDonald noted Sinclair's arrival at the fort:

> I am happy to find the poor Red River imigrants [sic] are safely arrived in this neighbourhood. Mr. James Sinclair left them the other day wending their way for Spokan &

came in here himself to see me & to make further arrangements for the prosecution of the journey downwards. He starts again today to rejoin them with more provisions. The party in all is now accommodated with 22 horses & two of our people are to go on till they meet the horses expected from Walla Walla.[38]

At this point, the party temporarily split up, with some of the older men and women travelling downriver by boat, while the horses and cattle were driven overland towards the Cascades. The others, including Sinclair and Maskepetoon, went by horseback to Walla Walla.

McDonald wrote to the trader at Walla Walla, saying that he wanted the settlers who arrived there to be sent downstream without delay. He did not explain, but the likely reason was that the territory was in an unsettled state and trouble with the Cayuse and other tribes was feared.

By this time, Maskepetoon was no longer familiar with the country, but Sinclair had taken a liking to him and invited him to accompany him all the way to the west coast. He was probably with the leader when they visited Colvile and was later referred to as Sinclair's "own Indian."[39] He was by Sinclair's side when they crossed the arid plains and reached the adobe buildings that constituted Fort Walla Walla. Here the situation was so bad that Indians were no longer permitted to enter the fort, but traded through a small opening at the gate.

"We arrived at Fort Walla Walla on the 4th of October," recalled Flett. "On the next day the fort was [accidentally] burned. Our party assisted the men of the fort to save their goods. The Indians were so numerous that it was not deemed safe to camp there, but we traveled down the Columbia until midnight."[40] Maskepetoon's instincts as a warrior came to the fore as they cautiously made their way downriver. His enemies may have been new to him, but he was prepared to do battle just as he had done with the Blackfoot tribes.

At daybreak, no enemies were seen, so the party continued on its way and in four days reached the gorge at The Dalles and stopped at the Methodist mission. Also in the area was a Catholic priest, who was labouring among the local Indians. While they camped for several days to rest their horses, the priest learned of Maskepetoon's presence and sought his conversion. The Cree chief politely refused and claimed his friendship was with the Methodists. When the local Methodist missionary, Daniel Lee, heard about the rebuff, he invited Maskepetoon into his mission and learned of his friendship with Rundle. Lee had been sent out by the American Missionary Society of the Methodist Episcopal Church, while Rundle was from the British Wesleyan Missionary Society, but both men shared the same goals in working among the Indians. Lee gave Maskepetoon a copy of the New Testament, which he carried with him for many years. Lee also wrote to Rundle, saying:

> There is an Indian with Mr. Sinclair who has received instruction from you. He had an interview with one of the Priests who labored to shake his faith in what you told him but he appears firm. I told him we had the Bible and what that taught us, we believed, &c.[41]

The Sinclair party made the dangerous river crossing at The Dalles, losing one horse by drowning, but everyone got through safely. The long and arduous journey ended at Fort Vancouver on October 13. Located on the northwestern side of the Columbia River in what is now Washington State, the fort was surrounded by cedar forests and was ninety miles inland from the Pacific. Some forty buildings were enclosed within a twenty-foot-high stockade, with twelve-pound cannon and formidable bastions providing protection. There were officers' quarters, men's quarters, warehouses and even a schoolhouse and chapel. This was the headquarters for the entire Hudson's Bay Company trade on the northwest coast.

Sir George Simpson was away when the settlers arrived, but on his return nine days later, Sinclair, Maskepetoon and the others met with him, as well as other notable figures of the fur trade—Peter Skene Ogden, John McLoughlin and James Douglas.

Sinclair's meeting with Simpson was said to have been a stormy one. According to John Flett, Simpson said:

> Our agreement we cannot fulfill; we have neither horses, nor barns, nor fields for you, and you are at liberty to go where you please. You may go with the California trappers; we will give you a fitout as we give others. If you go over the river to the American side we will help you none... If you go to the Cowlitz we will help you some. To those who will go to Nisqually we will fulfill our agreement.[42]

The settlers were disgruntled with the news. Joseph Kline left immediately for California with the trappers, while seven families went to Cowlitz and the rest to Nisqually. Sinclair decided to search the region to see if he could find a suitable place other than the ones offered by the Hudson's Bay Company. He arranged to take the steamer *Beaver* to search the coastline and took Maskepetoon with him. Maskepetoon was probably the first western Cree ever to set foot on an ocean vessel. The ship, owned by the Hudson's Bay Company, had been built in England six years earlier. It was a hundred feet long and twenty feet wide and was powered by two paddlewheels, one on each side, and carried four brass cannons. Maskepetoon had never seen anything like it before. He boarded the ship with Sinclair and rode up the coast as far as Whidbey Island, near the present Mount Vernon, Washington. Sinclair examined possible sites along the route, but as Flett recalled, "The Indians were found so numerous and war-like, that it was not deemed safe to settle in that region."[43]

One can only imagine what Maskepetoon thought as the paddlewheeler steamed along the coastline, stopping at villages where the inhabitants were belligerent and so numerous that they could easily have overwhelmed the ship. At the end of the journey, Maskepetoon asked Sinclair to write out an account of the trip; otherwise he would never be believed by his people back home.[44] Simpson learned about the request and described the situation in his own colourful style:

> After the arrival of the emigrants from Red River, their guide, a Cree of the name of Bras Croche, took a short trip in the Beaver. When asked what he thought of her— "Don't ask me," was his reply: "I cannot speak; my friends will say that I tell lies when I let them know what I have seen; Indians are fools and know nothing; I can see that the iron machinery makes the ship to go, but I cannot see what makes the iron machinery itself to go."
>
> Bras Croche, though very intelligent, and, like all the Crees, partially civilized, was nevertheless so full of doubt and wonder, that he would not leave the vessel till he got a certificate to the effect, that he had been on board of a ship which needed neither sails nor paddlers. Though not one of his countrymen would understand a word of what was written, yet the most sceptical among them would not dare to question the truth of a story which had a document in its favour.
>
> A savage stands nearly as much in awe of paper, pen, and ink, as of steam itself; and, if he once puts his cross to any writing, he has rarely been known to violate the engagement which such writing is supposed to embody or sanction. To him the very look of black and white is a powerful "medicine."[45]

One might speculate that the New Testament from David Lee and the letter from Sinclair made Maskepetoon particularly aware of the importance of writing and of the power it gave to those who possessed that talent. It was a lesson he would not forget.

Simpson raised the possibility with Sinclair of assembling another group of settlers from Red River, hoping the problems that beset the first emigrants would be resolved. With the influx of Americans to the region, it was of paramount importance to maintain Hudson's Bay Company and British control.

Following Simpson's instructions, Sinclair and Maskepetoon left Fort Vancouver in early December in hopes of crossing the Rocky Mountains before the snows blocked the trails. However, Sinclair had become exhausted by the gruelling trip, the efforts of placing the settlers on their lands and dealing with an uncooperative Chief Factor John McLoughlin. When they reached the Methodist mission at The Dalles, Sinclair became ill but insisted on pressing on. Although waited on by the ever-helpful Maskepetoon, it still took him a week to travel the fifty-five miles from the mission to Fort Colvile. When they arrived on December 17, Sinclair was immediately put to bed, told that the snows had come early, that the weather was becoming bitterly cold and there was little likelihood of crossing the mountains before spring. Eleven days later, however, Sinclair felt he was well enough to try, so he set out again. With him was his friend Maskepetoon, an Indian from the fort and an employee named LaGrise, who was supposed to take important dispatches across the mountains en route to Red River. According to Chief Trader McDonald at Fort Colvile:

> On the 28th of last month, Mr. Sinclair left this place in prosecution of his trip for east side, as well arranged for the undertaking as it was possible to be, but on account of the unusual depth of snow already on the ground, and the quantity of provisions it was indispensable to carry in the intermediate span to the next Estabt., he was reluctantly compelled to relinquish all hopes of

getting thro' the journey and accordingly was back here again his fifth day.⁴⁶

Writing to James Douglas, McDonald explained further:

> [They] had horses for the first two days to the foot of the mountains, but on equipping themselves there with all their train, their progress, even with the help of two extra Indians, became exceedingly slow, & indeed the journey altogether hopeless: the 4 miles they made that day [on foot] they retraced to the horses the next, & at the end of the fifth day were again back to us.⁴⁷

In fact, it was Sinclair's illness as much as the weather that drove them back, and when he reached Fort Colvile, tired, sick and freezing, he was to remain there until spring. But the dispatches still needed to be taken across the mountains, so the task was entrusted to the brave and dependable Maskepetoon. He would be accompanied by LaGrise with horses and supplies as far as the Tobacco Plains, then set out on his own on foot while the other man would return to the fort with the horses. As McDonald told James Douglas:

> The importance attached to Sir George's packet for Red River induced us to make a second attempt by the two men only, encumbered with nothing but their own scanty allowance of provisions for 15 days to take them to Tobacco Plains.⁴⁸

McDonald then gave instructions to Patrick McKensie, who was camped at the Tobacco Plains:

> You will afford Bras Croche every facility to get on with the packet and even if it be necessary let Lagrise himself continue on with him for some days till he falls in with

some one of his own people that will accompany him to the [Rocky] Mountain House. Mr. Rowand's man [LaGrise] however must absolutely be down here with the Canoes.[49]

Considering Maskepetoon's intimate knowledge of the mountains and his ability to travel more quickly alone, it is unlikely that LaGrise accompanied him. Rather, with Simpson's precious packet and a small quantity of dried meat, he successfully conquered the snow-clogged trails and the towering mountain pass before making his way safely down the mountain to the Bow River. From there, it was an easy run to Rocky Mountain House, where the packet was turned over to trader Harriott and dispatched to Fort Edmonton.

In his four months of travel, Maskepetoon's conquests were legion. He had shown white people a new crossing of the Rocky Mountains that resulted in their discovery of White Man's Pass. He went to the Pacific coast and travelled on a steamship—the first in his tribe to do so. He met such personages of the fur trade as Sir George Simpson, John McLoughlin, James Douglas and Peter Skene Ogden. And he made a midwinter crossing of the Rockies to carry dispatches for the Hudson's Bay Company. As Maskepetoon returned to his family and followers in the shadow of the Rocky Mountains, these acts undoubtedly had elevated his position with the fur traders and his own people.

CHAPTER EIGHT

Battle for Souls

While Maskepetoon was away, Louis Piche had begun to proselytize among his fellow Crees based upon his understanding of what he had heard in St. Boniface. In January 1842, trader Harriott learned of Piche's defection from the Wesleyans and the effect it was having upon the Rocky Mountain Crees. Writing to James Evans, the missionary at Norway House, he said:

> I wish I could say something favourable of this quarter but I am afraid . . . nothing satisfactory occurred in my trip to the mountain [Rocky Mountain House]. I only saw one Indian and from him I learnt that much of our friend Mr. Rundle's labour had been upset by that fellow Piche. I did all I could to convince him of this Error and have some hopes that it may have some effect upon them all.[1]

Meanwhile, Piche waited for the arrival of the priest whom Bishop Provencher had promised to send. The agreement was that Piche would meet him halfway.

There is no question that the Catholics were concerned that the Hudson's Bay Company had permitted Methodist missionaries to occupy their forts at Moose Factory, Norway House and Fort Edmonton. The editor of *Missions du Diocèse de Québec* stated:

> His Excellency, Bishop of Juliopolis [Provencher] announced to us [last year] that three Wesleyan ministers had been seen in the territory which was under his care; his Excellency expressed the hope that their predications would not achieve any success amongst the Indians . . . there is still hope that the light of the gospel will penetrate into the numerous nations of Indians to whom it was until now unknown, in spite of all the efforts of the enemies of the truth.[2]

The missionary designated for the Fort Edmonton area was Jean-Baptiste Thibault, a Quebec priest who had come to Red River in 1833 and was conversant in the Cree language. He set out from St. Boniface on April 30, 1842, and after an arduous journey, reached Edmonton on June 19. However, Piche was not on hand as promised and was nowhere to be found. The priest lingered around the fort for a month, baptizing many Metis, some of whom had previously "embraced the Wesleyan errors" of Rundle.[3] Thibault said that Rundle was dismayed upon his arrival. "Great was his anger at seeing the arrival of a cassock," the priest wrote, "as he knew of the magical effect this garment had on the minds of the Indians."[4] Rundle left no doubts about his reaction: "Reached the Fort early in the morning & found a Popish Priest there. My feelings can be better imagined than described . . . found that the Priest had made almost a dead sweep excepting the English. When will this system of lying vanities end?"[5]

By July 25, with Piche still missing, Thibault decided to go in search of him. With Gabriel Dumont as his guide and extra horses provided by Rowand, he followed a southwesterly course towards the Rocky Mountains. He wrote:

> After advancing for four days, we reached Gull Lake, where we found five Métis families who were very receptive to my teachings, and who made their confession.

> After four days of religious exercises, I left them with great regret, and a well marked path led me to the lodge of another Métis, named Paul Durand ... The following day I sent my guide in search of the Cree, who did not seem to be very far away. He came back two days later, accompanied by three Indians who invited me to visit those of their nation.[6]

From their camp, the priest continued on his journey, making a difficult crossing of the Red Deer River, and in another two days met a party of Metis who were going across the mountains to the Columbia River. They sent a message to Louis Piche, who arrived the following day with fifteen followers. The next morning, they set out on another day's march and finally reached Dog Pound Creek and a camp of sixty lodges, which Thibault said was made up of several bands. This was probably the entire Rocky Mountain Cree tribe and, as such, would have included Maskepetoon. Thibault wrote:

> I spent twelve days in the midst of this small group of people, busy from morning till night explaining to them the mysteries of our ancient religion, hearing confessions; and I had a hard time to take a few moments to pray and take my meals ... All of these Indians had already received a few instructions from the Methodists. A few were very attached to this sect, especially the bigamous ones ... I baptised a good number of children on this consoling mission.[7]

When Thibault left the Cree camp, Louis Piche accompanied him on the six-day return journey to Edmonton. There the priest continued to preach and baptize until he finally departed for Red River on September 18. He had been in the West for only three months, but in this time he had baptized 353 persons, mostly children, and performed twenty marriages, mostly

Metis.[8] In all, his missionary efforts were a decided blow to Rundle's work.

Not all Crees accepted the teachings of the priest. People like Maskepetoon and Lapotac chose to remain with the Methodists. Others were confused and went to Harriott for advice. He noted, "A good number of Crees kept aloof until I arrived to get my opinion upon the subject and you will naturally suppose I did not give it in favor of Mr. Thibault."[9] As time went on, Rundle found more and more parishioners who had stayed with him or, having succumbed to the excitement of Thibault's visit, lost interest once the priest left the region.

To what extent did the Crees understand Methodism and Catholicism and the differences between them? Probably not at all. What they understood was that two white men, two "medicine men" of considerable influence with the traders, had come among them and spoken of spiritual matters. Perhaps many of the Biblical stories would have been incomprehensible to them, but they did know about prayers, singing and mystical powers. Baptism could be compared to an elder blessing a child and painting his face to give good health and a long life.

As a result of this lack of knowledge, some confused interpretations of Christianity arose. For example, Maskepetoon told artist Paul Kane about an Indian who faced the problem of Christianity versus his native religion. Kane wrote:

> He told us that there was a tradition in his tribe of one of them having become a Christian, and was very good, and did all that he ought; and that when he died he was taken up to the white man's heaven, where everything was very good and very beautiful, and all were happy amongst their friends and relatives who had gone before them, and where they had everything that the white man loves and longs for.
>
> But the Indian could not share their joy and pleasure, for all was strange to him, and he met none of the spirits

of his ancestors, and there was none to welcome him, no hunting nor fishing, nor any of those joys in which he used to delight, and his spirit grew sad. Then the Great Manitou called him, and asked him, "Why art thou sad in this beautiful heaven which I have made for your joy and happiness?" and the Indian told him that he sighed for the company of the spirits of his relations, and that he felt alone and sorrowful. So the Great Manitou told him that he could not send him to the Indian heaven, as he had, whilst on earth, chosen this one, but that as he had been a very good man, he would send him back to earth again, and give him another chance.[10]

Father Pierre-Jean De Smet, when speaking to Crees and Stoneys at Rocky Mountain House in 1845, was told a similar story by an Indian who claimed that he had died:

> Immediately after my death I repaired to the heaven of the white men, or Christians, where the Great Spirit and Jesus Christ dwell, but they refused to admit me on account of my red skin. I then went to the country where the souls of my ancestors are, and there, too, I was refused admittance on account of my baptism. I am, therefore, come back to this earth, to renounce the promises I made in baptism and resume my medicine bag, hoping to expiate my former error.[11]

These stories circulated throughout the Cree nation and to adjacent tribes, causing many to continue in their attachment to their traditional religion and to "turn a deaf ear to the instructions of their worthy missionary."[12]

The Crees were aware that white people respected these preachers, so they believed their words must possess considerable spiritual power. But in choosing between Christianity and native religion, there were several other factors to consider, not the least of which was that many Metis already were Christians and mostly all of those were Catholic. This would strongly influence some Cree families, particularly those with Metis connections. Then there were the personalities of the preachers to be considered, the sincerity they exuded and their diligence in labouring among the people. Many had already responded positively to Rundle's efforts.

As early as 1843, the Rocky Mountain Crees were singing hymns, reciting a Cree version of the Lord's Prayer and, as Rundle said, "are accustomed to assemble themselves together for public worship on Sundays, even when absent from the Fort and scattered abroad in the woods."[13] As years went on, the knowledge of Christianity grew and along with it the sincerity of the conversions. However, none of the early missionaries claimed that conversions had taken place. And as far as Edmonton chief factor John Rowand was concerned, none of the missionaries was really welcome. "The worse thing for the trade," he wrote, "is those ministers & Priests; the natives will never work half so well now; they like praying & singing."[14]

The whirlwind visit of Thibault was highly successful among the French Metis. Within the Rocky Mountain Crees, however, only the direct followers of Louis Piche appeared to have remained steadfastly Catholic over the passing months. Thibault did not remain among them, as did Rundle, and thus his influence waned. As Rundle told Sir George Simpson, "Nearly the whole ... of the french half caste population have submitted themselves to the teaching of the Priest but I am glad to state that the greater part of the Indians inhabiting the woods remain still within the pale of Protestantism."[15]

Meanwhile, Rundle embarked upon a new venture that had a profound effect on Maskepetoon. His superior, James Evans, had perfected a simple system for writing in the Cree language. Through the use of syllabics, it was possible to translate religious or other works and for persons to communicate with each other in Cree. A historian described Evans' system:

He used a variety of triangles, angles, and pot-hooks—up, down, left, and right—to depict the thirty-six open vowel sounds which largely constitute the musical language of the Cree. Thus, an acute angle with the open angle up, down, left, and right represented "pay, pe, po, pah" respectively. In addition to these systems, Evans used a number of accent-like marks to indicate consonants used as terminals.[16]

Thus, Maskepetoon's name was rendered: L-shape ("Ma"), small inverted C ("s"), P-shape ("ki"), inverted V ("pi"), reverse C-shape ("to"), and small reverse C-shape ("n"). Hence: "Ma-s-ki-pi-to-n."

On October 30, 1841, Evans arrived in Edmonton to teach Rundle and Harriott how to use the system. He also brought with him copies of a Cree hymn book that came from his printing press. Evans spent two weeks teaching the system, copying texts and translating passages of the New Testament and the morning service into Cree. He then left the two men to continue the translating process.

Syllabics opened up a whole new world for Maskepetoon. He had come to appreciate the value and power of the written word from his trip to Fort Vancouver. Now it would be within his grasp to use the magic writing himself, either for reading or writing. Because of the "worldliness" he had acquired, he was among the first among the Rocky Mountain Crees to have access to syllabics, likely through his friend Harriott.

After a terribly cold winter, during which some people starved to death, the spring of 1843 brought warmth back to the prairies and woodlands. Violent warfare had erupted on the plains again between the Crees and Blackfoot, so the Rocky Mountain group stayed close to their traditional hunting grounds. During the summer, Rundle remained at Edmonton until the Blackfoot tribes had traded and left. On August 4, he set out for a pre-arranged meeting with the Rocky Mountain Crees south of the Red Deer River. Rundle passed Gull Lake, and when he reached the Crees, "found a good leather tent for my reception, prepared by my old friend [Maskepetoon]. In the evg. held prayers. About 23 tents in place."[17]

Rundle's "old friend" comment is interesting, as there is no evidence in his journal of any previous contact with Maskepetoon, other than baptizing some of his children. One can only speculate as to the nature of the contacts. In any case, the day after his arrival, Rundle baptized another son, John. The following day, disaster struck the camp. Louis Piche and a son were gambling with the sons of Paul Cayen, two half-Blackfoot Metis in Piche's band, when an argument broke out. Rundle described the scene:

> A day of horror! . . . Two murders committed in the morning near my tent, father [Louis Piche] & son *shot dead* by two half caste. What a shock to my feelings to be near such awful scenes. It arose from a dispute respecting gambling. The elder of the two was the son of a Canadian & an Indian woman. He came, in the morning, near the tents of the murderers, carrying an axe. His son was with him bearing a gun which I learnt afterwards was not loaded. The father was shot through the head whilst scuffling with an Indian for the axe & the son almost at the same moment was shot thro' the breast. The former never spoke afterwards, but the latter ran a few paces towards the tent saying only . . . "They have killed me."[18]

Rundle buried the two men in one grave, and the whole camp moved away from the awful scene. However, the missionary was disturbed when the killers, fleeing the wrath of the Piche family, took refuge in Maskepetoon's lodge. As leader of the camp, the chief could provide sanctuary, either until the matter was resolved by the payment of gifts to the dead men's family, or until they could safely get away. Tradition or not, Rundle spent an uncomfortable night with the two murderers.

Louis Piche had provided strong leadership to the Rocky Mountain Crees and shown the benefits of trapping and working closely with the fur-trading companies. His death had a number of far-reaching results. The Catholics lost a man who had preached on their behalf and gained firm support for the Catholic Church within his following. Piche's children, including Bob Tail and Ermine Skin, were too young at the time of their father's death to assume leadership of the band. As a family descendant recalled, "After Piche died they had no leader so some of his people went to Maskepetoon. They stayed with him for a while until they recovered, and then Bob Tail had his own people."[19]

Maskepetoon now became the acknowledged leader of the Rocky Mountain Crees. The band was made up of a number of families, each having its own leader. When they were off in the bush or hunting, that leader was solely in charge of his following. However, when several families joined together, one man would take control of the camp and its protection. That man was the resolute Maskepetoon.

He was thirty-six years old, had at least two wives and a number of children, and had proven his leadership and ability to both the fur traders and his own people. In 1843, Maskepetoon had two sons baptized, John and Joshua, and a year later, Benjamin; these were in addition to the earlier baptisms of Joseph and Peter. Nothing further was said of John in Rundle's diary, but three years later, Joshua was in a war party that raided the Peigans.

Maskepetoon realized the importance of the white man's education, so he turned Benjamin over to Rundle to learn their ways. Later, Maskepetoon wrote a letter in syllabics to Rundle:

> He-Who-Speaks-from-Above, I send you a letter. I shake hands with you. I want you to be here, to see you, I and the Assiniboines. There are twenty lodges. My son Benjamin, I want him to speak English. There are 164 buffalo. I tell you the news, my friend. I am Maskepetoon.[20]

In 1844, Rundle took Benjamin and two other boys—William Rowland and George Makokis—to travel with him and to be raised as Christians. They undertook such duties as looking after the horses and assisting with the meals. They also attended all services, said their morning and evening prayers and read from the Scriptures. Benjamin accompanied the missionary to Fort Pitt and Fort Assiniboine and presumably was learning English as his father had asked. Sadly, it all came to nought. In the spring of 1847, the boy became seriously ill as they made their way to his father's camp. When Rundle left, Benjamin stayed behind. "Saw poor little Benjamin for the last time," he wrote. "Gave Ben. one or two little things—tea, sugar, potatoes. Maskepetoon left kind indian to remain with Benjamin."[21] Some time later Rundle wrote, "Benjamin dead! What a changing world."[22]

One might wonder what effect this death had upon Maskepetoon. He had made a great sacrifice in giving his son to the church to learn the white man's ways. However, Benjamin's tragic death could not have shaken the chief's religious faith, as he had evinced no desire to become a Christian. It did not affect his personal relationship with the missionary, yet the pain was in his heart and in that of Sussewisk, the grieving mother.

At this stage of Maskepetoon's life, Rundle and his teachings seem to have had very little effect upon him. He saw the missionary only two or three times a year when he came to visit. The chief's life revolved around his family, his followers, hunting, trapping, his native religion and the protection of his camp. Except for the valuable knowledge gained from reading and writing in syllabics and benefiting from the spiritual powers of "He-Who-Speaks-from-Above" (as Rundle was called), Maskepetoon's daily routine was relatively unchanged after the missionary arrived. He saw Rundle primarily as a friend and ally, while Rundle initially viewed him as "a kind of chief" of the Rocky Mountain Crees.[23]

With the death of Louis Piche, the Catholics had lost an important ally in the Rocky Mountain Cree camp. Perhaps this is why Father Thibault changed his strategy and began to concentrate more on the Metis and northern tribes. He returned to the West in 1843, where at first he laboured near Fort Pitt in a small mission house a few miles upstream at Frog Creek. He then proceeded upriver to Lac Ste. Anne, where he established a mission for the Metis. While at Edmonton, he baptized a number of children, but the only Rocky Mountain Crees he would have seen were those who had come to the fort to trade. In the spring of 1844, Thibault was joined by Father Joseph Bourassa, who was assigned to the new mission at Lac Ste. Anne. From there, the two priests travelled mostly north and east to Lesser Slave Lake, Lac La Biche and Cold Lake.[24] While regular visits were made to Fort Edmonton, there is no record of either priest again pursuing the Rocky Mountain Crees into their home territory. As trader Harriott explained to Simpson, "The Priests do not interfere with his [Rundle's] Indian flock. They appear more occupied in tending their mission to the northward."[25] The one exception was the extended family of Louis Piche. Their conversion remained strong, and at least two descendants, Cecile and Catherine, were born at Lac Ste. Anne.

While the competition for souls had not ended, the presence of Christianity and the influence of missionaries had become a new element in the lives of the Rocky Mountain Crees. Their own religion still stood paramount over anything the churches had to offer. In most cases, Christianity was added to their native beliefs without replacing them.

CHAPTER NINE

Visitors

In 1845, Henry James Warre and Mervin Vavasour, lieutenants in the British army, were sent on a special spying mission by the prime minister of England. The Oregon Territory, which was under the control of the Hudson's Bay Company, had experienced an influx of American settlers whose presence threatened the British claim to the territory. To make matters worse, American president James Polk declared that his country would claim the entire west coast from Mexico to Alaska. At a special meeting in London, Warre and Vavasour were assigned to find a practical route for troops to travel across the North American continent in case of war and to examine the defences of the various Hudson's Bay Company forts along the way. Once on the coast, they were to determine how successful the British might be if they went to war over the Oregon question. To keep the purpose of their mission a secret, the two posed as gentlemen on an artistic and scientific excursion. Peter Skene Odgen, the senior Hudson's Bay Company trader, was appointed to accompany them.

When the two Englishmen reached the foothills of the Rockies, they needed someone to guide them through the mountain passes. Although not named in their records, that man was probably Maskepetoon. The guide in question was identified as a Rocky Mountain Cree with two brothers in the Cree camp. He led the party along a similar route as that followed by Sinclair in 1841 and used the same pass that

Maskepetoon showed to the earlier immigrant party. Peter Skene Ogden knew Maskepetoon, having met him earlier at Fort Vancouver. There was really no one else from the Rocky Mountain Cree camp who fitted the description.

Warre and Vavasour made a rapid trip from London to Montreal and then travelled inland to Fort Garry. There they joined a fur brigade bound for Fort Edmonton, which they reached on July 12, 1845. Looking at the post from a military point of view, Henry Warre stated:

> The Fort is tolerably well situated on a high bank overhanging the River, but is commanded by a Hill immediately in the Rear. It is surrounded by a twenty-foot Wooden Fence, with small Blockhouses at the Angles, and is crowded in the interior with Wooden Buildings. It is very Old, having been established in the time of the North West Company.[1]

The party learned that a serious state of warfare existed between the Blackfoot and Crees and that their trip to the mountains could be a dangerous one. With their new Cree guide in hand, they set out on July 15, following a southwesterly course through an area that Warre described as made up of dwarf poplar, small creeks and swamps. They camped the first night on Indian Sweatlodge River[2] and the next day travelled through "a thick and almost impassible barrier of Burnt wood, fallen in every direction, over which and round which we were obliged to guide our horses, and take care of ourselves floundering occasionally up to the Girths in the Swamps and blackened by the charred Wood."[3]

By this time they were in the vicinity of Pigeon Lake and were moving steadily when one of the scouts came riding back to the main party, saying that there were Indians ahead. Warre commented:

> As it is usual in this wild Country to consider all Strangers as Enemies until they have proved themselves friends, several of us galloped forward, leaving a few Men to protect the Horses and Baggage. Luckily our Scout had discovered that the Indians were accompanied by their Women and Children (certain sign that they were not on the Warpath). He therefore communicated with them; and on our arrival we held a "talk."[4]

The Indians were Rocky Mountain Crees, about fifty in number, who were hunting buffalo. The soldiers distributed tobacco and gifts to them, then "continued our journey, pushing on as fast as we could, into the rough forest land that borders the lower slope of the Mountains."[5] Unknown to Warre and Vavasour, however, they were being followed by a war party of Blackfoot. Warre later wrote, "Thinking we should probably join forces with the Crees, and remain with them, the Blackfeet deferred their attack until the night or following morning."[6] But because the two parties had separated, it was the Crees who bore the brunt of Blackfoot savagery.

The night raid caught the Crees completely by surprise, and in the brief affray at least four of them were killed, the camp robbed and the entire horse herd stolen, while the survivors fled to Edmonton for refuge.[7] Rundle noted a short time later, "On arriving at Edmonton, I found the Indians in great agitation in consequence of the murders that had been committed amongst them by the Slave Indians."[8] He identified one as a member of his flock—a son of Mikisiyinew, or Eagle Man.[9] Fortunately for the two English spies, no attempt was made by the Blackfoot to follow them.

Later that day, the English party reached Battle River, where they camped, and on the following day, handicapped by heavy rain and thunderstorms, they made only six miles before coming to a halt. On July 18, they crossed a creek that Warre called Prince's River, "from the circumstance of a Man of that name having been killed on its banks by the Blackfeet."[10] A few miles farther on, they came to the north end of Gull Lake and turned westward into a pine forest. All this time, the party was travelling a well-known path to Rocky Mountain House, yet no other travellers described it in such terrible terms. Either Warre was exaggerating or this was an unusual season for storms and forest fires.

At this point, the party branched off from the Rocky Mountain House road, their guide taking them south-southwest. The next day, July 19, they reached a height of land from which they got their first view of the Rocky Mountains. Warre was disappointed. He felt the Rocky Mountains could not "bear comparison with the Alps, either in size or magnificence of outline."[11] They crossed the Medicine Lodge River, where they paused to dry out their equipment. While he waited, Warre shot a few prairie chickens to add to their larder. "We have been living on bad Buffalo Meat, dried and made into Pemican, Hams and Biscuit," he wrote.[12] The next day, their hunter shot an elk and others killed geese and prairie chickens. All were "a very acceptable addition to our scanty stores."[13]

From the Medicine Lodge, they crossed the Little Red Deer and came to the main stream of the Red Deer River. During all this time, the men were travelling within the hunting grounds of the Rocky Mountain Crees but in areas best suited for winter trapping. Across the river, however, the landscape changed. Their guide led them to a broad plain extending far to the south. On July 22, they saw plenty of signs of Indians and were constantly on the watch. When they saw a column of smoke, they feared the worst, but investigation proved it to be from an abandoned camp. That night they reached the welcome banks of the Bow River and followed it upstream the following day. That was when they met their second band of Indians. Warre wrote:

> We soon came up with the Indians, who proved to be Strong Wood Crees and Assiniboines on a Hunting expedition... We found them very friendly, and of great assistance. Among them were two Brothers of our Guide. They had killed a Buffaloe Bull of the Strong Wood kind, much more savage than those usually found on the plains, and were moving their Camp to the neighbourhood of its Carcase.[14]

When the party came to the carcass of the buffalo, they saw women and children cutting it up and loading the meat on their dogs. These were sent to the camps. Some dogs, said Warre, "seemed more inclined to partake of than to carry their loads."[15]

The party crossed to the south side of the Bow River on July 25 and encountered burned fallen timber and sharp stones that lamed some of the unshod horses. Passing over a neck of land, they descended by a very long, narrow pass under an almost perpendicular mountain. The next morning, they followed a narrow valley to an open plain, where their hunter killed a moose and Warre caught a couple of dozen trout. That night they camped on another small prairie, having made thirty-two miles during the two days. They were now deep in the mountains, probably in the Banff region. There, Vavasour made a sketch of Cascade Mountain and part of Mount Rundle.

Warre's description of his historic trek over White Man's Pass was very matter-of-fact. He stated:

> Sunday, 27th July, 1845. A very Cold night with hard frost. At half past 6 o'clock a.m. commenced the ascent of the height of Land; toiled up a very steep scarp of about One thousand two hundred feet to a small Lake, about a mile from which we came to another small Lake from which we found the Waters running to the West, but the View was still impeded by the surrounding Mountains. They appear higher and grow more beautiful in Shape as

we advance. We occupied four and a half hours to cross this ridge, descending the stream we again reached the thick woods.[16]

Once on the other side, they followed a route similar, if not identical, to the one along which Maskepetoon had led the Sinclair party four years earlier. On the evening of July 28, they reached the Kootenay (or McGillivray) River, which Warre wanted to follow, but their guide warned them against it, "so we determined upon the known route, across a high ridge to the Head Water of the Columbia."[17]

Crossing the height of land, they reached Sinclair Canyon, Radium Hot Springs and the open valley of the Columbia River. From there, they went south past Lake Windermere and Canal Flats, ultimately arriving at Fort Colvile. There was no mention of taking on a new guide once they had crossed the mountains; like the Sinclair expedition, they may have kept their Cree guide until they reached Colvile.

Warre and Vavasour continued on to Fort Vancouver, where they continued to play the role of wealthy gentlemen while they examined the military situation. They observed the increasing number of American settlers, particularly in the Willamette Valley, and the unsuitability of the Hudson's Bay Company posts to serve as military defences. They concluded that sending troops across North America was not feasible and stated so in a secret report. However, by the time the report reached London, the prime minister had already decided that Oregon was a lost cause, and the area south of the forty-ninth parallel was ceded to the United States.

CHAPTER TEN

The Life of a Chief

During the late 1840s and early 1850s, Maskepetoon became well established as leader of the Rocky Mountain Crees. As he moved through his late thirties and early forties, his children formed the nucleus of his own extended family, augmented by others who were attracted by his leadership qualities. According to an elder, only four of Maskepetoon's sons reached manhood, and later all were killed. Maskepetoon had numerous descendants through his son Joseph, but an elder said, "I don't know about any daughters."[1] However, as Paul Kane met Maskepetoon's son-in-law, he must have had at least one daughter.

As leader of the entire Rocky Mountain Cree group, Maskepetoon determined where to hunt, where to travel and how to protect the camp. He listened carefully to suggestions and complaints from his council, which was made up of leaders from other families. From time to time, questions might have arisen about young men leaving on a raid or concerns about a hunting party that had failed to return. Perhaps the camp had to be moved because the horses needed better grazing, or an invitation might have been received to meet another band to travel together to trade. On matters where a decision was needed, Maskepetoon used his abilities as an orator to gain a consensus of the council, rather than making decisions unilaterally.

As a leader, Maskepetoon was respected for his skill as a hunter, his generosity and his wisdom. People were attracted to him because he was considered to be a "lucky" chief, a man who found buffalo on the edge of the plains and who avoided unnecessary conflicts with their enemies, but who also protected his camp like a mother grizzly with her cubs. He welcomed visitors to his lodge, honoured them and presented them with gifts on their departure.

His wives were important in maintaining his prestige. They performed the usual duties of tanning hides, making beautiful clothing ornamented with porcupine quills, minding the children, preparing meals and performing the multitude of tasks that befell a woman in a Cree camp. Besides being the wives of a chief, they attended to guests who often stayed in their lodge, made gifts of clothing for presentation and one of them, probably Sussewisk, accompanied her husband on official visits to friendly or enemy tribes.

In their daily lives, Maskepetoon and the Rocky Mountain Crees followed their familiar routine of trapping in the winter and hunting on the edge of the prairies in summer. These practices were affected by forest or prairie fires, starvation, warfare or other occurrences. Any incident could cause a disaster among the group, and many did. In the autumn, they waited until the supply boats had arrived at Edmonton before visiting the fort. Then they traded their furs, paid their debts and obtained their winter supplies. In spring, they returned with their furs, dried meat and robes. Besides necessities such as bullets, powder, clothing, snare wires and knives, there were other items that many considered just as essential to their well-being. Among these were tobacco and liquor. Tobacco came in the form of a long twisted rope and was sold by the fathom. The men with their long-stemmed stone pipes and women with their stubby little ones would no more think of going onto their traplines without tobacco as they would go without ammunition. A gift of rum or brandy was given to the Crees when they arrived at a trading post, after which everyone had a one- or two-day binge. When they sobered up, the regular trading began. Men could get more liquor, but often they were satisfied with the one debauch.

The Rocky Mountain Crees were not considered to be problem drinkers like their plains cousins. Murders and fights occurred, but less frequently. People were cautioned not to drink near the trading post itself, so when visiting Edmonton, the Crees retired across the river to the appropriately named Drunken Lake or went south to Whitemud Creek.

Maskepetoon had a fondness for liquor, and when he drank he sometimes became belligerent and difficult to control. In 1845, he almost killed Baptiste Brenow while they were drinking at Whitemud Creek, and a year later he slapped a man while the Indians were trading at Fort Edmonton. On another occasion, he attempted to scalp his favourite wife, Sussewisk, during a drunken rage.[2] He made a slice across her forehead and temples but did not remove the entire scalp. Instead, as one person recalled, it flopped in the front. Sussewisk was obliged to wear a scarf or other covering on her head to keep her scalp in place and to hide the disfiguration.[3] Typically, when Maskepetoon and his band came to the fort, they immediately began to drink, or as a clerk wrote, "they had a booz." Two days later, the same clerk added, "Mr. Maskepetoon still on a booz with some Crees."[4] But, like most other chiefs, once he left the fort, he remained sober until the next visit.

Cree elders spoke of daily life during this period.[5] One said that people lived in leather tipis, but unlike the tipis of the plains tribes, theirs did not have wings at the top to draw out the smoke. Because mosquitoes and bulldog flies were so numerous at certain times of the year, the people preferred a smoky, bug-free tipi where the smoke gradually curled its own way out the top. The fire was kept burning during the day, but at night the coals were covered with ashes and the fire could be restarted the next morning. At night, regardless of the weather outside, the people wrapped themselves in their buffalo robes, secure from the wind and the cold.

By this time, the Rocky Mountain Crees were being identified by other names, as they spent less and less time in the shadow of the Rockies. They were variously called Strong Wood Crees, Bush Crees or Woodland Crees, the latter including other Crees living north of the North Saskatchewan River from Edmonton to Fort Pitt. At a later date, they also were called the Pigeon Lake Crees. John Palliser described the tribe in the 1850s:

> They [Strong Wood Crees] travel about in small parties, using horses and dogs for transport in summer; both of these animals carry their loads on their backs, but in winter the dogs draw a long light sleigh over the snow. These Indians have regular tracks cut through the woods, wide enough to allow a pack-horse to pass. During the open weather, they live by the chase of the moose-deer, carriboo, or thickwood reindeer, the wapiti, small deer, and bears; but in winter they are compelled to depend chiefly on rabbits, which are very abundant in some parts of the country. Though occasionally in autumn they make short excursions to the plains for buffalo, when the herds come close to the edge of the woods. They often suffer great privation during their long winters, as they are then confined to the dense woods, and are employed in trapping the marten, minx, fisher, and other fur-bearing animals...
>
> As a rule these Indians are hard working and docile, and in manner silent and self-possessed. They are extremely hospitable, though it is seldom they have more than the barest necessities of life. They trade their furs and dressed deer skins for ammunition, tobacco, and clothing; and but few of them care to waste the fruit of their hard toil on liquor.[6]

Warfare continued to be of concern to Maskepetoon during this period. In 1844, Blackfoot warriors attacked a Cree trading party right outside the gates of Fort Pitt, killing two men and taking their furs and horses.[7] Closer to home, the Blackfoot attacked a camp of twenty lodges between Edmonton and Fort Pitt, killing two men, eight women and two children.[8] A few days later, a party of Blackfoot tried to kill a Cree and a trader just across the river from Fort Edmonton.[9] When traveller Frederick Graham visited the fort in 1847, he noted, "There are now at the fort a poor woman and a man of the Crees, who were badly wounded by the Peigans a few days ago. The woman has the side of her face blown off, and the man has been shot through the thigh."[10]

Maskepetoon's policy on war remained firm. If they were fighting with the Blackfoot tribes, he made no attempt to stop his young men from going on horse raids, but in times of peace, he banned such attacks and closely guarded the camp to prevent raiders from sneaking away. He had been an active warrior himself in his younger years and knew of the eagerness of the youngsters to make a reputation for themselves, but he weighed that against the best interests of the band. Generally, if they could remain peaceful, the chief preferred it that way.

Meanwhile, events were taking place far to the south that ultimately affected Maskepetoon and the Rocky Mountain Crees. On the Missouri River plains, the Blackfoot tribes were keeping busy protecting themselves from enemies that seemed to attack them from all sides. Early in the 1840s, sixty men in a Peigan war party were killed when they attacked a small band of Flatheads. A year later, Crows killed a leading Blood chief, Walking Crow, and in 1844, Crees made off with six hundred Blackfoot horses. In the same year, the Small Robes band of Peigans was almost completely destroyed by the Flatheads, who took 160 women and children as captives.[11] These actions tended to draw the Blackfoot tribes southward as they gathered to protect their hunting grounds.

Fort Benton was built on the Upper Missouri River in 1847 and did a thriving business. During its first year, the traders bought more than $20,000 worth of furs and robes and cleared their trading shelves.[12] The American traders provided a ready outlet for the bulky buffalo robes that the British traders eschewed. The Siksikas, who had seldom ventured very far south of the Bow River, now found it profitable to take some of their furs and robes to the Americans in the Missouri, where the range of goods was often more appealing than that offered by the British. All these factors meant that the Blackfoot were not often seen on the edge of the foothills, which provided an opportunity for Maskepetoon to extend his range onto the plains.

During these years, Rundle was continuing his work as a Methodist missionary. He liked to make an excursion each summer to see Maskepetoon and his people and had been on such a trip in 1843, when Louis Piche was murdered, and in 1844, when he baptized eleven-year-old Samson[13] and other members of the Maskepetoon family. In 1845, Maskepetoon came to trade at Edmonton in March, bringing with him twenty men and one woman, probably Sussewisk. He visited the missionary and helped to prepare a map of the Cree hunting grounds south to the Bow River. When Maskepetoon left two days later, Rundle accompanied him almost to White Mud Creek before turning back. Presumably the chief had purchased liquor at the fort, for after Rundle left him, the Crees had a debauch at the creek and got into a fight. Exclaimed the missionary, "O this drink! What poor souls has it murdered."[14]

In April, Rundle wrote to Maskepetoon and gave the letter to a party of Crees and Stoneys who were going back to their hunting grounds. The missionary himself did not follow; he travelled east that year to Fort Pitt and Fort Carlton, where he remained until mid-August. When he returned, he made no attempt to visit the Cree camps, possibly because Maskepetoon was with the Warre and Vavasour party crossing the mountains. Instead, he chose to go to Rocky Mountain House to labour from there and visit with his fellow Methodist John Harriott. He set out for the fort on September 23, reaching Gull Lake four days later. At Three Hills, he met a hunting party of Stoneys and on the following day, a small Cree camp under Eagle Man, whose son had been killed by the Blackfoot who had been following the Warre and Vavasour party. The family joined the missionary, and they arrived at Rocky Mountain House at the beginning of October. There, Rundle found another of his parishioners, Peace Maker, as well as the Piche family. Another visitor at the fort was Father Pierre-Jean De Smet, whom Rundle came to admire in spite of him being a Jesuit priest. De Smet had come to the plains in an attempt to find the Blackfoot and arrange a treaty with them and the mountain tribes. When De Smet heard about the conflict between Louis Piche's sons and his murderers, he offered to mediate between the Catholic families. He stated:

> Two Crees, of the same band and family, father and son, had been killed in a quarrel two years since. The presence of the offending party for the first time since the perpetration of the murder, rekindled in the others that spirit of rancor and revenge so natural to an Indian's breast, and which only the Christian religion is able to mollify, and there was every reason to apprehend fatal consequences from the old feud.
>
> With the approbation of Mr. Harriote [sic], I assembled them all in the fort; the Governor himself had the kindness to be my interpreter. He made a long discourse on the obligation and necessity of their coming to a sincere reconciliation; the matter was discussed in form, each Indian giving his opinion in turn, with a good sense and moderation that surprised me. I had the pleasure and satisfaction of seeing the calumet passed around the assembly. This is the solemn pledge of peace the token of Indian brotherhood the most formal declaration of the entire forgetfulness and sincere pardon of an injury.[15]

During the month Rundle was at the fort, he conducted services, baptized children and gave religious instruction to the occupants, as well as to Crees and Stoneys who came to trade. Among the Cree visitors were Peace Maker, Green Leaves and Thunder Bird. During his sermons, the missionary spoke about such subjects as the Day of Judgment, the love of God and the Lord's Supper and instructed his listeners to "work out your own salvation with fear and trembling."[16] He also entered a cryptic message in his journal: "Heard dreadful news about [Maskepetoon's] son; what a wretch!"[17]

On his return to Edmonton, Rundle spent the winter conducting services and instruction at the fort. He made no further mention of Maskepetoon until February of 1846, when he directed the Hudson's Bay Company to send the man two bundles of twist tobacco at the missionary's expense. The chief arrived at Edmonton in mid-June and was there when a Blackfoot trading party arrived. Rundle wanted to speak with the Blackfoot, so Maskepetoon took him to their camp and acted as interpreter. Like many Crees, he knew their language, particularly as his wife Sussewisk appeared to be from that tribe. This was a brave act in itself, as Maskepetoon was a well-known leader and there was no formal peace treaty between the tribes at that time. To kill such a man in a time of war would have been a great feat. To the Blackfoot he was Manikapina, Young Man Chief.

By this time, Rundle considered Maskepetoon to be among his best friends. The man had no interest in being baptized, but neither did he object to his children going through the ceremony. He could communicate easily by syllabic writing and read the various religious passages that the missionary gave him. Rundle had plenty of ideas for the future of the Rocky Mountain Crees, and the chief was part of them. Not only did he want to open a permanent school but also a mission station far from the trading posts. Although he had examined a number of places, Pigeon Lake was his final choice for a mission station, even though it was uncomfortably close to the route the Blackfoot took when going to Edmonton to trade.

In the spring of 1847, Maskepetoon and some of his followers again came to Edmonton to trade. A couple of weeks after they left, Rundle followed them, looking for an escort south and into Peigan territory. He found Maskepetoon camped near the Red Deer River with most of his band. After a brief visit, they set out for the south with some of Maskepetoon's followers, including Walking Bear and Horse. They crossed the Red Deer River, passed Horn Hill, near the present town of Innisfail, had breakfast the following day at the Lake Where the Sarcees Were Killed and camped at a spring near Eagle Hill.

By this time, Maskepetoon and his companions were far out on the open prairies. To the west, the wooded forests of the foothills rolled back to the very base of the Rocky Mountains, which were, as Rundle said, "like clouds this ev'g."[18] To the east, the prairie undulated in its grassy mantle, disappearing into the hazy horizon. The weather was warm, and as it was now late May, meadowlarks could be heard in the deep grass while curlews flitted about. Overhead, the shrill honking of geese could be heard as they wended their way north in their familiar V-shaped formation.

When the party reached Dog Pound Creek, north of the present town of Cochrane, they came to the sad burial place of one of Maskepetoon's children. Beyond that was Writing (or Pictograph) Coulee, which led down to the Bow River. All this area was familiar to the chief but new to the missionary. Proceeding upstream near old Peagan Post, they crossed to the south side of the river, where Rundle observed, "The Broken Arm was kind in getting my things across; it was hard about the raft as wood was not near."[19]

As was usually the case, the party had set out without extra food, planning to hunt along the way. They were unlucky at first, and by the time they crossed the Bow River, their food was scanty. Rundle prayed, and Maskepetoon went hunting with his son and brother. Either or both approaches worked, as a deer was killed by Maskepetoon's son. As they travelled south, they passed Fish Creek, Moose Mountain and Red Deer Lake, all southwest of the present city of Calgary. The next day, Maskepetoon's son killed a moose to fill their larder.

This was the southern part of Maskepetoon's territory, usually occupied when the Peigans were far out on the prairies hunting buffalo. In the fall and winter, when they and other Blackfoot tribes came back to the foothills to their winter quarters, the Crees discreetly withdrew into their primary trapping areas east of Rocky Mountain House. When there was peace, it may have been safe for the Crees to hunt in the Highwood region, but treaties often were best honoured by tribes avoiding each other. Coming together too often would surely end up with a young warrior taking a horse from the other tribe, stealing a woman or getting into an argument over gambling. Any of these could destroy peaceful relations, particularly if someone was killed.

When they reached the Highwood River, the Crees were joined by a party of Stoneys, including a number of children. Jimmy Jock Bird, who was travelling with the Blackfoot, arrived a short time later with a chief of the North Peigan tribe, who issued an invitation for all to come to his camp. According to Rundle, "Before we reached camp, stopped on or at hill. Arrived at Camp; went into Bull's Head tent, Principal chief of this party of Peagans. Lodged at Mr. Bird's tent." The next day he wrote, "In this camp at present, 24 tents Peagans, & 25 tents Crees & Ass. Mr. Bird's makes 50 tents in all."[20]

During the weeks he was in the Peigan camp, Maskepetoon was treated as a guest of honour. He was invited to one feast after another, joined in long discussions and received many gifts. All knew that at another time and another place, the Cree chief would treat Peigan chief Bull Head in exactly the same fashion—and at other times they would be at war.

Rundle's diary contains a couple of comments about Maskepetoon's son, or sons, which have little meaning without the story behind them. On May 28, he wrote, "Young man seen who went with Broken Arm's son." Is this a reference to the son killed during a trip to the Kootenais? And, "Spoke thro Wm to Broken Arm's son." Why mention that he spoke through William and not directly?[21] Was the son unwilling to speak to the missionary? Questions, but no answers.

Maskepetoon and family stayed in the area for more than two weeks, travelling with Rundle. While on the trail, Bird pointed out where two major battles had taken place—one in the 1700s, with the foothills Indians fighting those from across the mountains, and another in 1846, when the Peigans battled the Kootenais quite close to where Maskepetoon was camped. Over the next few days, the mixed camp of Peigans, Crees and Stoneys roamed through the area south of the Highwood, including the Old Woman's Buffalo Jump, west of the present town of Cayley. Impoundments near that place were being used by hunters, but with little success.

As a result of Rundle's exposure to the Peigans and their daily life, he had grave doubts about their religious practices. "The Slave [Blackfoot] Indians are gross idolaters," he wrote, "having gods many & lords many. The Sun, moon & stars are all worshipped by them with many objects in the animal creation & also perhaps a host of gods besides. Great importance is attached by them to dreams & perhaps it may be said that according to their dreams, so they worship."[22]

In mid-June, the Maskepetoon family separated from the Peigans and Stoneys. This is when Joshua, Maskepetoon's son, and three companions slipped back to the Peigan camp and stole a number of horses. Fearing that this would result in conflict, the Crees moved quickly towards the Bow River. Sure enough, six days after their departure, a dispute arose in the Peigan-Stoney camp. As a result, a horse owned by Stoney chief Chiniki's wife was shot, and the camp was in an uproar. The next day, there were rumours of trouble, but nothing further happened. At last, Rundle and party reached the upper waters of the Elbow River, forded it and then crossed the Bow.

Some time after leaving the camp, Maskepetoon and his family separated from Rundle and let the missionary travel with his Stoney flock. When Rundle got back to Edmonton on July 20, he learned that during his absence, the Blackfoot had attacked a party of Crees on Battle River and eleven were killed. Among them were Bozilla, Big Man's son, and one of Maskepetoon's wives, while a man named Mutakayk was shot in the thigh and was lame.[23] The wife in question may have been Matonnow-a-cap, whose early death would explain why her name was unfamiliar to modern informants. While Maskepetoon was travelling peacefully with the Peigans, his followers were being attacked by another branch of the same nation.

Rundle's comments about the idolatry of the Peigans might have implied that the Rocky Mountain Crees followed none of these practices, which to a certain extent was true. As a woodland people, they did not have the leisure time of their buffalo-hunting neighbours to develop secret societies and complex rituals. Their religion was more individualistic, and while they believed in spirits, these often were personal spirit helpers that could guide and protect them in their daily lives. In the woods, there were good and bad spirits. There was the *pakakos*, a skeleton figure that punished careless hunters; the *wetigo*, a creature with a heart of ice that roamed the forests; the *mantokan*, which protected people crossing rivers; and the "little people," who lived near whirlpools and made stone arrowheads for the Crees. And there was the pipe that was at the centre of their prayers. As an elder stated, the Woodland Cree "asked for health, long life, and for achievement of his ambitions."[24]

"The first thing in the morning," the man stated, "the elder . . . gave thanks to the Father of All for the privilege of seeing another day, another sunrise, and prayed for health and strength to tide him over the day ahead. He never failed to give thanks before meals. If he was a smoker, after lighting his pipe he would point the stem upwards in humble supplication and call on the spirits of his forefathers . . . to share with him the pleasant aroma of his smoke."[25]

Those Woodland Crees with individual spiritual powers treated the sick, foretold the future and protected people from "bad medicine" and any mysterious forces of nature. This belief in the spirit world extended beyond rituals and recognized that some people possessed special powers. An elder recalled, "Whenever an Indian had this certain power, he was well respected, or scared of. The people believed in them, but this power was very bad if used for the wrong purpose."[26] This gave rise to the terms "good medicine" and "bad medicine."

The elder told of a war party setting out on foot in the fall to raid the Blackfoot horse herds. Among them was a stranger from another woodland band. Several days later, they were crossing an open plain when a horde of Blackfoot Indians suddenly swooped down on them. The Crees ran into a coulee and hid in a grove of bushes. There, they were surrounded and two of their men killed in the exchange of gunfire. Meanwhile, the Blackfoot camp was moved to the site, and tipis were pitched all around the trapped men. The Crees felt they were doomed.

Then the stranger took his pipe and passed it around. "Now," he said, "you will have to do whatever I will have to say if you want to live. There is something mysterious happening and when I get up, take a hold of each other and on to me. You will follow me. Whatever you do, do not look at a person (meaning them Blackfoots) even if you come abreast of them. If you such as take a look at one they will spot us right away and kill us all."

The man began praying, and as he did so, the wind blew up a gale and heavy snow began to fall. While this was happening, the man arose, and the rest followed him out of their hiding place. "The Blackfoot were so close walking around them," said the elder, "but they still walked in between them. They passed the teepees even though they were pitched so close together. So they made their getaway. When everything had calmed down, the Blackfoot lost them altogether. There wasn't even a track of them even though it had snowed."[27]

Maskepetoon's younger brother, Samson, had his share of extraordinary experiences. He told of the time when a camp of ten lodges of Rocky Mountain Crees had travelled south to the Oldman River, with the belief that the Blackfoot were far out on the prairies. One evening, Samson rode downriver to catch some fish. When he was almost there, he saw a man walking towards him along a buffalo trail. When they met, the stranger said, "I will tell you one thing; that is why I came to meet you. When you are done fishing, you will go home. When you arrive at your camp, you will immediately prepare to move your camp towards the mountains. If you do not move your camp, in the morning, when the sun rises but a little, many people will be advancing towards you."

After delivering his message, the man walked away, and as Samson watched in amazement, he turned into the shape of a buffalo. Samson was truly scared. He thought it was an illusion; nothing like this had ever happened to him before. So he went home and told the people of the amazing things that he had seen and heard, but they didn't believe him. That night, people could hear the coyotes howling nearby. There was a man among them who could understand the animals, so they asked him what the little wolves were saying. He told them, "They said prepare immediately, run towards the mountains, if you do not run, tomorrow when the sun rises but a little, many people will advance towards you. This is what the coyotes had said when they called out."

But the people did not believe him either, so they didn't run away. The next morning, just when the sun was rising, they were attacked by a large war party of Blackfoot. Samson escaped, but almost all the others were killed and their horses stolen. They had not listened to the warning of the buffalo spirit. "This is true," said Joe Samson, Samson's son. "It had happened a long time ago when the people were alone on this land."²⁸

Another story about Samson tells that shortly after he was married, he made a pledge to go into the woods and leave an offering to the buffalo spirit. He vowed to do it right away, but eventually summer turned to autumn and he had not yet fulfilled his promise. Joe Samson said:

> One day, the two of them, my father and mother, had left to go see some friends. They had one horse. By the evening they were already a long ways off when they saw a buffalo. My mother told him to go kill it so they could eat some meat when they made camp. So Samson went towards it and shot it, but he didn't kill it. It started to come towards him in anger, so the old man ran away towards the woods. This buffalo was furious and would bellow because he was so angry.
>
> Samson remembered the offering he had promised to give. He had not given it so he knew that was why the buffalo was angry. So the old man Samson ran away. He had so much speed and he used all of it as he ran to the woods. But he could not outrun the buffalo. When it caught up to him he took to a big willow tree and he climbed it. That is what he did.

Perched in the tree for hours, Samson regretted not having left the offering, so at last he quietly spoke to the buffalo. He said that before there was snow on the ground, he would give what he had promised. As soon as he said this, the buffalo left. Then, when it was far away, Samson came down and ran to the place where he had left his wife. "I have angered the buffalo; he might return," he told her. So they hurried away, riding double on the one horse. They ran for a long time and for a long distance. The buffalo never did come after them, and eventually he gave to it what he had offered.²⁹

A third story told by Joe Samson occurred at Pigeon Lake during winter. His father went with his dog to track a lynx he had seen earlier. He succeeded in killing it and was on his way home in the bitter cold when he heard a sudden loud cry from a squirrel nearby. It surprised him, so he put down his gun and chased after it. When he caught it, he decided not to kill it but played with it for a while. Eventually the squirrel got tired, and so he set it free.

A short time later, the Crees moved towards Buffalo Lake to kill buffalo, and there they encountered a large herd near the present town of Bashaw. There, at the west side of the lake, were rolling hills covered with buffalo too numerous to count. Said Joe Samson:

> The snow was deep and it was very cold. It was about 50 or 60 below. In the morning there was an attempt to move camp. The women moved the camp of about ten tipis altogether. The men left on horseback before everyone else. They went ahead to give chase. These men had guns, the kind that you load from the muzzle. They saw some buffalo while moving camp. They gave chase on the ice of the lake and it was very cold.
>
> The women who were moving camp would sometimes start a fire to warm up. Soon they set up camp close to the lake near the chase. Then one of the men arrived in the camp and reported that they had killed ten or more buffalo. He also said that my father, the old man Samson, had also given chase and all his fingers were frozen. He had loaded his gun eight times and these were the old style muzzle loaders. So he could not shoot his gun any more because his hands were so frozen.

When he got back to the camp, Samson reported that he had killed five buffalo. When a Native doctor looked at his hands, he told Samson he would lose all of his fingers. His son said:

That night no one could really sleep. This was partly because of all the meat they had eaten but also of the thought of the old man Samson losing his fingers. This one was the man who was heavily relied upon for protection, food, and leadership. That was why all the people were concerned about his situation.

It was near morning when Samson finally went to sleep. Soon he was dreaming that someone had come to see him from above. And then he was asked, "Do you feel the pain on your hands where you froze them?" "Yes," he said, "I feel the pain." It spoke to him again. "Do you think that you will never use your hands again?" he was asked. He replied, "I will never use my hands again." He was asleep while he was talking to the one who came to see him. He was told, "Nothing will be wrong with you; you will heal quickly."

That is when Samson realized that it was the squirrel he had played with that was talking to him. The creature pitied him because the man had let it go. When Samson awoke, his hand gradually healed.[30]

A fourth story told by Joe Samson was not about his father or his uncle Maskepetoon but about a dog that was with four men who were going to hunt buffalo near Sakahikanihk Lake. Samson recalled:

> In the evening they set up camp but they did not know that they were being followed by a Blackfoot war party. They did not know anything. That night the Blackfoot moved in. First they took all their horses. They were still sleeping and in the morning they were still sleeping. Their tents were knocked over and soon they were all killed; no one was alive. Only the dog was left alive. He had run away as soon as he heard all the shooting. But he would

return often to where his owners were killed. He stayed there for a long time but finally left this place.

The lonesome dog travelled around, looking for people from his owners' band, but he could not find them. He went to Whitefish Lake, but they were not there. He went out on the plains, where he found another camp, but they too were strangers. As he lay down beside a woman, he said to her, "I am all forlorn." The woman was surprised and asked, "Whose dog is this? It talks. It has said that it is lonely."

No one knew the dog, but it stayed with these people. At last, a visitor recognized the dog and realized that its owners must be dead. With some urging, the dog led them to the place where the men had been killed, but all they found were their bones. Now everyone knew why the dog had been so lonesome that it had to speak.[31]

CHAPTER ELEVEN

Out to the Plains

In the autumn of 1847, Maskepetoon made one of the most important decisions of his life. Increasingly, the buffalo herds were concentrating farther east, and the animals were seldom coming within easy range of his hunting grounds in any great numbers. When he looked at the situation, Maskepetoon knew he needed to take drastic steps to look after his followers. He made the decision to leave his traditional lands in the foothills and find a place closer to the herds. By moving almost two hundred miles northeast, he was close to the woodlands north of the North Saskatchewan River, where people could still trap. Nearby were such friends as Little Hunter, who usually ranged from Whitefish Lake south to Two Hills. Maskepetoon now camped in the same region for summer hunts and for mutual protection. In winter, some of his people returned to the Pigeon Lake area, while others stayed with the chief on the edge of the plains.

The move had been made after careful consideration, for the foothills had been the hunting grounds of Maskepetoon's followers for generations. The ancestors of his people were buried there, and the hills held places of spiritual significance and places filled with memories. Yet the harsh reality was that the buffalo were withdrawing, and although the Crees had known starvation before, it had never seemed as devastating as during the winter of 1846–47. The foothills area could still support a number of trappers and hunters, but not as many as it had earlier.

The Crees under Stephen Piet Eagle chose to remain near the foothills, as did Maskepetoon's younger brother, Samson, and the Piche sons.[1] They were satisfied with trapping, fishing, hunting big game animals and killing any buffalo that strayed into the region. In summer, if the herds were close and the Blackfoot far away, they had no hesitation in venturing onto the plains. But Maskepetoon was different. From his new campsite, he was taking the first steps to becoming a Plains Cree, or at least a Cree who spent most of his time on the plains.

Other Woodland Crees, particularly those under Little Hunter, usually spent the winter just north across the river, but during the winter of 1847–48, they too were drawn to the edge of the plains by hunger and were only about six miles east of Maskepetoon's camp near Raft Lake.[2] These camps could assist each other in the unlikely chance that Blackfoot war parties might brave the winter cold, and they also offered welcome companionship. Previously, Maskepetoon and his followers would have been spread out on their individual traplines in sight of the Rocky Mountains. Now they were in a single camp from which they could hunt buffalo and also travel north of the North Saskatchewan River to trap. This was a different kind of winter for them. No longer were they isolated and alone, eking out an existence in the bush. The women in particular loved having others close by with whom they could visit, gossip and share their workloads. The men, too, found time to gamble and perform religious ceremonies that had once been only a summertime experience.

From his winter camp, Maskepetoon sent a syllabic message to Rundle saying that he would return to Fort Edmonton in the spring. Rundle responded with his own syllabic letter, together with tobacco and some sugar for Sussewisk. These were easily delivered, as Maskepetoon's camp was close to the main trail from Fort Pitt to Edmonton. On one occasion, James Simpson, a clerk and mailman, stopped by to pick up two letters from Maskepetoon and put them in with the packet from Fort Pitt.[3]

There is no indication if any further communication or contact ever took place between Maskepetoon and Rundle, and by July of 1848, the missionary had left for England, never to return. The separation was not one of minister and adherent, but the parting of two friends. Maskepetoon had not yet become a Christian and appeared to have no desire to do so. This was made abundantly clear early in 1848, when artist Paul Kane visited Maskepetoon's winter camp. Kane wrote of his interview with the chief:

> Amongst other topics of discourse, he began talking about the efforts of the missionaries amongst his people, and seemed to think that they would not be very successful; for though he did not interfere with the religious belief of any of his tribe, yet many thought as he did; and his idea was, that as Mr. Rundell had told him that what he preached was the only true road to heaven, and Mr. Hunter told him the same thing, and so did Mr. Thebo, and as they all three said that the other two were wrong, and as he did not know which was right, he thought they ought to call a council among themselves, and that then he would go with them all three; but that until they agreed he would wait.[4]

Two points were made: Maskepetoon did not try to convince his followers to accept Christianity, and he was skeptical about its success among his people. He was a follower of his own religion but gladly accepted the knowledge, education and friendship of the Methodist churchman.

Kane's visit to the chief was an interesting one. The artist was on his way to Fort Kipp when he came to the camp of about forty lodges. "We went to the lodge of the chief named 'Broken Arm,'" said Kane, "who received us very kindly, spreading buffalo robes in the best part of his tent for us to sit on and placing before us the best his stock afforded. After supper, the chief having cut some tobacco and filled a handsome stone pipe, took a few whiffs from it himself, and then presented it to me. On my doing the same, and offering it to him again, as is the custom, he told me that he wished me to accept it as a gift."[5]

When others in the camp learned of the visitor, they flocked to the lodge, anxious for any news from the Edmonton area. "Amongst our visitors," said Kane, "was the son-in-law of the chief; and, according to the Indian custom, he took his seat with his back towards his father and mother-in-law, never addressing them but through the medium of a third party, and they preserving the same etiquette towards him . . . I remarked that one of the leggings of the young man was spotted with some red earth, and the other not: on inquiring the reason, I was told that the spotted leg had been wounded, and the red earth was intended to indicate blood."[6] The image presented by Kane was one of a respected chief, surrounded by his family and living in comfortable winter quarters.

Meanwhile, Maskepetoon's trip across the mountains with James Sinclair was destined to be repeated. Sinclair had spent the winter of 1841–42 at Fort Colvile, then returned to Red River, where he resumed the business of being a private trader. In 1849, he decided to return to Oregon, and when the Hudson's Bay Company heard about his plans, it engaged him to inspect some of its trading posts on the west side of the Rockies. Sinclair left the Red River Settlement in the summer of 1850, and when he arrived in Fort Edmonton, he re-engaged his old friend Maskepetoon to be his guide.

Little is known about this trip. Travelling with a few men and pack horses, they retraced their path along the edge of the foothills to the Bow River, then followed their old route over White Man's Pass and down to Radium Hot Springs. Historian D. Geneva Lent wrote, "Once more the Cree Indian proved reliable as a guide, and Sinclair appears to have crossed the Rockies again with little trouble, reaching Fort Colvile well before snowfall."[7]

From there, Maskepetoon returned over the pass to his hunting grounds, while Sinclair went to California, travelled through the Isthmus of Panama and was back home by 1852. There he was asked by Governor Simpson to take a second group of immigrants to Oregon and to take charge of Fort Walla Walla when he arrived there. Late in 1853, Sinclair wrote to Simpson on the question of a guide. "I should like to get the service of La Grace for as far as the Crossing Place on the Kootenai River," he said. "I think he is now at Carlton. He knows the route well and will act as interpreter should we meet any Blackfeet."[8]

Simpson replied, "I . . . sent a letter to Mr. Rowand, the officer in charge of Carlton, requesting that La Graisse may be attached to the party to act as guide as far as the Kootonais River crossing place."[9] Baptiste La Graisse (or La Grace) was a well-known guide who had spent considerable time on the west side of the Rockies and later was with the Palliser expedition.

When Sinclair was ready to leave Red River Settlement on May 5, 1854, his party consisted of about a hundred people, of which twenty-eight were men and eleven of these heads of families. They used two-wheeled carts drawn by oxen, each man carrying a Winchester rifle. They went via the Qu'Appelle River and across country to Fort Carlton where, according to historian D. Geneva Lent, "Sinclair secured the guide that he had especially requested . . . This was a shrewd, dried-up little Métis, known as 'La Graisse.'"[10] At the fort, they learned of hostile Blackfoot activity in the area, so they travelled along the north side of the North Saskatchewan to avoid their war parties.

At Fort Pitt, no Indians were permitted inside the fort, all transactions being handled through a wicket in the gate. Moving on, the Sinclair party proceeded westward and were a couple of days on the trail when they encountered a Cree encampment. This proved to be Maskepetoon and his followers, who were located at approximately the same place where Kane had seen them two years earlier. John Campbell, a member of Sinclair's party, recalled:

This party of the Crees traveled along with us until we came to Fort Edmonton. We hired the chief of this band of Crees, whose name was Mackpictoon, or broken arm, to act as guide. These Cree Indians were very friendly to our party. They used to accompany some of our party when they went out hunting buffalo, and kept all the party supplied with fresh meat.[11]

There were nearly a hundred Crees in the band, and they acted as escorts during the day and guards at night. This was obviously at the direction of Maskepetoon, who undoubtedly was happy to see his old friend and was prepared to accompany him over the mountains even if the settlers already had Baptiste La Graisse as their official guide.

Campbell was impressed with the skill shown by the Crees in buffalo hunting and with the huge herds they saw between Pitt and Edmonton. He stated:

> The last day that we saw the buffalo was on a Sunday. We were travelling along as usual, and we could see a black mass moving towards us. These were the buffalo travelling towards the north and we had to stop to let them by. When they came up to us they separated, some going ahead of our carts and the others behind. We had to stop and let them by and go around our loose cattle and horses as they wanted to follow the band of buffalo. We were obliged to remain at that place for over two hours to let them go by us. Just as far as the eye could see there was nothing but a black mass of them and they were going on a small lope.[12]

The plentiful supply of buffalo was the reason why Maskepetoon had chosen to camp east of his old hunting area. Significantly, Campbell makes no further mention of seeing buffalo herds as he travelled westward to Fort Edmonton and the foothills.

When the party reached Edmonton, they were surprised to find the gates to the fort closed. As they approached, they raised a flag to indicate that they were friends, and men came out to greet them. Sinclair learned that a large Blood war party had defeated the Crees three days earlier and were thought to be still in the area. In the days that followed, however, there was no sign of them, and the traders concluded they had returned south to the plains.

The Sinclair party set out from Edmonton in mid-August, keeping to a route east of where Sinclair had gone in 1841. Travelling was much easier, as they were partly on the plains. They must have had reason to believe they had nothing to fear from the Blackfoot tribes, perhaps because they were escorted by Maskepetoon's band. They passed the Bear Hills, Battle River, Blindman River and Red Deer River without incident. After camping on the south side of the Red Deer, Donald Whitford recalled, "In the morning we travelled along & came in sight of the Ridge on the road where the Indian told us the Rocky Mountains could be seen... We travelled hard all day & we came in sight of the Ridge that the road went over & came up to a hill & all the party came on ahead with carts to look at the mountains... & behold we saw the Mountains all white like winter."[13]

Continuing on south, they passed the Lone Pine, a solitary landmark just west of the present town of Olds, went over Dog Pound Creek and then down to the Bow River. As they travelled, they suspected they were being followed; the proof came one night when seven cattle came bawling into camp with arrows sticking out of their bodies. Two died on the spot. All belonged to John Moar and Roderick Sutherland, who also lost three horses. Sinclair said, "I think the cattle were shot by four young scamps, and that they were prevented by some others from molesting us."[14]

The next morning, they learned that there had been about forty Blood warriors following them. "I presume they saw that we were on our guard," said Sinclair, "and that it would not be safe to molest us. They therefore kept their distance, of which we were not sorry."[15]

When they reached the mouth of the Kananaskis River, the Crees left the caravan but Maskepetoon stayed. They also met a hunting party of Stoneys, and two were hired as guides. This now gave Sinclair four men he could count on to take them to the Columbia River.

From their camp on the Bow River, they prepared to cross the mountains over Kananaskis Pass. However, an examination showed that the difficult route could not be used by carts, so it was necessary to abandon them and use pack animals. According to Whitford, "We camped down in the flat & there is the place we stayed about 10 days, the people making pack saddles for the horses & oxen to pack all the things we needed to see us through the Rockies. The people sawed wood all day till they had made the pack saddles strong."[16] Finally, they were ready to start, the horses and oxen serving as pack animals. This proved to be a daunting task. Campbell said:

> It was quite a sight to see the young steers with the first saddles on their backs . . . It was a grand sight to see their capers and there was not but one or two in the whole outfit that knew anything about packing. We had to stay in camp longer so as to get the young stock broke in to their job, but we had the time of our lives when we started traveling through the timber. In the narrow trail a steer would bump his pack onto a tree and then he would do some bucking to get that pack off; then we would have a time catching him to put the pack onto him again. We had to go very slow to get the stock used to their work. Some of the women had to ride on the back of the old oxen, as there were not horses enough for them, but these had to be led, as they did not guide very well with just the halter lines.[17]

Some days they did not make more than seven or eight miles, and the whole of September was spent in getting through the mountains to Canal Flats. It was an experience Sinclair would not soon forget. He wrote:

> Our rascally Guide took us by a pass over the Mountains (known only to himself), which he represented as the best and shortest, but which took us 30 days and this with hard work in cutting our way and hunting after cattle through a dense forest, wind-fall timber, deep ravines, steep side hills, following up one River (the Strong Current River, which falls into the Bow River near the old Fort) to its source, and following down another, the Kootonais, to this point where it is 200 yds. wide. Altogether it is the worst road I ever travelled.[18]

This "rascally guide" probably was La Graisse, the official guide of the expedition,[19] since Maskepetoon preferred White Man's Pass and knew that it would be simpler to travel over that route. Sinclair wrote, "Had we taken the Route by the Red Rock, my old Route, we should now have been near Walla Walla... I am only surprised we were able to bring a single animal here. Had I seen the road before I should never have dreamed of driving Horned cattle by such a rascally route."[20]

After two days at Canal Flats, Maskepetoon and the Stoneys went back across the Rocky Mountains to their own country, while some Kootonais at Canal Flats were taken on as guides for the trip to Fort Colvile. From there, Sinclair continued his journey to Fort Vancouver.

By 1855, a number of changes had taken place on the frontier. Father Thibault, worn out from his labours at Lac Ste. Anne and in the north, had retired to Red River and was replaced in 1852 by Father Albert Lacombe. This young missionary soon became one of the most popular figures in the West. As a Methodist minister said, "This ecclesiastic presented a decided contrast to many of the Romish clergy, being most courteous and urbane in his general deportment. There is a frankness and freedom about him that makes one lament that such a person should stand connected with such a system."[21] Lacombe concentrated initially on the Metis at Lac Ste. Anne and gathered a faithful flock to his side.

After Rundle left in 1848, the Methodists had only a lay reader, Benjamin Sinclair, to keep the mission at Pigeon Lake open, but later he abandoned it and moved to Lac La Biche. Some Woods Crees continued to use Pigeon Lake as a gathering place under the leadership of Stephen Piet Eagle, but they did so without any missionary presence.

In 1855, a new Methodist minister arrived in the person of Thomas Woolsey, an Englishman. He settled at Fort Edmonton, although he made no secret of the fact that he wanted to be out in the field, working with the Crees and other tribes. He made Pigeon Lake his base and set about repairing the abandoned buildings. If he met Maskepetoon during these first few months, he made no mention of it. In fact, more than a year passed before he referred to Maskepetoon by name in his journals. At that time, he wrote:

> Received a note from Maskepetoon, a Chief, presenting his compliments and requesting me to be diligent in praying for him. He says he is endeavouring to instruct his band to be earnest for what is good. He concludes thus, "Nothing more. It is I."[22]

The letter had been written in syllabics, so the missionary "returned in a brief epistle on the things belonging to his eternal good."[23] Woolsey did not mention the chief by name at any other time during his entire stay in the West, although he was similarly lax in identifying other Indians. In 1860, he did speak of a chief who "is greatly attached to our work and is resolved to co-operate with us to the utmost extent." He then said the chief was the person who had visited the Methodist mission in Oregon and still carried a New Testament given to him by the Rev. Daniel Lee.[24] That could only be Maskepetoon. In spite of seldom being named in the Woolsey journals, Maskepetoon and the missionary must have known each other well, for in later years Woolsey called him "my old friend" and commented, "We have frequently traversed those plains together, amidst vicissitudes too strange for ordinary language to portray. Occasionally, being somewhat acquainted with the vernacular of the Blackfoot people, he has acted as an interpreter to that people."[25]

When Woolsey first arrived at Fort Edmonton, he was told that some Woods Crees were camped nearby and went to visit them. He noted:

> Our arrival was speedily announced to the Crees by an old Indian named Stephen, who at once introduced us to the best tent, where a large buffalo robe was spread for our accommodation. The chief men of the camp then took their seats around us. The sacred pipe, or calumet, was speedily passed, each one taking a whiff. I then addressed them at some length.[26]

On September 28, a trading party of Blackfoot arrived, and after a welcoming ceremony, arrangements were made for a peace pact between the Crees and Blackfoot. This was a common event, organized by the Hudson's Bay Company to assure some degree of peace while the two tribes were in close proximity to each other. The missionary described the event:

> The different tribes assembled in the hall, when energetic addresses were delivered by the Blackfect, which were made known to the Crees, through an interpreter, who made a suitable reply. Each tribe then placed the calumet (or sacred pipe) upon the table, forming an angle, after which the pipes were lighted and handed round by one

of the Blackfeet to each of the Crees. Then followed another, giving to each Cree a piece of lump sugar, first touching his own lips with it, and then applying it to the lips of the other. Then followed a third, who kissed each Cree; and then a fourth, who shook hands with them.

This was followed by a recognition on the part of the Crees, three or four of whom presented several small parcels of tobacco to the Blackfeet chiefs, as presents for other chiefs of their tribe, with whom they expected to meet shortly. All these acts were preceded by a very expressive oration. The Blackfeet expressed themselves most enthusiastically and eloquently.[27]

The Hudson's Bay Company trader opined, "It is to be hoped that this may continue long," but it was not to be. Barely a month later, the same trader reported that his men had "met with a party of Crees who dogged the Piegan Indians who were here lately towards the Rocky Mountain House and run away with some of their horses. This is an infraction of the late compact of peace and betrays the thievish propensities of the Crees."[28]

Maskepetoon had not been at the peace ceremony. It is likely he had been on his way there to participate, for he arrived a day after it was concluded.[29] He and others stayed at the fort for a couple of days, and on October 4, the clerk reported that "The Indians now are all away to their hunting grounds."[30]

Meanwhile, most of the Blackfoot tribes had left the area and were congregating at the confluence of the Missouri and Judith rivers in Montana in anticipation of the peace treaty with the United States government. The need for a treaty arose in 1853, when authorities proposed that a possible railway route from the Mississippi River to the Pacific Ocean would go through Blackfoot territory. This was also a good opportunity to bring peace among the warring tribes. Negotiations were supposed to have begun in early August 1855, but treaty goods and gifts had failed to arrive because of low water on the Missouri, so the talks were postponed to the autumn. Those scheduled to sign the pact were the Peigan, Blood, Blackfoot, Gros Ventre, Nez Perce and Flathead.

The Crees were represented by only one man: Broken Arm from Turtle Mountain. He had come to the treaty grounds as a witness with Little Dog, a Peigan chief, and carried tobacco as a mark of friendship from the Crees and Assiniboines downriver.[31]

Some historians have speculated that the Cree representative was Maskepetoon of the Rocky Mountain Crees. However, the Rocky Mountain Cree chief had left Fort Edmonton about October 3 to hunt, and just thirteen days later the American treaty was signed. Most delegates had been on hand for many days prior to that date. To travel more than five hundred miles mostly through enemy territory in less than two weeks would have been an incredible task. Also, when Maskepetoon came back to Fort Edmonton on November 26, the most important news he carried was that he had narrowly escaped a prairie fire and had brought in furs to trade valued at 50 MB.[32]

Because of the fear of the Peigans, many Woodland Crees spent the winter of 1855–56 near Fort Edmonton. Only Stephen and a few other resolute souls returned to their hunting grounds, while Maskepetoon and his followers remained downriver and hunted on the plains. The buffalo were so plentiful that the chief concentrated on supplying fresh meat to the fort. In January, the trader at Fort Edmonton noted, "This morning 8 men with 32 horses were sent for meat to Maskepitoon's camp. Mr. John Sinclair accompanied the party with rum and other articles to trade with the Indians."[33] In the spring, Maskepetoon brought in a hundred buffalo robes, with some wolf and fox skins to trade.[34] These were the products of a plains hunter, not a woodlands trapper.

Meanwhile, Woolsey visited Stephen's band in the spring and found that, unlike Maskepetoon's followers, they had little to eat. "In consequence of a scarcity of provisions," he wrote, "we proceed to the plains."[35] At first they subsisted on "wild plants and inner bark of trees,"[36] but as they travelled, they killed moose, deer, porcupine and beaver, and gathered duck eggs and berries. They stayed in sight of the mountains, but found the area to be completely devoid of buffalo. Finally, in mid-August, the Crees suggested to the missionary that he return to Edmonton, "as they are fearful of want of food and do not wish me to suffer."[37]

The situation had not improved by autumn, so the Pigeon Lake Crees under Stephen were forced to go onto the plains for their fall hunts. They killed a moose and a deer to ward off starvation, but more than a week of travel passed before they found a few buffalo. They killed three, but misfortune continued to dog them, for wolves devoured two of the carcasses during the night. They pressed on to the east, taking refuge during a blizzard, and after almost a month of travel, they came upon a large herd of buffalo. Here they encountered other Crees and a few Sarcees and happily began to decimate the herd.

Meanwhile, Maskepetoon had been out on the plains at a different location with Lapotac, chief of the Beaver Hills Crees. In September, he notified Fort Edmonton that they had meat on hand. Reported the trader:

> 13 men ... with 7 Carts & 27 pack Horses were sent off this morning to Laputuque's & Maskepetoon's camp to assist them in bringing their provisions of which they have more than they can bring in with the few horses they have, & as it is an object to secure all the provisions we can, this party is started merely to assist the Indians in with their provisions & not to trade with the Indians—will be paid here when they come themselves, which I suspect will be a few days after the return of our people.[38]

Ten days later, after the meat had been received, the trader announced the arrival of the Crees. He stated:

> The Chiefs Laputuque & Maskepitoon with their respective bands came this afternoon on a trade. They were received with a Salute of 3 Guns each. Laputuque has been recognized as a chief of the first rank. After the customary speechifying & smoking the Calumet was gone through, the chiefs got a present of a Suit of Clothes & a Keg of mixed Rum each. They appear to be well satisfied with this treatment. Laputuque has promised to be one of our Hunters.[39]

The Crees drank all that night and into the following day. The fort was closed up, and the Hudson's Bay Company refused to trade with them until all their rum had been consumed. Three days later, the trader confirmed that Maskepetoon and his band were now sober enough for business, while Lapotac's band traded the following day. However, both bands took rum in trade, so they were immediately ferried across the river to be as far away from the fort as possible.

Meanwhile, Woolsey had travelled with the Pigeon Lake people when they went to the plains, and at the beginning of December he returned to the lake to see those who had stayed behind. He found they had been subsisting on fish, but when they learned about the success of their comrades, they too left for the plains. So, during the winter, the former Rocky Mountain Crees were divided into three groups: Maskepetoon with the Plains Crees, Stephen in a large camp on the plains, and the remainder who chose to stay near Pigeon Lake and their traditional hunting grounds.

After they left the fort, Maskepetoon and his people went to a location out on the plains called Point que Bas to build a pound. The herds remained plentiful, and before the end of the year, the chief notified traders that he had taken four hundred buffalo. He sent a messenger with the news, also informing the fort that free traders from Lac La Biche would be descending upon them and that they should send out men for the meat.

"Maskepitoon deserves some credit for this," commented the trader.[40] Clearly, the chief favoured the Hudson's Bay Company over free traders. In response, the Hudson's Bay Company sent twenty-two sleds to pick up the meat. Other meat came from the camp of the fort hunters who were at a place called Salt Lake. Lapotac was their leader, and Sayakimat of the Rocky Mountain Crees was one of his crew.

CHAPTER TWELVE

The Buffalo

Many Crees were turning away from their traditional trapping activities to become meat suppliers as part of a wider international trend. As buffalo became scarce at such places as Fort Pelly and Fort à la Corne on the eastern edge of the plains, traders had to rely more and more on places like Edmonton and Fort Pitt to supply the needs of the fur trade.

In fact, buffalo herds were decreasing all across America. There were an estimated 60 million buffalo at the time of Columbus' landfall, and the figure had remained steady as long as they were hunted only by Indians seeking food and robes. But as Europeans arrived, the market for buffalo robes and meat increased steadily. By 1820, there were no more buffalo east of the Mississippi River, and a decade after that, the total population was estimated to have dropped to 40 million. The slaughter continued in order to meet the steady European and American demand. In 1840, the American Fur Company sent 67,000 robes down the Missouri River from the Blackfoot trade, and in 1848, some 110,000 robes were sent. There was also a demand for buffalo tallow and tongues. In 1848 alone, 25,000 buffalo tongues were exported from buffalo country. In many cases, the buffalo had been killed solely for their tongues. In the 1850s, about a quarter of a million buffalo were being slaughtered every year just for robes.

At the same time, the fur-trading companies required large amounts of dried meat and pemmican to supply their northern posts. Over a ton of fine pemmican was needed every year just to take care of Norway House and the lower forts. The Hudson's Bay Company's demands were clearly indicated in the minutes of the Northern Council in 1830:

> That Gentlemen in charge of Districts & Posts be directed to use their utmost endeavors to collect large quantities of Leathers dressed, and Parchment, Buffalo robes, Pack Cords, Snow Shoe line, Sinews, tracking Shoes, Leather tents, &c., &c., as these are articles absolutely necessary for the trade in many parts of the Country and cannot be purchased in Europe or Canada.[1]

The buffalo usually were found just south of the North Saskatchewan River, but their movements were unpredictable. Prairie fires might keep them away, weather conditions could affect their movements, and sometimes they just seemed to have an ornery streak and failed to show up. In 1849, for example, a fur trader's wife wrote that at Edmonton, "the Indians are starving in every direction & of course the dividends will be small. Even the Buffaloes have left the Saskatchewan & there will be no dried Meat nor pemican for next year."[2]

With the overhunting, the quest of the Americans for robes, and the Crees supplying large amounts of meat and robes for the trade, the buffalo population was destined to recede from the edges of their grazing lands. As historian Arthur Ray commented about the needs of traders:

> In order to obtain the supplies of dried buffalo meat, fat, and pemmican which they required, the Indians living adjacent to the parkland-forest border found it necessary to travel greater distances during the latter half of the nineteenth century as the bison range contracted ... Therefore, it was becoming impractical for many of the ... bands to trap furs in the late autumn and early

winter months and hunt bison during the middle of the winter also.[3]

One of the results of this thinning of the buffalo herds was that the Crees had to go farther and farther south to reach them. This took them directly into Blackfoot territory and led to inevitable conflict. Maskepetoon may have been peacefully inclined before, but there is no evidence that he had been a peacemaker while living near the foothills. Rather, it was only after he moved to the plains while hunting in close proximity to enemy tribes that peacemaking became so important to him.

During the winter of 1856–57, Maskepetoon became acquainted with chiefs from the Plains Cree tribes downriver: Sweet Grass, Little Hunter, Little Chief and others. In the spring, his elevated status was noticed when he and others came to trade at Edmonton.[4] A trader commented that six Crees came in advance of the main party to receive tobacco for greeting ceremonies. He said they were "from a band of thirty tents of Crees coming in on a trade. They will be here to-morrow & all the big bugs among them are coming such as Sweet Grass, Maskepetoon, Laputuque & some others. They bring plenty of Robes."[5]

While the chiefs were together, they discussed the possibility of a peace treaty with the Blackfoot. Already that spring, a fight had taken place near the Elbow and seventeen Crees had been killed.[6] Missionary Henry B. Steinhauer at Lac La Biche heard of a proposal for a peace conference on the plains. He said:

> For some time back an attempt has been made to establish peace among the various tribes, such as the Crees, the Assiniboines, Blackfeet, Sarcees, the Blood, Peagans, and some other tribes of Indians. During the last summer it was partially established, but not so far confirmed as all to be free from apprehensions. The last winter was a very severe one to all; starvation and sickness prevailed to a

great extent, and took off a great many; and I believe that this has done a good deal toward mollifying the various hostile tribes.

    I received a note lately from a Cree Chief, informing me that there is to be a general assembly of the Indians at some central point on the plains, for the purpose of settling and confirming the peace among themselves.[7]

The situation remained tense throughout the summer of 1857, and although enemies and allies sometimes congregated in the neutral area around a fort, a fight could break out at any time. Then Maskepetoon made a bold move, sending a messenger to Edmonton with tobacco "for the Blackfoot, Blood Indians, and Circees."[8] This was given to a Blackfoot chief coming to trade, and two weeks later, Maskepetoon arrived at the fort to meet with the enemy tribe. Presumably they discussed the terms of a treaty and a place where they could meet on the open plains. Maskepetoon and Little Chief notified their own people about the forthcoming pact and found the other Cree bands ready and willing to abide by any terms that might be established. A month later, Maskepetoon and Little Chief went south to the meeting place, and when they rode back to Fort Edmonton, they made a triumphant entrance accompanied by "the usual ceremony giving Horses and firing salutes."[9] At last there was peace again on the prairies.

As described by Steinhauer, this was a great treaty, encompassing all the tribes of the Blackfoot Confederacy. They had come together on the plains, smoked their pipes, sang, kissed and feasted together. This was not just a temporary treaty to allow tribes to hunt in peace for a few weeks, but one that was meant to last. In fact, it lasted for almost three years, which was something of a record between those tribes. Also, it must have been one of the largest treaties in many years, embracing all four tribes of the Blackfoot nation, Sarcees, Plains and Woodland Crees, and perhaps even the peaceful Stoneys. This meant that hunting parties did not worry about surprise attacks, and no one feared being waylaid en route to a trading post. The women could tan hides and care for their children without having one eye on the horizon, and the responsibility for guarding the camp could be left to young boys, giving the older men a chance to hunt.

No one could predict how long the peace would last. Some previous treaties had been tragically short, ending just days after they were concluded. Almost inevitably, the breach was caused during a routine horse-stealing expedition, when either a raider or camp protector was inadvertently killed. As long as there was no loss of life, the people could put up with a few horse raids, as long as they didn't get out of hand.

Chiefs like Maskepetoon had to exert firm control over their followers. If young men were suspected of planning a horse raid, the guards would be cautioned to be alert and to stop anyone drifting away from the camp with only a lariat and a bag full of extra moccasins. If caught, they would be brought before the chief, or perhaps the council, and punished for threatening the peace.

Everyone was happy with the treaty, including the traders, who could now get on with their business of taking robes, furs and meat in exchange for tobacco, rum, knives, beads and other items in their large stock of wares. Within days of the treaty, the Edmonton traders were able to report that the fort was crowded with "Crees, Blood Indians, Blackfeet and Circies."[10] A few weeks later, a "party of Blackfeet arrived, they & the Crees had a booze at night."[11]

By 1857, Piche's old band had been taken over by his son Bob Tail. He had found that hunting buffalo on the prairies was more desirable than starving in the bush, so his followers joined Maskepetoon's camp to be with other families that had given up trapping. Along with Bob Tail was his younger brother Ermineskin, neither of whom were as peace-loving as the other Rocky Mountain Crees. In later years, Ermineskin spoke at a Sun Dance about a fight in which he was involved. "During the fight," said a reporter, "he was in a rifle pit and saw a gun sticking out of another pit occupied by a Blackfoot. He grabbed the gun and was pulled into the pit. He cut the Blackfoot with his knife and escaped, taking the gun with him."[12] Bob Tail also had the reputation of being an aggressive warrior and a strong leader.

Prior to the treaty, the Pigeon Lake Crees had spent the summer of 1857 on the plains, but had avoided the enemy. At their farthest point, they were almost two hundred miles east of Pigeon Lake and a hundred miles south of the North Saskatchewan. This would place them close to Sounding Lake, which later became a focal point for Cree bands. These Pigeon Lake Crees met small groups of hunters from other Cree bands and often camped with them. They seldom stayed in one place for more than a week, moving frequently in order to follow the moving buffalo herds and to avoid coming to the attention of enemy tribes. According to Peter Erasmus, who accompanied the hunters:

> There was a definite assignment for each member of the tribe. The elder men acted as guards and buffalo hunters. The young men were given regular duties scouting or locating buffalo or enemy camps; they were being trained to be the eyes and ears for the camp. They travelled in a wide radius of the camping grounds and some of them would stay out several nights if there was any suspicion of strangers within reach of their people. The women were always busy tanning hides or making moccasins, leather clothing for the men, and their own clothes. Even the young boys in camp had to go through a course in physical training which took the form of wrestling, jumping, and racing... Their elders made them bows and arrows, and I was surprised at the proficiency which these young boys developed in their use.[13]

These Crees returned to Pigeon Lake in the fall, loaded with pemmican, dried meat and robes. Woolsey, who could see the day coming when there would be no buffalo, urged them to turn to farming. He put in a garden at the mission, and a few Crees planted grain. Unattended all summer, the tiny plots of land still produced a quantity of potatoes, other vegetables and barley. Woolsey also ordered an iron plough, but he realized that as long as there were buffalo on the plains, the Indians would not settle down to farming.

During the winter of 1857–58, the Pigeon Lake Crees remained in the foothills.[14] With a plentiful supply of dried meat and pemmican, supplemented with fish, moose and deer, they were able to follow their usual pursuits as trappers. Stephen took advantage of the treaty to go south and spend time with the Blood Indians. Maskepetoon went back to his buffalo-hunting grounds, and when Steinhauer went to visit the Crees on the plains, he said that "the old Chief, Mas-ka-pe-toon gave me a hearty welcome."[15] The chief's mother was baptized at Edmonton in the spring, but there is no indication that he was present.

The peace treaty held firm over the passing months, although it was severely tried. In the spring of 1858, Crees stole two horses belonging to The Sun, great chief of the Siksika, while he was trading at Edmonton. In response, two days later the Siksika stole two horses that some Crees were bringing to the fort. However, when The Sun learned that they were Woolsey's horses, they were quickly returned.[16] In the spring of 1859, a Cree war party took six horses from the Siksika; they were pursued and eight Crees were killed. "The peace is now broken," opined a trader,[17] but he was wrong, for sane heads prevailed and the treaty held.

An English visitor to Edmonton noticed the tension between the two tribes. He wrote:

> The Crees & Blackfeet regard each other distrustfully & the latter who are at present few in number slept within

the Fort a few nights ago, hearing of a large war party of Crees being near. One of their Chiefs, however, held in much dread by them having killed some of them for disobeying his orders, told them they were old wives & borrowing a pistol from us slept in his own lodge. He is a fine fellow & his name, Natoos [The Sun], known far & wide.[18]

At the end of the season, after the summer hunts were over, Maskepetoon and his followers visited Edmonton with a supply of robes and pelts to trade. The clerk at Edmonton wrote, "The Crees headed by the Little Chief & Mas,kipitoon [*sic*]arrived to day, about 100 men besides women & children. They came in with the usual ceremonies, giving Horses & firing salutes, &c., &c. Their Horses were paid for, and they got a quantity of Rum to drink."[19]

The items brought in by Maskepetoon reflected his Plains Indian status. At the spring hunt, he and his people traded 238 wolf skins, 190 prime buffalo robes, 5 common robes, 3 dressed (tanned) half robes, 2 whole dressed robes, 211 red foxes, 1 cross fox, 39 kit foxes, 11 badgers, 2 wolverines, 2 skunks, 20 martens, 48 parchment hides, 150 pounds of dried meat, 495 pounds of pounded meat, 800 pounds of grease, 60 pack cords and 26 buffalo tongues.[20] The bulk of the goods, of course, came from the buffalo: robes, parchment, meat, tongues, grease, etc. The woodland animals, such as martens and wolverines, were scanty. These probably came from a few members of his band, perhaps old men who had memories of their earlier days, who crossed the North Saskatchewan to do a little trapping.

Maskepetoon continued to supply meat to the fort, but not the quantities he had provided a couple of years earlier. As Woolsey noted during the winter of 1858–59, "The buffalo have been so remote from Edmonton House and Fort Pitt during the past winter as to cause considerable difficulty in obtaining provisions for the respective establishments."[21]

Maskepetoon sent word to Edmonton in the spring that he had eight buffalo cows ready to be bartered. This is a far cry from the four hundred carcasses he had traded three years earlier. Two weeks later, traders were back to his camp for another supply, but the number was so small that they didn't even send sleds, but used pack horses instead.[22]

By summer, the shortage of buffalo was apparent to everyone. For a while, even Lapotac, the fort hunter, was obliged to go to the bush to hunt for moose. In August, a trader said, "A few Crees came from the beaver lake, no buffalo in that direction. The Crees are starving. Those who are here are very troublesome. They are continually trying to thieve."[23] By September, however, some Crees were able to locate the herds, and scanty supplies of meat began trickling into the fort again. Maskepetoon and Lapotac came a month later to trade but brought very little provisions with them. Nevertheless, "they had a booz" and were joined by some visiting Sarcees. Maskepetoon and his party drank for the next three days.[24]

There are a number of descriptions of drinking at Fort Edmonton, none of them very pleasant. An American, John Jones, recorded what he saw in 1858 when some Blackfoot came to trade. He wrote:

> The announcement being received by the Indians that the Master of the fort was now ready to receive them, they formed themselves into an irregular line with the chief at the head leading a horse as a present to the Chief Trader. At the gates of the fort the Indians were received in due form by the Hudson's Bay officials. The Indian chief after a brief address presented the horse and received in return a military coat after the same pattern he wore, as also an invitation to dine with him (the chief only), which is considered a great honor.
>
> Not understanding the proceedings we had recourse to our interpreter. He informed us that the chief was to be

the recipient of the periodical entertainment given to all the chiefs when they called at the fort. The doors were now closed; and the Indians dispersed. Our informant stated that while at the table the chief is plied pretty freely with rum; and if in consequence he becomes somewhat obstreperous and obstinate, they dose the rum enough with laudanum to put him to sleep; and in this insensible and maudlin state he is turned out and given over to his followers.

The gates are now closed, and the portholes are opened. There is but just room enough to pass your hand through. The furs are now rapidly passed through the aperture by the thirsty Indians; and the rum is distributed in the same manner with equal rapidity; and then follows a scene of drunken revelry that beggars description. Braves, squaws, and children are all huddled indiscriminately. Virtue and decency finds no resting place while in their bacchanalian orgy. Such a sickening and disgusting sight I never wish to behold again.[25]

Colonel William F. Butler's description of the ceremony in Edmonton is similar to that of Jones. He wrote:

The fire-water for the Crees was composed of three parts of water to one of spirit, that of the Blackfeet, seven of water to one of spirit, but so potent is the power which alcohol in any shape exercises over the red man, that the Blackfeet, even upon his well-diluted liquor, was wont to become helplessly intoxicated. The trade usually began with a present of fire-water all round—then the business went on apace: Horses, robes, tents, provisions, all would be proffered for one more drink at the beloved poison ... But things did not always go so smoothly. Knives were wont to flash, shots to be fired—even now [1870] the walls of the Indian rooms at Fort Pitt and Edmonton show many traces of bullet marks and knife hacking done in the wild fury of the intoxicated savage.[26]

Just after Maskepetoon's visit to the fort, a party of Blackfoot came to trade. The clerk described the scene:

> They came in *en ceremonie* to day & gave in 1 miserable Horse that will not survive the winter. They got some Rum as a present, a little in a Keg to each chief. They were very troublesome & quarrelling in the Indian House; they wished to Trade through the port hole in the Indian House, the same as the Crees do, and gave them a trial but found them so bad that we shut them out & traded through the Bastion port Hole, or another port Hole in the Stockade. They should never be allowed to drink in the Indian House.[27]

One can sympathize with Rundle when he lamented, "Oh that murderous shameful drink!"[28]

Over the winter of 1859–60, the buffalo were far out on the plains, and starvation again was commonplace. Some Crees coming in from the plains went directly into the bush, hoping to survive on fish from one of the nearby lakes; Maskepetoon and his followers who stayed on the plains had to travel four or five days before they could reach the herds. In the spring, the chief notified the fort that he had meat to trade, so twelve pack horses were sent on the long journey, with the chief expected at the fort shortly after they returned. But in mid-April, a trader reported:

> A Cree arrived from the Plains today from Maskepetoon's and Lapotack's camp, with a message for some Ammunition, and with news that the Buffalo have been less numerous across the Battle River and that instead of coming in to Trade at once as they had intended . . . they are to go & hunt and try to get some provisions.[29]

When the traders heard the news, they sent a man to their camps with ammunition and tobacco to tell the Crees to obtain as much provisions as they could, but they would have to bring in the meat themselves, as the fort's horses were in such poor condition that it was impossible to send them out.[30] Ten days later, the trader returned with Lapotac in tow but not an ounce of meat.

Stephen's followers were suffering just as badly as those camping near the fort. They decided that their only option was to head out to the plains themselves to search for the elusive buffalo. Woolsey heard they were gone and set out from Edmonton to find them. Travelling ten hours a day, he finally caught up with them at the Iron Stone, close to the present town of Lougheed. This is about a hundred miles east of Pigeon Lake and seventy-five miles south of the North Saskatchewan River. They were in a large camp with a number of bands present. They had not yet found the buffalo herds, and the people were hungry, subsisting on ducks and wild berries. Travelling for another week, the missionary was impressed by the fact that since his arrival in their camps they had killed no less than five thousand ducks.

At last they reached the buffalo, or as Woolsey called it, "the land of plenty."[31] Soon the people were feasting on real food, rather than birds and berries, and there was happiness all around. Then their joy knew no bounds when Maskepetoon and his followers arrived at the camp. At last, the Rocky Mountain Crees were together again! By now, one group was living on the plains and the other in the woods near Pigeon Lake, but they were still one people with relatives in both camps. Fires were lit, meat boiled, feasts given and people travelled from lodge to lodge renewing acquaintances. The gamblers were out in force, their melodic singing and drumming providing a joyous background for the happy camp. Judging from the size of the camp, many other chiefs probably were there with their bands, including Little Hunter and Lapotac.

An old man from Stephen's camp went through the village and called upon everyone "to avail themselves of the privilege of receiving religious instruction" from their missionary.[32] A chief invited Woolsey to see the Iron Stone, a meteor of almost pure lead that sat on a nearby hilltop. "The pagans regard this metallic substance as a mun-e-to," said the missionary, "and have placed sundry offerings under it, such as beads, buttons, broken earthware, arrow-heads, tobacco, red cloth, and feathers."[33]

By now, Christianity had been accepted by many of the Pigeon Lake Crees and some of the plains people. One chief, baptized two years earlier, told the assemblage how hard it had been for him to accept the new religion. He had two wives and liked to drink and felt he was unworthy of the faith. Then he had a vision in which he saw people in great agony for their sins; when he awoke, he was determined to give up drinking. He said:

> I resolved to do and therefore, before we went to trade the next time, I told my band that, according to my usual custom, I would on entering the fort precede them, as their chief, but I was resolved to give up drinking rum. My young men besought me with tears to change my resolve but I stood firm and trust to be able to carry out my resolve.[34]

Maskepetoon had not yet accepted Christianity, but he read the Bible. According to his nephew:

> He was one of the first to have the great writing (syllabics) and he was very fond of this writing . . . [He was] a proper human being through and through. He was a creative thinker. He made friendships with his fellow humans. He would pray and he would ask the Great Spirit to give them good tidings on this earth, along with the people he was living along side with at the time. He

would do whatever he could in everything that he did to assist his people.[35]

As for his leadership, his nephew said, "People from throughout the land would seek refuge and protection from him. He was a leader who led a good life amongst the people who lived along side him at the time. That was why he was the chief. There were many Cree who would always travel with him to wherever he thought of moving his camp so that they could hunt the buffalo."[36]

Maskepetoon was at the peak of his career. He was a respected chief and a proven peacemaker. He was wise, strong and a natural leader. He inspired others by his personal life and family and by the seemingly effortless way he was able to encourage confidence in others. His band, once made up of a segment of the Rocky Mountain Crees, had grown dramatically because of him. Families from other bands, observing his successful leadership, flocked to his side and accepted him as their new chief. Woodland Crees, Plains Crees and even some Metis families were now part of his band.

CHAPTER THIRTEEN

War Again

Maskepetoon's great peace treaty of 1857 had held firm in spite of a few setbacks. By 1860, however, it was starting to come apart at the seams as the Crees penetrated farther and farther into Blackfoot country and as large camps decimated the buffalo herds. In late July, the Blackfoot came upon some Crees who were gambling and killed two of them. About the same time, a large band of Blackfoot was preparing to attack a Cree village when their chief stopped them and reminded them of the treaty. Then there was a rumour that a Metis hunter had been killed by Sarcees near the big Cree camp. As Woolsey said, "This proved too true, as shortly after all came home bringing the bloody corpse of the poor fellow. I shall not soon forget the shrieks of the immediate relatives of the deceased."[1]

While the Crees were still camped near the Iron Stone, the Blackfoot staged a nighttime horse raid. Many of the Crees wanted to go in pursuit but were stopped by their leaders because of the danger of going out in the darkness. In the morning, they discovered how lucky they had been when they found places where the Blackfoot had lain in ambush. Anyone venturing from the village would have been killed. Some young warriors wanted to retaliate and attack the Blackfoot; again, they were stopped by their chief. When Woolsey was returning to the fort, this leader said, "Tell the great chief at Edmonton that we would have been at war with the Blackfeet ere this, and

I at the head of them, had you not urged us to submit rather than avenge the deeds perpetrated."²

As news spread of the Blackfoot and Sarcee raids and subsequent deaths, many Crees became intent on revenge. To them, the peace treaty had been irrevocably destroyed, and retaliation was the only answer. Leaders like Maskepetoon and Lapotac might have called for restraint, but this was not the case at Fort Pitt, where the Cree chief was either powerless or unwilling to restrain his young men. A war party under Koominokoos headed for Fort Edmonton, where they knew the southern prairie tribes came to trade. When they arrived, the Siksika were camped west of the fort, so the Crees pitched their lodges on the east side. There they waited until they saw some Siksika going to the fort to trade and opened fire on them. Woolsey noted in his diary that "a deadly feud took place between the Crees and Blackfeet close to the gates of the establishment ... when a Siksika chief was shot and barbarously scalped before the vital spark had fled." A Siksika elder identified the chief, saying "the Blackfeet was attacted [sic] by the Crees ... and a great war chief was killed, his name was Eagle Leggings (Peta-soye-kwa)."³

Two days later, a band of Sarcees arrived at the fort, unaware of the latest conflict. According to Woolsey, they had just crossed the river "when a war-party of Fort Pitt Crees fired upon them and killed one instantly; the others fled throwing off their robes which had been perforated by bullets so that, doubtless, others are wounded. The Crees then scalped the victim and brought it to the Crees near the fort; both scalps were triumphantly tossed about for some days."⁴

The Blackfoot, intent on revenge, attacked three employees of the fort, who narrowly escaped with their lives. According to trader Henry Moberly, the Blackfoot also threatened to attack and burn the fort, saying the traders favoured the Crees and were protecting them.⁵ Added Woolsey, "They seemed resolved to take revenge on anyone. The fort gates have been subsequently closed and a guard on duty every night lest the

Blackfeet should cross the river and attempt to do damage to the whites."[6]

The anger of the Blackfoot spread to Fort Pitt, where they attacked a Cree camp. In a pitched battle, twenty Crees and four Blackfoot were killed. Other Blackfoot who were leaving Edmonton set the prairies on fire to drive the game away.[7] Fearing a bloodbath, more than half of Lapotac's followers fled to the woods near Whitefish Lake and Lac La Biche, while the chief, with about forty lodges, bravely returned to the uncertainty of the plains. Maskepetoon, who had been on the plains when the Edmonton attacks occurred, chose to stay out until mid-December, when he arrived with twenty-six men and thirteen women. They had a number of dogsleds loaded with products of the chase including grease, dried meat, fresh meat, pounded meat, pemmican, tongues, and the pelts of wolves, foxes, lynx, beaver, wolverines, badgers, bear, fisher and muskrats.[8] Once the trade had been concluded, the chief went out to the plains and came back again just before the end of the year. Said a trader on December 29, "Maskepetoon, Little Chief, &c. &c. with 40 Men and as many women arrived today loaded with provisions & grease, pounded meat, &c. Gave them a little Rum to drink at night."[9]

By this time, winter was upon them, so there was little to fear from the Blackfoot. They would be in their camps along the river valleys, close to the buffalo. The snow and bitterly cold weather would keep them from making horse raids while they concentrated on hunting and surviving. The death of one notable Cree did occur early in 1861, but presumably from natural causes. A trader reported:

> [The freemen] brought the melancholy news of the death of our greatest and best Chief Lapotack. His body was brought here for burial. He fell down dead suddenly. It is supposed by the Crees that he had been poisoned by some of the Ft. Pitt Crees, but upon this head we can't give an

opinion. The general opinion here of the old Freemen is that he was not poisoned, but died from the bursting of a blood vessel, as he bled a great deal from the Mouth. He was a good man in every way and always did his best for the Whites. He was a sober man, never tasted a drop of Liquor; his loss to Edmonton House is irreparable. His Family are left to the Charity of the HBCo and right well do his children deserve to be taken care of.[10]

Lapotac, chief of the Beaver Hills Crees, had become an influential chief partly through his good relations with the traders. He was an official hunter for Edmonton, and when he was not doing that, he and his followers were providing meat to the fort. In the eyes of the traders, he was the greatest chief in the area, while on the plains, such men as Maskepetoon and Sweet Grass were considered to be much superior. With the death of Lapotac, the leadership of the Beaver Hills Crees fell to Little Chief and later to another Lapotac, a son of the fallen chief, but neither gained the stature of their predecessor. The only great leader in the Edmonton area now was Maskepetoon, and although perhaps not the first choice of the traders because of his independence, he was accepted as the successor to Lapotac. He also was recognized for his self-appointed role as a peacemaker among the Crees.

When the spring of 1861 arrived, so did the threat from the Blackfoot. What would happen? Would they wreak vengeance throughout the plains and attack the trading posts? Would wiser heads counsel for peace? No one knew, so there was fear. There might be a horse raid on an unsuspecting camp, a few warriors lying in ambush along a trail, or a mass attack on a trading post. In preparation, Rocky Mountain House was abandoned. The clerk at Edmonton said, "They now threaten openly to kill whites, Halfbreeds or Crees where-ever they find them, and to burn Edmonton Fort. All this is owing to the Blackfoot Chief, that was killed here last Fall by the Crees."[11]

Maskepetoon and Little Chief came in from the prairies on April 1, before Blackfoot war parties were in the field. They had about twenty men, women and children with them and admitted frankly that they were worried about the Blackfoot. But Maskepetoon probably had already made overtures regarding peace, for ten days later, Little Sarcee Chief, leader of the Sarcees, came to the fort, bringing tobacco and seeking a truce. Maskepetoon joined them a few days later, and together they went to the Sarcee camp, where a pact was made.[12] But this agreement involved only the Sarcees—there were still the Siksikas, Bloods and Peigans to consider.

A month later, an advance party of six Siksikas carrying a large white flag arrived at the top of the hill on the south side of the North Saskatchewan River. Not sure if they would be welcome, they waited until the traders hoisted the Hudson's Bay Company flag. Then they rode down to the riverbank but were afraid to cross until one of the traders came to meet them. "The red Gentry seem to be very much afraid of us," said the trader.[13] Obviously the fear of retribution had existed on both sides, the Crees and the Siksikas. The next day, the main party of some ninety Indians was welcomed, with caution, and peacefully traded their buffalo robes.

There were several good reasons why the Blackfoot tribes did not carry out their threats of extermination. Perhaps the most important was the influence of their chiefs, who wanted to end the bloodshed. Another was a more practical reason. In the south, gold had been discovered, and some merchants were abandoning the Indian trade to supply the hundreds of miners invading the upper Missouri and mountain areas. The future of the Blackfoot's southern trading base was in jeopardy, so the tribes could not afford to alienate their British suppliers of ammunition, tobacco and trade goods. To add to the uncertainty, the gifts promised by the American government as part of its 1855 treaty had failed to arrive because the steamboat carrying them had sunk. This made some Blackfoot wonder if the Great Father in Washington had abandoned them and if the peace treaty with the mountain tribes was over.

Whatever the reason, an uneasy peace returned to the plains for the summer. But now, sensing the reluctance of the Blackfoot to attack, the Crees became the aggressors. In September 1861, a trader at Edmonton reported that some Indians had arrived. "They proved to be Blood Indians, Blackfeet & Piegans. Several Crees here; we had hard work to prevent them from killing or taking their horses. The Indians all slept in the fort. We made them make peace."[14]

The trader's comment makes it clear that the peace was forced upon the tribes and was doomed to fail. Only two days later, a Cree or Stoney shot a Peigan in the leg, then on the following day, a Sarcee was killed by someone from Maskepetoon's camp. On the third day, wrote a trader:

> Finished trading and the Blackfeet, Piegans, Blood Indians and Circees crossing. As the two last boat loads were pushing off from the shore, a party of twenty or more of Crees made a rush to massacre all that were in the boats, but as fortune would have it, all the Men of the fort were under arms. We rushed to meet them & managed to stop them by some good words and some by menaces so that our friends the Blackfeet got clear.[15]

There were eight hundred Indians camped around the fort, many of them drinking. Yet it was to be their last drunken hurrah, for the Hudson's Bay Company had finally decided to stop selling rum or any other liquor at its western posts. According to a Red River newspaper, "The last drop of rum at Edmonton House was served out to the Indians in December [1861]."[16] Maskepetoon had imbibed all his adult life, but when the Hudson's Bay Company discontinued the sale of liquor, he made no attempt to buy it from any of the free traders who showed up from time to time.

Meanwhile, the Crees had become the most troublesome group at Edmonton. Only through persuasion and tact were the traders and some of the chiefs able to get the bands to finish their trade and return to their hunting grounds. The Crees and Sarcees supposedly still had a peace treaty, so when they left, they decided to go together to a pound to kill buffalo. A Sarcee who was a boy at the time described what happened:

> The Sarcee made a truce with the Cree and established a common camp at a buffalo pound that the Cree had built. As soon as the buffalo drive ended, however, they moved away, taking with them a certain Blackfoot Indian who had temporarily joined his fortunes to theirs. Before they departed, some Cree who were friendly with my father advised him to camp apart, because their people were planning to attack the Sarcee; and, as we moved away someone in the Cree camp did fire a shot that wounded the Blackfoot Indian in the leg. My father, with two or three kinsmen, therefore detached himself from the rest of our people and set up his camp a few miles away.
>
> The following morning the main body of the Sarcee again moved camp. The warriors and the women rode ahead; behind them travelled a score of children in the charge of an old man, and in the rear of the train another band of about ten children conducted by a second old man. Suddenly the Cree rode down on them from behind, killed the two old men, carried off the children, and attacked the warriors and the women as they were pitching their tents. Both sides suffered many casualties, the Sarcee far more than the Cree. Finally night put an end to the battle and the Sarcee escaped in the darkness.[17]

The war continued sporadically for the next year. At Red Deer Lake, east of the present town of Ponoka, the Crees fought with the Blackfoot and killed one of their leaders, Bull

Straight Hair. Another Blackfoot, Sleeps on Top, was killed when he wandered away from his camp, the raiders taking his horse, gun and scalp.[18] And in another fight, Crees wiped out a significant part of the Sarcee tribe. As they were travelling along the Vermilion River, Sarcee hunters were suddenly attacked by a large force of Fort Pitt Crees. The Sarcees fled, but they were overtaken and killed one by one. A Sarcee boy recalled the incident:

> A hand-to-hand melee ensued, in which the women fought as desperately as the men; but hardly one of the party succeeded in reaching the tents. Meanwhile some of us were piling poles, travois, bags and other things around the tents to form a barricade, while others dug holes in the ground for cover. I was hurried away with a party that carried two large tents to the shore of the lake where we should be protected in the rear. There our enemies soon surrounded us . . . some armed with guns, the majority with bows and arrows. The noise of their guns was deafening, and their arrows pattered on the water like rain.

While the women and children huddled behind the tents, their leader, Bull Head, and two other Sarcee chiefs led the defence. Whenever the enemy came too close, one of them would charge and repel them. At nightfall, Bull Head called for a charge, and the Crees finally withdrew. When it was over, the Sarcees counted their losses. They had, said the Sarcee informant, "lost at least twenty families, including women and children. Never again did they recover their earlier strength."[19]

The Crees, seemingly emboldened by the lack of aggression on the part of the Blackfoot tribes, continued to harass them when they came to Fort Edmonton, causing a trader to comment that the Crees "give us more trouble than all the rest."[20] Early in 1862, they raided a Blackfoot camp, killing eight, taking all the Blackfoot horses, and losing two of their own men. A short time later, they killed a Blackfoot just across the river from Edmonton.[21] In March, two trading parties, one Cree and the other Blackfoot, arrived at the fort at the same time. Because of the threat of open warfare, the Crees were shut up in a dwelling house and the Blackfoot in the Indian House. When one tribe finished trading, it was sent on its way before the other was released. With Edmonton now being the focus of warfare, both sides decided to avoid the place, and not a single person, Cree or Blackfoot, came to trade during the six months from March to September.[22]

In this climate, Maskepetoon appeared unable to bring about any reconciliation of the tribes, so he stayed on the plains, hunting buffalo and bringing dried meat and grease to the fort.[23] But as tempers cooled and confrontations declined, the chief again pursued the goal of peace. In December, the trader at Edmonton said:

> 50 Crees, headed by Broken Arm, Sweet Grass, &c. arrived, sue for peace with Blackfeet, brought a letter from Lower Crees (Ft. Pitt & Carlton) all asking for peace to be made with Blackfeet and wish to see the Blackfeet here. Agreed to send Tobacco and a message to the Blackfeet to ascertain their feelings on the matter. Blackfeet are anxious for peace also.

A day later, he wrote:

> Sent Mr. Brazeau off to meet the Blackfeet with Tobacco from the Crees to make peace. Conditions of coming— all arms (Guns & Knives) to be delivered up by both Parties before meeting. If the Blackfeet won't agree to this, not to come here until the Crees are done Trading & away. Crees agree to give up arms & do nothing if the Blackfeet will make peace & do the same. If not, Crees

agree to go off home quietly for the present & not to molest the Blackfeet at Fort or going off.

Then, the next day:

> Mr. Brazeau arrived with the Band of Blackfeet, Blood Indians, Piegans & Circees, 50 men besides Women & Children . . . Received them in the Indian House, took all their Guns from them, and then introduced the Crees with their Chiefs to them. All passed over well and the Peace made, as great deal of speeches made on both sides and no want of promises to keep the peace well.

An observer estimated that some five hundred Blackfoot and eighty Crees were on hand for the ceremonies.[24] Then, on the fourth day:

> The Peace was finally satisfied to day in the mess room, the Chiefs of each of the Tribes being present. Delivered a paper to each Chief confirming the Peace made, signed with the names of all the Chiefs present. Tobacco exchanged & sent to Slave Indian Camps & Cree Camps, all parties saluted each other with a Kiss, shook hands and the Crees went off quietly at once. Long may it last.[25]

Although the details of the treaty had been arranged at the fort, gaining commitment from all the Crees appears to have been done beforehand. With Maskepetoon representing the Fort Edmonton Crees and Sweet Grass the Fort Pitt Crees, full support was assured.

Peace treaties came in various forms and offered vastly different results. Least permanent were the temporary treaties relating to the hunt. Two opposing parties might come together, particularly in times of hunger, and agree not to harass each other during a hunt. This meant that both sides could kill buffalo without fear of an attack from the other. Once the hunt was over, so was the treaty. Another type of pact was one made between two tribes, such as the Beaver Hills Crees and the Bloods. This was binding only upon the two groups and did not affect others in their nations. Under such a treaty, the Fort Pitt Crees were still at liberty to attack the Bloods, and the Beaver Hills Crees could raid the Peigans. Considering the similarity of clothing and campsites, it would be easy to mistake one band for another, so such treaties, although common, were usually short-lived. Those that lasted were the ones where the principals who made the treaty sent messengers to their allies asking them to honour it.

A treaty could be arranged by the Hudson's Bay Company. Even though there might be no strong desire on either side to come together in peace, they did so because of the presents offered by the traders and the threat of limiting their trade if they refused. Such treaties were made with tribes that happened to be at the fort at the time and did not necessarily include other bands. This type of treaty was usually successful while the opposing tribes were together at the fort. They visited each other, smoked together and drank together. When they left the fort, the durability of the treaty depended entirely upon how strongly they felt about it. To what degree bands not participating in the treaty would honour it depended on their leadership, their control of their warriors and their wish for peace.

The most desirable treaty was one that embraced all warring nations: Woodland Crees, Beaver Hills Crees, Plains Crees, Fort Pitt Crees, Siksikas, Bloods, Peigans and Sarcees. Maskepetoon's 1857 pact, for example, lasted for three years because it included everyone. When such a treaty was being considered, messengers carrying sweetgrass and tobacco were sent to the enemy. If the sweetgrass was burned and the tobacco smoked, this indicated a willingness to negotiate a treaty. The messenger returned with sweetgrass and tobacco and a suggested time and place to meet. A peacemaker, such as Maskepetoon, would go from band to band among his allies or send messengers, seeking their support. If they agreed, they gave him a pipe that signified their approval. Meanwhile, the opposing tribe, such as the Siksika, followed a similar procedure among its allies. At the appropriate time and place, either on the prairies or at a trading post, the warring sides came together and the treaty was concluded with smoking, prayers and kisses.

An old warrior once said that treaties were made by the old and broken by the young. The desire for adventure and prestige made it difficult to keep teenagers in camp, so when a band was located within easy range of an enemy, the camp was closely patrolled to halt any young raiders who might try to slip away. Sometime they eluded the guards, sometimes not. If they got away and were successful in a simple horse raid, the treaty remained secure. In some instances, a peaceful chief might even send the stolen horses back to their owners. But if there was a loss of life on either side, the treaty was in danger of being destroyed. One way to prevent the situation from getting out of hand was for the offending band to move away to avoid a revenge raid.

Maskepetoon was concerned about the success of the 1862 treaty. The following May, he asked a white visitor, "Well, my friend, do you think that the peace between the Blackfeet and ourselves will last for any time?" In response, the friend replied:

> I said I feared that it would soon be broken because they all traded at one fort, if for no other reason. They were led in this way to steal horses from each other, and in my opinion the first that will be killed will lie at the fort. You should, I said, have your own fort to trade in, and not go trading to the same fort as the Blackfeet. Each tribe is large enough to make it worth while to establish amongst them a small trading post; and thus seven nations which are always at war, would not be forced to trade at the same place, giving them, as it were, an opportunity of killing each other.[26]

One group that remained relatively unaffected by the war was the Pigeon Lake Crees, under the leadership of Stephen. Staying in the bush, trapping and venturing onto the prairies only when necessary, they avoided much of the mayhem that was occurring farther east. A Cree explained that they were a peaceful people: "Our chief has always adopted a peaceful attitude to all the tribes. We have never stolen their horses or committed a warlike action in our memory."[27] Stephen and his council were bound by the ethics of their Christian faith, but this pacifist attitude meant their young men were often held in contempt by other bands. Said Peter Erasmus, "The pride of these young men, the persistent training and watchfulness in guarding their camp, was at variance with the declared policy of peace at any price held by the elders... I sympathized with their independent spirit and their determination to protect their own hunting grounds."[28]

Methodist Church authorities considered Pigeon Lake to be too dangerous during the troubled times and ordered that the mission be moved to safer grounds. The site selected was sixty miles downstream from Edmonton, and it was named Victoria mission. It was an ideal location for Maskepetoon, as it was close to his hunting grounds, but not for the Pigeon Lake Crees. They refused to follow the missionary and continued to live and hunt in their traditional area.

CHAPTER FOURTEEN

The McDougalls

Woolsey had been a missionary among the Crees for almost ten years when, in ill health and worn out by the harshness of prairie life, he retired to Ontario and was replaced by George McDougall and his son John. Unlike their predecessors, the McDougalls were an ambitious pair who decided to tame the West in their own fashion. They extolled the agricultural virtues of the region, looked to its imminent settlement and shamelessly promoted the Methodist cause and their own mission work. One of their goals was to select a symbol of their success in the West. That symbol was Maskepetoon. It did not happen immediately, but over time they praised his peacemaking efforts, his leadership and those of his virtues that compared favourably with Methodism, or at least with Christianity. Had he not been such an outstanding man, Maskepetoon might have become a puppet of the church, but he maintained his integrity and independence all his life. Yet he was still the subject of homilies about choosing peace over war, forgiveness of one's enemies and bravery in the face of danger. These sermons reflected well on him and on those who claimed him as their own.

When the McDougalls arrived, Maskepetoon had not been baptized, and in an 1863 speech to George Flett, he appeared to be in no rush to take the step. Maskepetoon said:

> I heard the chief Nee-ta-me-na-hoos, or Little Hunter, say to the Interpreter, Mr. Monkman, that his heart was much troubled about religion. He wished to join the

church, saying that he stood as between two—one telling him to pray, and the other telling him not to pray. I, too, wish to pray, but I am frightened to fall again. I am troubled night and day whether I will join or not.[1]

Maskepetoon had been influenced by Christian teachings for more than twenty years, and no doubt accepted many of the tenets of the faith. However, both Rundle and Woolsey had respected his reluctance to abandon his old religion and made no attempt to baptize him. His friendship with the missionaries was sincere, and he valued them as friends. But he was wise enough to know the difference between friendship and religious commitment.

Upon their arrival in the area, one of the first persons the McDougalls wanted to meet was Maskepetoon, so they decided to visit him on the prairies. They left the site of Victoria mission in mid-August 1862, several weeks before the great peace treaty was signed. Because the area was still in a state of war, they travelled cautiously, reaching the large Cree encampment at a bend in the Battle River four days later. Maskepetoon, carrying a flag, came out to meet them and escorted them into the camp in company with a Cree cavalry. There were several in McDougall's group, including his son John, Woolsey, Steinhauer and interpreter William Monkman.

The camp consisted of some seventy lodges which, on the basis of seven persons per lodge, meant that between four hundred and five hundred men, women and children were at the place. The buffalo were near and food was plentiful. "Women were dressing skins, scraping hides, rendering tallow, pounding meat, making pemmican, slicing up the fresh meat and hanging it on the stages," the younger McDougall wrote. "Some were cooking; some were sewing, with awl for needle and sinew for thread."[2]

When a council meeting was held in the outdoors, Maskepetoon arose and gave the following speech, as recorded in part by the missionary Woolsey:

We are very glad to see you all, but especially our chief Minister. Other persons traverse our country but we are comparatively unnoticed by them. It is not so with you: here you are as our great friend. I am now 54 years of age and have seen many changes in that time. I remember when the buffalo was so numerous as to be amply compared to the blades of grass around us, when contrasted with the present number. What you see of them now is but the remnant.

This tract of country may be divided into three sections, the Indians occupying the outer portions and the buffalo the centre of it. In order to subsist, we must meet our enemies on one common hunting ground, subject frequently to loss of life and property. Now as you perceive, we are always in danger of the Blackfeet who already murdered many of our people. We are compelled to have sentinels on duty continually and to tether our horses every night lest they should be stolen from us.[3]

George McDougall responded by saying that the religion of the Bible was the only remedy for the world's troubles, but he followed this with his own secular message that expressed his vision for the future of the West. He told his audience that white people would be coming, that the buffalo would soon be exterminated and that the tribes would be dealt with fairly by the British government. He warned them that they should turn to farming and prepare themselves for a great change in their mode and manner of life. "In all probability," he told them, "they would soon have many white men crowding in among them and were to avoid giving offence in any respect and never be guilty of any depredation whatsoever."[4]

This blunt message and lecture must have come as a surprise to the assemblage. There is no indication that anyone, fur trader or traveller, had previously spoken to them about losing their lands to white settlers. In addition, many among his audience could never accept the possibility that the buffalo, their staff of life, could disappear. If the talk upset Maskepetoon, there is no indication of it in missionary records, but the message did get around. A year later, an Edmonton trader stated, "Sweet Grass and a few followers arrived from Fort Pitt quarter, come to enquire if the report of the Company having sold their Lands & that their Fort, etc. were to be given up, were true."[5]

The treaty of December 1862 held firm over the winter. The Blackfoot killed two Stoneys, but they were not part of the peace pact, so they didn't count. With the treaty in place, the Blackfoot were no longer afraid to go to Edmonton or Fort Pitt and kept the traders busy throughout the winter months. At the beginning of April, a large contingent of Blackfoot was joined by a trading party of Beaver Hills and Fort Pitt Crees under Sweet Grass and Little Chief. There was tension for a while when two Blackfoot horses went missing, but they were later found to have simply strayed from the camp.

At Fort Pitt, a similar tranquility existed. A traveller, Dr. W.B. Cheadle, noted in late April:

> Peace had just been concluded between the Crees and the Blackfeet; large camps of both nations were within a day or two's journey of the Fort. From these there was a continual going and coming of visitors, all anxious to avail themselves of the rare occasion of a peace, generally only of very short duration.
>
> On these state visits by the members of one tribe to those of the other, the men adorned themselves in gaudiest finery and brightest paint. Scarlet leggings and blankets, abundance of ribbons in the cap, if any were worn, or the hair plaited into a long queue behind, and two shorter ones hanging down on each side of the face in front, each bound round by coils of bright brass wire; round the eyes a halo of bright vermilion, a streak down the nose, a patch on each

cheek, and a circle round the mouth of the same colour, constituted the most effective toilet of a Cree dandy.[6]

While Cheadle was at Fort Pitt, news came in that a Cree woman had been killed in the Blackfoot camp.[7] There was some momentary concern, but in the end all decided to treat it as a domestic affair. The woman had gone to marry a Blackfoot, but another man took a fancy to her. The two men began to argue but then decided that their friendship was more important than the woman, so they killed her.

About this same time, Maskepetoon was in a camp near the Victoria mission with some sixty lodges of followers. He found the location to be convenient, particularly when the Hudson's Bay Company built an outpost there. To further cement their relations with the chief, the missionaries opened their home to him. Wrote John McDougall:

> Both father and mother have taken a strong liking to Maskepetoon, and have given the old gentleman a room in the new house, of which he is very proud. In this room he leaves his papers and books and clothes, and into it he often goes to read his Bible. His manly, courteous and kindly behavior makes it pleasant to have him in the house.

Such an accommodation was of obvious benefit to the chief, but it also placed him directly under the care and custody of the missionaries—something that neither Rundle nor Woolsey had ever tried to do. McDougall added:

> In every good work he is as the missionary's right hand. It is well it is so, for at this time the missionary needs all the help he can secure. This strange, promiscuous, turbulent crowd need careful handling. Men who have quarreled about a horse or a woman bring the case to the missionary to settle. Women whose husbands have, as they say, "thrown them

away," come to him to reinstate them in their husband's favour and lodge. Widows who have been robbed by their late husband's relatives pour their complaints into his ear, and look to him to adjust their claims.[8]

If the younger McDougall's assertions are correct, then his father must have brought about a complete reversal of roles. Rather than the missionaries, it normally would have been Maskepetoon who would sit in judgment and offer solutions to his people's problems. Not only was he a respected chief fulfilling a traditional role, but he had soldiers to enforce any decision he might make. In a few brief sentences, young McDougall seems to have reduced the chief to a servant to the missionaries.

A case that reflected the real situation occurred at Victoria mission some time later. A gold prospector named Gowler missed the tools that he had left by the river where he had been panning. As reported:

> He could only suppose that an Indian was the thief. He therefore complained to the chief. At once the young men of the camp were called together and addressed, the thief being asked to give up the stolen tools. No one responded. Mas-ki-pi-toon then called upon them to pass before him in review, and asked each individually if he had the white man's property. Some hundred or so had passed when the chief stopped an Indian who had just denied the theft, and raising his knife, threatened to kill him if he did not bring the tools. They were forthcoming. Mas-ki-pi-toon had selected the culprit, and Gowler was bothered no more.[9]

Maskepetoon was wise enough to know that he needed the missionaries. The traders concentrated only on company profits, while passing groups of travellers or gold prospectors were of no help at all. As Maskepetoon said about the missionaries, "They know that we are poor, and that we are as children knowing nothing. We are as if our eyes were covered, and cannot see as white men see." He had agreed with Woolsey a few years earlier when the missionary wanted to introduce farming to the Pigeon Lake people, but this would be a difficult transition. As Maskepetoon and fellow chief Little Hunter said, "I wish to sow, but how can I get my young men to take a hoe and dig up new sod? I cannot get the young men to work at new ground while the good buffalo meat is so near. How hard it is to change the mind of the Indian!"[10]

He also asked the missionaries for a school, praying that children could get the kind of education he had desired for his son Benjamin many years earlier.

Maskepetoon had suffered the loss of several children over the years through illness and warfare. Although he had a number of relatives—brothers, nephews and nieces—his nuclear family was relatively small. Only four of his sons reached manhood: Joshua, Joseph and two others. Of these, Joseph was described as "big, solid and staid—a man you could depend on."[11] One of the other two was murdered by a fellow Cree. He had gone to the Kootenai Indians to buy horses, and on the way back had been slain by his companion. When the man returned to the camp, he claimed the young man had been killed in an enemy attack. Later, the truth was discovered. At first, Maskepetoon threatened to kill the murderer, but in the end he forgave him.[12] This capacity for forgiveness, whether inspired by Christian teachings or his own culture, also extended to a Blackfoot who killed Maskepetoon's father during a time of war. During a peace treaty, the two happened to be in the same camp, and there was fear that when Maskepetoon learned of the man's presence, he would kill him and wreck the treaty. According to McDougall:

> When he heard it he sent for his best horse, had him saddled and accoutred as for war, fastened him at his tent-door, and ... sent for his father's murderer. The man, an elderly warrior, came as to his death, and Maskepetoon

waved him to a seat near himself in the tent. Passing him his own adorned chief's clothes, made of leather, decorated with beads and quills and fringed with human hair, he said to him, "Put those on." Again Maskepetoon spoke: "You deprived me of my father, and there was a time when I would have gloried in taking your life and in drinking your blood, but that is past . . . You need not fear; I will not kill you. You must now be to me as a father; wear my clothes, ride my horse, and tell your people when you go back to your camp this is the way Mon-e-guh-ba-now [Young Man Chief] takes revenge."[13]

Maskepetoon showed great leadership in ignoring his personal feelings, and he opted to keep the treaty intact. This was the mark of a great chief, but his actions were not unique, as there were examples of other leaders showing the same kind of forgiveness. For example, when a party of Crees went to the Siksika and Blood camps to make peace, the Siksika were willing but the Bloods were not. They threatened to kill the peace party, so the Crees prepared to leave under a Siksika escort. Two young Crees, however, decided that they would risk death by going to the Blood camps themselves to speak to the chief. When they got there, the chief greeted them, knowing that they were Crees, and sent for an interpreter who could speak their language. The chief said, "These two young men have killed the anger in me by coming to my tent like this, in the early morning. If they are willing, I will take them as my relatives. I thought that I could never be friendly to Crees, for they took the lives of two of my sons. But these have killed the anger in me. They will be my sons." Like Maskepetoon, the chief gave them his best clothing and invited them to live in the Blood camp. They stayed until the Bloods moved south, then returned to their people, taking with them gifts of horses from the chief.[14]

By the late spring of 1863, the Indians had moved out of their winter quarters, and the peace treaty soon was in jeopardy.

Because of the shrinking herds, the Crees and Blackfoot were simply too close to each other on the plains. Under such conditions, young men could not resist slipping away to round up a few enemy horses. In May, fur-trade reports confirmed that horse stealing had started again, and by August, the two tribes were back at each other's throats. A trader commented, "The Blackfeet & Crees are again at war; this will have some effect on our Trade at Edmonton as the Blackfeet will be afraid to visit that Post on acct. of the Crees being always on the watch for them."[15]

Maskepetoon stayed on the plains over the summer and in the autumn took robes and meat to the fort. Afterwards, he settled near Victoria mission for the winter of 1863–64. A few buffalo herds were close, so the hunting was good. In January, men from his camp brought in dried meat, tongues and grease to trade, but only five buffalo robes and twenty-eight wolf skins—a far cry from the numbers of earlier years.[16] Only a few minor skirmishes took place over the winter; however, in the spring of 1864, fighting broke out anew.

The first incident occurred when a hunting party from Maskepetoon's band was attacked by the Blackfoot. According to McDougall:

> The Crees were surrounded and kept for two nights and nearly two days in the pits they had dug with their knives. The Blackfeet were ten times their number, and kept them well under cover, but did not muster courage sufficient to rush in, or the Crees would have been cleaned out in short order. As it was several were killed. Of two I knew, one was killed and the other shot in the breast but recovered as by a miracle.[17]

About this time, a large party of some seven hundred Siksika and Bloods came to trade at Edmonton. They had been there for a couple of days and were packing up to leave when a war party of Fort Pitt Crees under the leadership of Little Pine attacked the few who were still in front of the fort gates. The Siksika returned the fire but were forced to retreat down the hill, leaving their horses behind. One Blood who was seriously wounded was dragged inside the fort by his wife, who had their little child on her back. The Crees captured the loose horses but were forced by the traders to return them to the Siksika. Meanwhile, the plains people assembled on the south side of the river and hurried away to their camps, but they lost everything they had received in trade, such as tobacco, ammunition, cloth and blankets.

The Blood inside the fort had been shot in the chest and was in serious condition. Father Lacombe, who was at the fort at the time, took the wife and child to St. Albert mission for safety. When the man died, they stayed under the protection of the missionaries for a couple of weeks. Later, a head chief of the Bloods, Rainy Chief, came to find out what had happened to them. He smoked a pipe with the traders, was given gifts and took the two survivors back to their own camp.[18] Others in the tribe weren't so forgiving. A war party of Bloods was observed near the fort, ready to take revenge on any Crees that might show up. Forewarned, however, they stayed away until the war party finally left.

Maskepetoon had seen all that was taking place. He was sad that his peace treaty had lasted for such a short time, but even a few months of peace had allowed his people to hunt and probably had resulted in the saving of a few lives. However, when his own horses were stolen in the early fall, the chief did not hesitate to try to get them back, in spite of the war. With his fifteen-year-old son and a few companions, he and his party travelled south until they reached the Battle River. They were just coming up a hill when they met a Blackfoot hunting party riding up from the other side. Both parties were surprised as they met at the brow of the hill. Most of the Crees scurried into hiding, leaving only Maskepetoon and his son to face the enemy. Wrote George Flett:

Immediately on getting sight of the Crees, the Blackfoot threw off blankets, got ready their guns, and rushed on to fight. To their amazement there was no one to fight with. The Cree Chief, whom they did not recognize, was in the road, with his son on horseback by his side; but so far from making any warlike demonstrations, the old hero had taken out his New Testament, which he appeared to read with great composure. He was as cool as a cucumber. This unlooked for event, so entirely out of accord with Indian practice, struck the impetuous Blackfoot with astonishment, which caused them to halt suddenly, and then, seeing the unaltered bearing, fearlessness and peaceful attitude of the chief they became awed, believing that this must be a great medicine man who was under the protection of the spirits. Seeing that he was not in the least afraid, and that he declined either to fight or fly, they at last called out to him, "who are you?"

"Mas-ke-pe-toun," was the reply.

All the Blackfoot knew of the famous Cree peacemaker, and their mood immediately changed from aggressive to conciliatory. They set aside their guns and gave father and son a friendly greeting. Maskepetoon called to his companions to come forward, and one by one they crept out of the bushes, to the great amusement of the Blackfoot, who contrasted their cowardice with the bravery of their leader. The Cree party accompanied the Blackfoot to their camp, where Maskepetoon's horses were restored to him.[19]

A story has circulated that this incident took place near the city of Wetaskiwin and resulted in the naming of the Peace Hills. This is at variance with what elders have said. George Mann, the Indian agent at Hobbema at about 1900, was told about the real source of the name. He wrote:

> Louis Bull of Bull's Reserve says he was a young lad at the time but remembers quite well the incidents of the two

peace compacts entered into. His story I am sending you as it is in substance practically the same as all the others whom I have interviewed.

About the year 1860 a small Band of Blackfeet who had been hunting in the North, camped on the way south on the north side of a small hill near the present town of Wetaskiwin. On the south side of the hill a Band of Crees were also in camp, and each Band sent out a young chief to reconnoitre. The two chiefs met on the top of what is now known as Peace Hills. There the two Chiefs made a peace and smoked a pipe together.

But this pact was of very short duration as the Blackfeet on their way south, fell upon a party of Crees camped on the Battle River where the Mission now stands on the Samson Reserve and massacred the party with only a few exceptions, among whom were the late Kinnewitts of Ermineskin Reserve and old woman Okaine, now living on the Samson Reserve, who substantiated the story as told by Louis Bull. It was not until some seven years after the above had taken place that a real and presumably permanent peace was made in 1867.[20]

In September 1864, a number of Fort Pitt Crees went to Edmonton to see about making peace.[21] No Blackfoot trading parties appeared there, so two months later they tried again, Sweet Grass sending a gift of tobacco to Edmonton.[22] The offer was accepted just before the onset of winter. Not included were the Stoneys, who made a foray near Edmonton shortly thereafter and took thirteen Cree horses.[23] In retaliation, five Crees, with Maskepetoon's young son among them, set out to raid the Stoney camps. They found them at Pigeon Lake, so they asked John McDougall if they could spend the night at his mission. This request was granted—no doubt Maskepetoon's son was welcome there. That night, when everyone was asleep, the Crees crept into the Stoney camp and took a dozen horses.

It should have been a grand experience, but it wasn't. The horses were in no fit condition to travel fast and for a long distance. Some had to be left along the way, and the rest were abandoned when angry Stoneys on foot caught up with the Crees, who had to flee.[24]

The buffalo were plentiful and close during the winter of 1864–65. In January, the trader at Edmonton stated, "Two Crees arrived from the Cree Camp, say they have plenty of Buffalo & want us to go out on a Trade; ordered them to go to Victoria & Trade there as we sent supplies there for them. Sent Tobacco to the principal Crees."[25] There were no serious infractions of Sweet Grass' treaty, and by spring the Crees were well stocked with food.

But then another enemy appeared on the horizon—not a Blackfoot raider, but an epidemic of measles and scarlet fever that swept the plains, killing more than a thousand Blackfoot in its path. By spring, it had spread to the Crees and to families at Fort Edmonton. When Sweet Grass came to the fort, there were sick children in his camp, so traders would not allow them to come across the river. Instead, men were sent to trade with them.[26] Word came from Rocky Mountain House that the disease was rampant there, and the Blackfoot coming to the fort were blaming the white people for the disease and threatening to kill any they met.

The disease also struck Maskepetoon's camp, in the vicinity of Victoria mission. Like the Blackfoot, many blamed the Europeans for bringing the disease, and the Plains Crees in particular were arrogant and in a bad mood when the McDougalls tried to visit them. "Indeed," said John McDougall, "if it not were for Maskepetoon and his own people, many a time our Mission party would have suffered."[27] Eventually the epidemic passed, and the Crees buried their dead and went on with their lives.

CHAPTER FIFTEEN

A Christian Leader

Labouring alongside George McDougall during the measles epidemic, Maskepetoon finally agreed that it was time for him and his wife to join the Christian church. On April 16, 1865, he was baptized Abraham Wood Maskepetoon, age fifty-eight, while Sussewisk became Sarah Maskepetoon, age fifty-five.[1] Almost a quarter of a century had passed since the chief had first met Rundle, and over the years he had faithfully read his Bible and other tracts that were given to him. He absorbed the stories told to him about Christianity and what it was to be a Christian, many of them dovetailing with his own beliefs and practices. According to his nephew, "I have heard that he would gather his fellow Crees together. On Sundays he would read to them from the writings that he had."[2] One day when the elder McDougall visited the chief, "he was found reading the eighth chapter of Romans from a copy of the New Testament which had been given to him by the Rev. Thomas Woolsey."[3] Christianity did not make Maskepetoon a new man, rather, it affirmed the qualities, attitudes and beliefs that he already possessed.

A short time later, John McDougall accompanied Maskepetoon and his people to the plains for the spring hunt, where he immediately noticed that most of the band was non-Christian. Decrying the situation, he lamented:

> Here was paganism intensely conservative, the outcome of many centuries of tradition. And here were its high priests,

and the novitiate following which thronged after them, seeming to me as "the blind leading the blinder," if this were possible; the whole causing a devolution which was lowering the range of thought and life and ideal, and all the while producing a profundity of ignorance as to things moral and spiritual which in turn, as a logical sequence, affected the physical and material life of this people.[4]

Some leaders, such as Maskepetoon, Little Hunter and Stephen, had accepted the Methodist teachings, while Sweet Grass, Kehewin and Bob Tail had welcomed the Catholics, but the majority remained with their old ways. The belief that Christian conversion could be attained by converting the leaders was probably true, as the adherence of the leading chiefs would have an effect on the others. Already, quite a number of Maskepetoon's followers considered themselves to be Christian, while Stephen's flock at Pigeon Lake possessed a strong nucleus of believers.

The success of the Methodists was of great concern to the Catholics. The Oblate priests who had concentrated on the Metis and northern Indians found they were losing out on the prairies. Their missions at Lac Ste. Anne and St. Albert were too far from the plains tribes and had not been effective. But in 1864, Father Lacombe had been assigned "the mission of coursing the prairies to try and reach the poor savage Crees and Blackfeet."[5] One of his first actions was to establish a new mission, about fifty miles upstream from Fort Pitt. Named St. Paul des Cris, it was in the heart of the Fort Pitt Cree hunting grounds. Until this time, Bob Tail had camped with Maskepetoon near Victoria mission, two of his children having been born there, but he was among the first to accept the Catholic mission as his own.

The Hudson's Bay Company traders did not like the mission site. One trader commented, "The main cause of the failure of the Fort Pitt Trade is the Establishment of a Roman Catholic

Mission, two days above Fort Pitt for the benefit of the Fort Pitt Crees, whither they went ... last Spring and fall, and [did] little or nothing in the way of collecting Provisions."[6]

Inter-tribal war broke out anew during the spring. In May 1865, a trader reported that a fight had taken place in which six Crees, four Assiniboines "and a good many Blackfeet" had been killed.[7] A more tragic confrontation took place a month later when a Blood war party of eighty men attacked a Cree camp near a place called Round Timber. A Blood leader described the scene:

> We covered the fronts of our light-coloured horses with buffalo robes and made the party look like buffalo. We walked our horses towards a certain hill that was between us and the camp. Several times we had to take to open prairie, but we walked slow, like buffalo, and all lowered our heads and horses' necks, and reached the hill, behind which all of us painted and made ready for action.

The Bloods counted twenty-nine Cree women who were going for water, with a young lad as their guard. On a signal, the Bloods attacked and the women fled screaming towards the camp. But they never made it: the war party surrounded them, and one by one they were cut down until all thirty lay dead on the prairie. They were scalped and their clothes taken. The Bloods headed for home, pursued by angry Crees, but as the Blood leader said, "We went slow, allowed them to catch up to us, then turned and charged them, killing their leader."[8]

Stung by the savage massacre, the Crees vowed revenge. Most of the Blackfoot tribes had gone south for a new treaty with the American government, so there was no chance for a swift reprisal. A man from the Fort Pitt Crees lost a daughter, Broken Wing, in the attack, so he travelled from camp to camp urging the people to take revenge. One group that listened and acted was Bob Tail's band, and they were perhaps joined by others from the Pigeon Lake Crees, who were on the prairies for the autumn hunts. They had been a peaceful people, perhaps too much so. Said Peter Erasmus, "The contemptuous attitude the other tribes held for the Pigeon Lake Indians on account of their declared policy for peace was growing irksome to these trained young warriors, and I feared they would break out in open defiance."[9] He was right, and under the leadership of Bob Tail, they joined a huge revenge party, mostly from the Fort Pitt area. In December 1865, men, women and young boys from the Cree, Assiniboine and Ojibwa tribes danced for three days and then set out for the Battle River, where they knew the Siksikas were settled in their winter camps. Thunderchild, a Cree patriarch, was a young boy at the time, and he recalled the event:

> Scouts went out before us, and on both sides, and there was a general shout when three riders appeared. Two of them were scouts, the third was a Blackfoot woman, very pretty. The scouts had killed her husband, and they gave her to Short Tail [Bob Tail], the brother of Ermine Skin. But they warned us that one Blackfoot had escaped and would give the alarm, and that there might be an attack that same night. We would have to be ready.[10]

When they reached the enemy camp late at night on December 4, they crossed the river and set up a camp among the poplars. From there, some warriors went out and captured a few Siksika horses. It was obvious that their presence was undetected. The camp belonged to Natos, The Sun, a prominent leader of the tribe, but what the Crees didn't know was that Father Lacombe was visiting and was sleeping in the chief's lodge.

At 2 a.m., the Crees attacked, focusing on the chief's large painted lodge. Father Lacombe recalled what happened next:

> Suddenly Natous started up, and seizing his gun, cried out in a wailing tone in the language of the Black-Feet

"*Assinaw! Assinaw!* The Crees! the Crees!"¹¹ He had scarcely uttered these words when a frightful peal of musketry was heard, and our tents were pierced with balls. That of the chief was the one most exposed to danger . . . I am utterly unable to express what I saw and felt on that fearful night . . . My chief, with his family, had dashed out of the tent he inhabited, and encouraged his men to defend themselves valiantly. On the first discharge, two poles of our tent had been broken, and I saw the blazing wads from the guns fall at my feet.¹²

Soon there was the cry of the wounded on both sides as the Siksika hurried to defend their camp. They had only sixty guns, and the onslaught of the Crees' superior firepower forced them back. But The Sun stood firm and rallied his men to hold off the attackers. He was succeeding when a bullet struck him in the leg and put him out of the battle. An Assiniboine dashed into the chief's lodge and grabbed the priest's breviary, but a Siksika who witnessed the action shot and killed the man, scalped him and recovered the book. As the Siksika retreated to the far edge of the camp, the victorious Crees invaded it. Recalled Thunderchild:

> By now the Blackfoot had fled back to their camp, and there were war yells, and the cries of women and children. I ran forward to the line of Crees facing the Blackfoot camp. One of the Crees ran into the camp and hit a Blackfoot tent, shouting out, "I am called the son of *O-ka-mai-ka-na-wa-sis*." Then the others ran forward too, one after the other, and I ran with them.
>
> They began to cut the tents open and pull them down, but the Blackfoot had run in amongst the trees, where there were more tents, and they were digging pits in the soft ground of the fire places. They shot and killed some of the Crees at the edge of the bush . . . Someone began to yell, "If anyone can take that shield near the tents, he can

have all these women." And another sang, "I am *O-pe-po-noik*. Cover me, fellow-children. I will take it." And he walked over and took it; but it was a drum, not a shield.[13]

The battle raged all that night. The Siksikas counterattacked and drove the Crees back, but then retreated again. Three times they attacked, and three times they were repulsed. When it was daylight, Lacombe tried to halt the fighting, waving his red cross flag, but was pulled to safety when a spent bullet ricocheted and struck him on the forehead.

Meanwhile, the gunfire had been heard downriver, where other Siksikas were camped. Under the leadership of Crowfoot, they surged into the battle, forcing the Crees to withdraw. "The wounded and dead were carried back to our encampment," said Thunderchild, "though the dead who were close to the Blackfoot tents we had to leave. I walked beside my wounded friend and wet his lips with snow." The Siksikas followed them, but they were afraid to come close and finally called off the pursuit to look after their dead and wounded.

The Siksikas had twelve killed, fifteen wounded and two children stolen. More than two hundred horses were captured, twenty-five lodges destroyed and virtually everything inside taken as plunder. The Crees lost ten men and had fifty wounded, some dying later. The father of one dead Cree warrior said, "My son has been in the games, and has been beaten. We will leave his body here." Thunderchild said of another casualty, "Before he died, he gave his three horses to his aunt, and he asked her to care for his dog which had waited at the camp for him, and had stayed beside the dying man. Then the woman sang of her nephew, of his manliness, and of the love that his dog had for him. She wept for him, and the women mourned aloud. And the dog searched the camp for the man he had followed faithfully."[14] In spite of their losses, the Crees believed they had taken revenge for the slain water carriers, and they triumphantly returned east to their hunting grounds.

Battle of Four Ponds

Artist Frederic Remington depicted Father Albert Lacombe trying to stop a battle between Blackfoot and Crees in 1870. Many of Maskepetoon's followers took part in the attack. The image appeared in Harper's Weekly, October 18, 1880.

Fort Edmonton

This is how Fort Edmonton looked during Maskepetoon's time. It is where he brought his buffalo robes, meat and other goods to trade for ammunition, powder, knives and other items. The painting was made by Paul Kane following his visit to the fort in 1847 and is now in the Royal Ontario Museum, Toronto.

The Rev. Robert T. Rundle was the first Protestant missionary to visit Maskepetoon. He also introduced him to the system of syllabic writing that made it possible for him to communicate with the missionary and other chiefs.

John Edward Harriott, a trader for the Hudson's Bay Company, became a good friend of Maskepetoon. He was in charge of Rocky Mountain House, where the chief often traded, from 1834 to 1853.

RM House

This 1847 painting by Paul Kane shows a Stoney camp with Rocky Mountain House in the background. The fort was used by Maskepetoon and his followers and was run by the chief's old friend John Harriott.

Fort Vancouver

This is approximately how Fort Vancouver looked when Maskepetoon visited it in 1841. It was located near the mouth of the Columbia River in the present state of Washington. It was sketched by John Mix Stanley about seventeen years after the chief's visit.

SS Beaver

When Maskepetoon travelled to the west coast in *1841*, he had the opportunity to ride in this Hudson's Bay Company steamship, the SS Beaver. It left Fort Vancouver and went up the coast as far north as Whidbey Island, near the present Mount Vernon, Washington, looking for settlement sites. On his return, Maskepetoon asked for a paper proving he had actually ridden on the boat so that he could show it to others when he returned home. This is a view of the boat in Burrard Inlet in *1888*.

Maskepetoon Letter

This letter was written in syllabics by Maskepetoon to missionary Robert T. Rundle on December 28, 1844. It states, "He-Who-Speaks-From-Above [Rundle's Cree name]. I send you a letter. I shake hands with you. I want you to be here, to see you, I and the Assiniboines. There are twenty lodges. My son Benjamin, I want him to speak English. There are 164 buffalo. I tell you the news, my friend. I am Maskepetoon."

Eyes on Both Sides

Eyes on Both Sides, seen here in 1832, was a Cree chief from the Upper Missouri River who was taken on a trip to Washington in 1831–32, where he met President Andrew Jackson. His other name was Maskepetoon, or Broken Arm, the same as the Canadian chief. He was painted in 1832 by George Catlin.

MASKEPETOON'S CAMP—(See page 188).

Maskepetoon's Camp

Maskepetoon and his Cree warriors are shown escorting a group of missionaries to the chief's camp. According to John McDougall, this was a huge camp made up of Woodland Crees, Plains Crees and people from other tribes. The drawing was made by J.E. Laughlin for McDougall's book Forest, Lake and Prairie.

Woolsey

The Rev. Thomas Woolsey came west in 1855 and opened a mission at Pigeon Lake. In later years, he recalled that he and Maskepetoon "frequently traversed those plains together, amidst vicissitudes too strange for ordinary language to portray." This engraving is from "a photograph taken soon after his return from the North-West." It was published in John McDougall's Saddle, Sled and Snowshoe.

Maskepetoon and Wife

Borrowing from images of eastern Canadian Indians, this unknown artist depicted Maskepetoon and family in sombre tones. It was used as an illustration in missionary Egerton R. Young's Indian Life in the Great North-West.

George McDougall

The Rev. George McDougall, Methodist missionary, first met Maskepetoon in the summer of 1864. McDougall was the minister who pressed the chief to become a Christian and baptized him Abraham Wood Maskepetoon a year later.

Maskepetoon and Son

Maskepetoon and his son are depicted by artist J.E. Laughlin in an incident where the chief bravely faced attacking Blackfoot. When the attackers learned who he was, they praised and honoured him. The image was used as an illustration in John McDougall's Saddle, Sled and Snowshoe.

John McDougall

The Rev. John McDougall, son of George McDougall, was a friend and sometime companion of Maskepetoon. He was an ardent Methodist and nationalist.

Samson

Samson, seen here in 1886, was the younger brother of Maskepetoon. He was chief of the band when they settled on their reserve.

Erasmus was saddened by the death of the Crees, particularly those from Pigeon Lake. "I was never again to see many of these young men," he lamented. "Under a war chief from Fort Pitt, they were drawn into battle with the Blackfoot. Although they won the battle, many of the Pigeon Lake men were killed, and the tribe so decimated that living at Pigeon Lake so near to Blackfoot territory made that area unsafe for many years."[15]

After the raid, bad luck plagued the Crees for the rest of the winter of 1865–66. The buffalo, usually plentiful just south of Victoria mission, failed to appear. One reason for this was that a huge fire that engulfed the northern plains during the fall had destroyed their winter pasture. Another was that the herds were simply getting smaller because of overhunting. By late January 1866, Maskepetoon and his followers were starving. In addition, bitterly cold weather made long-distance travelling on the plains impractical. The traders at Rocky Mountain House were living on rabbits, and Fort Edmonton was expected to be on short rations by spring.[16]

With a shortage of food at Victoria mission, John McDougall set out in January to find Maskepetoon, who was said to be 150 miles southeast, past Birch Creek. When they found no signs of Indians or buffalo, they turned eastward, eventually catching up with Maskepetoon just as he was leaving for a new campsite. "We were disturbed to find," said McDougall, "that these people were living from hand to mouth—that while the buffalo were within from sixty to one hundred and fifty miles distant, they had not yet attempted to come north."[17] Not wanting to venture any deeper into Blackfoot territory, Maskepetoon had waited and hoped the buffalo would come to him. They hadn't, and now the starving Crees were forced to move closer to the herds. Finding no food for the mission, McDougall was reluctantly preparing to go home when Maskepetoon sent word to the lodges, asking people to donate meat for the mission. This was done, in spite of their own starvation.

"Tell your father," said Maskepetoon, "that we are still hopeful of the buffalo taking a turn northward, and of making robes and provisions and coming into the Mission in the spring well loaded. Tell him to pray for us."[18]

But the buffalo never did come, and by March, Maskepetoon's camp was too close to the Blackfoot for comfort. Neither wanted war, as they were too busy trying to survive, but the situation remained tense. In March, a Fort Edmonton trader said, "The Indians are everywhere on the Plains about here, and Victoria, and we have daily arrivals of Starving Creatures, begging for food and Ammunition. Rabbits are fortunately fairly numerous, or some would most certainly starve to death.[19]

About this time, a Cree came to Fort Edmonton, hoping that the Blackfoot would be there so that peace could be made. When they didn't show up, a few Crees contacted Father Lacombe at St. Paul des Cris and explained that their camp was within a day's march of the Blackfoot. "The Crees, dreading vengeance from the Black-Feet," he said, "besought me to go to these savages to appease once more their wrath." The priest first visited the Cree camp, where he was assured of that tribe's peaceful intentions and was given tobacco to take with him. He continued:

> I then went to the camp of the Black-Feet, who were much surprised to see me. I remained five days amongst them. They consented to make peace with the Crees; the tobacco of the two nations was cut up together, and the large calumets of peace were brought out. They smoked them as indications of concord. I represented the Crees.[20]

This treaty remained firm for a brief time, giving the Crees and Blackfoot a chance to recover. But both sides were angry about their losses and only waited for spring to get their revenge.

The appearance of Father Lacombe on the prairies, with his assistant Brother Constantine Scollen, reawakened the competition for souls that had been more or less dormant for more than two decades. Now, since St. Paul des Cris and Victoria missions were fairly close to each other along the North Saskatchewan River, each missionary began to rail against the other. George McDougall wrote:

> The Papacy, the man of sin, is powerfully represented in this country. There are five priests to one Protestant missionary. They are anti-British in their national sympathies, and if we may judge the tree by its fruit, anti-Christ in their teachings. Their converts have a zeal, but their fervor prompts them to propagate a system and not a Saviour. By them the Sabbath is desecrated, polygamy tolerated and the Bible ignored. Their churches are the toy shops where the poor heathens get their playthings, such as idols, beads and charms.[21]

Constantine Scollen was equally direct:

> It is only in a country like this that one can rightly witness the glorious triumph of truth over error. Here you may see the Protestant Minister with the bible in one hand and the mammon of iniquity in the other, proclaiming aloud that this large book with its gilt-edge is the "book of God," and he that believes in it shall have a few shillings from the Preacher. Thus whilst in theory he preaches abnegation, in practice he preaches quite the opposite... The poor Indian is indeed very ignorant, but he... sees that the religion preached by the Protestant Minister is full of alloy and therefore cannot be from God who is infinitely pure.[22]

In 1866, Maskepetoon's followers finally split on religious grounds. The Catholics under Bob Tail resorted to St. Paul des Cris, where they met with fellow converts Sweet Grass and

Kehiwin. In 1867, the St. Paul des Cris journal recorded, "Several prairie Indians arrived—Kiskayu [Bob Tail]."[23] And two years later, the priests recognized Bob Tail as a chief when they noted, "Kiskayu and his band have arrived."[24] Maskepetoon continued to camp near Victoria mission, and his followers, many non-Christians among them, were identified with the Methodists. This separation was strongly supported by missionaries on both sides. Usually, however, larger camps were a mix of the two groups, with no apparent animosity. Some time later, Scollen visited a camp on the plains that was composed of "about 70 lodges, of which 40 were Roman Catholics, 13 were Protestants, and the remaining pagans."[25]

Maskepetoon appeared to be unaffected by the factionalism that was becoming evident in his camp. Two of his best friends were Sweet Grass and Kehiwin—both Catholics—while his friend Little Hunter was a staunch Methodist. Religion played no part in Maskepetoon's leadership; he was concerned with maintaining order in the camp and on the hunt, protecting his people from their enemies and doing all he could to put food in the lodges.

By the late 1860s, the Crees needed a strong leader, as it seemed their world was quickly falling apart. The buffalo were diminishing in great numbers, people were starving, gold miners were tramping through their territory and the Blackfoot had become violent against everyone—Crees, Stoneys, Americans, fur traders and missionaries.

The renewed Blackfoot hostility originated along the Missouri River and centred on the village of Fort Benton. Murders, confrontations and bloodshed became commonplace as the Blackfoot resisted the influx of white people into their lands. One of the earliest incidents occurred in the spring of 1865, when Bloods stole some horses at Benton. The local citizens retaliated by murdering the first Indian who came to town—a Blood chief. When his tribe heard about it, they attacked a party of eleven woodcutters and killed them all.

During the following winter, four North Peigans were murdered by drunken miners, and in response, tribesmen swept into the Sun River area, destroying the government farm, killing an employee, slaughtering the cattle belonging to the Catholic mission and murdering the herdsman.

From that time, any "northern" Blackfoot Indians (Bloods and Siksikas) risked their lives in coming south. In the autumn of 1866, Benton citizens killed and scalped seven Peigans who came too close to their town. In 1867, a freighter was killed, robbed and his body peppered with bullet holes. This was followed by two other killings and several horse raids, while the settlers responded with equal viciousness. Mountain Chief, head chief of the Peigan tribe, was attacked when he went to Fort Benton, causing him to flee for his life. When the Peigans heard about it, they raided Virginia City, where they took eighty horses and escaped from an angry posse. The citizens, in turn, ambushed twenty-one Peigan youths and made them prisoners. They were then turned over to the army at Fort Shaw, where they were held as hostages until the stolen horses were returned. The people of Montana called this the "Blackfoot war."[26]

In the face of this kind of mayhem, many Peigans and Bloods were afraid to visit the trading posts on the Missouri. Their option was to go to Edmonton, Rocky Mountain House or Fort Pitt. But among their trading parties were young Blackfoot warriors whose hatred now extended to white people everywhere. This became apparent in the summer of 1866, when the Blackfoot attacked Fort Pitt. According to a trader:

> A day or two after the departure of the Brigade from Fort Pitt, that Post when garrisoned by only 5 men, was visited by a war party of 200 Blackfeet, who managed to force an entry into the Fort & pillaged the Trading Shop and Men's Houses of all they could ... Leaving the Fort the same party fell in with the Fort Hunters & pilfered them of Clothing, Horses, carts & lines ... A week

later, a Blackfoot fired at McDonald at Carlton House (wounding him severely in the right side and through the left arm).[27]

Late in the summer of 1866, the Blackfoot tribes came to Edmonton under the leadership of The Sun. They traded peacefully but were ambushed when they left the fort and a number of them killed. "Said act, if true," said a trader, "may considerably affect us as regards provisions as probably the Slave Indians may be afraid to come in a trade to this place."[28]

A short time later, a party of Bloods came north, wanting to trade but afraid to come to the fort because of the Crees. In response, the factor sent out carts of goods to them at Battle River. While the Bloods waited, they were joined by a number of Siksikas, who pillaged the carts when they arrived and wanted to kill the Metis drivers. However, the Bloods defended the Metis and saw them safely returned to Edmonton.[29]

Maskepetoon had heard that this Blood trading party was coming and went with fellow chief Kehiwin to Edmonton to greet them and to see if they could make peace. The Bloods, of course, were not there, but as soon as the two chiefs arrived, their horses were stolen by their one-time allies, the Stoneys. The chief had to make his way back to the Victoria trading post on foot, where he was chagrined to learn that, in his absence, the Blackfoot had struck his own camp and taken seventy-seven horses. They had cleaned out the camp; not a horse was left. Not only that, but they had killed a man and his wife and cut them to pieces.[30]

The whole camp was furious, and Maskepetoon among them. While he had been away trying to make peace, the very people who could profit by peaceful relations were out to destroy his camp. Food was in short supply, and now his people would not be able to travel with any speed the long distances to the buffalo herds. Instead, they would have to rely on their dogs and sleds. After the raid, a trader noted, "The Crees are preparing for a formidable attack on the Blackfeet, so we may have, or rather may hear of a repetition of last 4th & 5th Decr."³¹ That was when the Crees had attacked the Blackfoot while Father Lacombe was in their camp.

The Crees had to delay their retaliation until the spring of 1867 because of the bitterly cold and stormy winter. In March, a huge war party of 1,200 Crees set out to gain their revenge; they discovered a Blackfoot camp containing ninety warriors, which they attacked. The small force responded vigorously, many of the Blackfoot probably armed with repeating rifles. When it was over, three Blackfoot had been killed, two wounded and a woman taken prisoner. The Crees, on the other hand, lost ten men and had several wounded.³²

Soon, nothing seemed the same on the plains. Seven lodges of Stoneys fought with eight Crees, while Peigans fought with their fellow Siksikas and killed twenty of them. Conflict had reached a point where one could hardly tell friend from foe. A trader commented, "The Indians are getting very bad, Crees & Blackfeet, and I think it is just a question of time when they will turn on the Whites & endeavour to massacre the whole. The Blackfeet say they plainly see they are to fall before the advance of Whites & Civilization & they don't care how soon."³³

Information was circulating that cast the future of the tribes in doubt. The buffalo were rapidly disappearing, rumours continued to be spread that their lands would be taken from them, the McDougalls and other missionaries were talking about farming being a way of the future, and more and more white traders, miners and travellers were flooding their territories. The Indians had good reason to be angry and depressed.

Maskepetoon could do nothing about the changes or the reluctance of the tribes to seek peace with each other. None of the Blackfoot tribes was amenable to a treaty, and even if one was made, it probably would not have been honoured by other branches of the nation. Instead, he focused his attention on seeing that his people were fed. During the summer, they travelled to the plains in force, maintained a close guard and dried the meat for later use. From time to time, they were visited by Metis hunters, free traders, missionaries and travellers. One visitor, James Gibbons, who was staying with the Methodists at Victoria mission, set out with John Whitford to bring back a supply of meat. They travelled to where the town of Vegreville now stands, but did not see a single buffalo. His partner turned back, but Gibbons travelled south for another 125 miles until he found a Cree camp of about a hundred lodges. Although Sweet Grass was there, the camp may have included Maskepetoon. Because they had no horses, his people were using impoundments to kill buffalo.[34]

During this time, Maskepetoon's camp included some Rocky Mountain Crees and others who had flocked to his side because of his leadership. There also were families from the Beaver Hills Crees, Fort Pitt Crees and Woodland bands that normally hunted north of the North Saskatchewan River. The rest of the Rocky Mountain Crees stayed in the Pigeon Lake area under the leadership of Stephen and, after he died, of Samson. They hunted for furs and lived off deer, rabbits and fish, although Samson did take them to the plains whenever it was possible to hunt buffalo. Sometimes they found a few scattered herds and old bulls fairly close to the woods, but more and more they had to go all the way to Maskepetoon's camp before they could find sufficient supplies to fill their needs. The buffalo, tens of thousands of them, still coursed the plains south of the Bow River, but they refused to come north in any significant numbers.

By the spring of 1867, the Pigeon Lake people had barely enough meat to feed themselves and little to show for their winter's work. As McDougall said, "About the end of March Indians began to straggle in, bringing little or no provisions, but glad to fall back with us on the food supply of the lake."[35] Some turned to gardening to provide vegetables and grain for the fall. After the crops were planted, Samson set out again for the plains, so McDougall and others joined him in the hunt.

They passed the Red Deer River and were 150 miles from the lake before they found a herd of a hundred buffalo. "Here we remained for several days," said McDougall, "going out and killing and bringing the meat home, all the time constantly on guard to prevent our horses being stolen or our camp attacked, for we were now on the outer fringes of the great herds of buffalo and might come across enemies at any time."[36]

The fall hunt was moderately successful, as it was in Maskepetoon's camp. Other chiefs, such as Sweet Grass and Kehiwin, hunted farther east, where no large herds were found. The devastation was everywhere. During the winter, two Crees died of starvation right outside St. Paul des Cris, and the priest in charge admitted that he "could not look on calmly at his inability to help the starving Indians begging for help."[37]

By the spring of 1868, Maskepetoon's camp was in the first throes of breaking up. Some families were returning to their original bands, while many of the Rocky Mountain group decided they would prefer to face starvation in the foothills, where there was a good chance of finding fish in the lakes and rabbits in the bush. Furs were fetching good prices and were exchanged for tobacco, cloth and other goods. By this time, Fort Edmonton and other posts had accepted the fact that the halcyon days of unlimited food from the plains were over, and the traders were readjusting their lives accordingly.

Interestingly, the savage warfare between the Crees and Blackfoot eased off for several months while families concentrated on food gathering. There were small raids and horse stealing, but no wholesale slaughters were taking place. Enemy camps were often within a day or two from each other, and the chiefs cautioned their young men against causing trouble. But the tension was there, and any little incident might touch off a maelstrom of violence. Maskepetoon, the proponent of peace, trod a thin line between war and peace, between starvation and plenty, and between a difficult today and an unknown tomorrow.

CHAPTER SIXTEEN

Death on the Plains

During the winter of 1868–69, Bob Tail lost a number of horses that had either strayed or were stolen. A group of Maskepetoon's people, including women and children, went to search for them, and after some days they arrived at a Sarcee camp. Because the two groups had an uneasy peace, the party entered the camp cautiously, but they were greeted in a friendly manner. The Sarcees did not have the missing horses nor had they seen them. The Cree leader asked if there were any Siksikas in the area and was told there was a camp on the Battle River. However, the Sarcees advised them not to go there, saying that the Siksikas were angry after a run-in with another group of Crees. Most agreed to bypass the camp, but a man named Six Fingers said, "We are looking for our horses and need to make our way in that direction anyway."[1]

So while the others camped, Six Fingers and a friend went to the Siksika camp. He also wanted to visit his sister, who was married to a Siksika. When they arrived, they ignored the angry and hostile glances and rode directly to the sister's lodge. They were just getting off their horses when a Siksika asked the sister if she knew who they were.

"No," she answered, "I don't know them." She realized that because of the hostility in the camp, she would be killed if she admitted that one of them was her brother.

The two men had made a fatal mistake in going to the sister's lodge rather than directly to the chief. Had they done so, he probably would have offered them sanctuary and admired their bravery in entering the camp alone. But there was no chief present, so young Siksika warriors immediately attacked the two Crees. One was killed on the spot, but Six Fingers managed to mount his horse and flee for his life. He was hotly pursued and was trying to cross the Battle River when his horse became mired in the mud. He too was killed.

The rest of the Cree party had camped nearby, and when they heard the gunfire, they rode off to engage their enemies. In the camp, a little boy, his sister and their grandmother could hear the sounds of battle. They knew it was over when the shooting and war whoops stopped. A short time later, they heard drums and the victory songs of the Siksikas. All the Crees were gone, except for a couple of women and children. While they wondered what to do, a Siksika found their hiding place. Fortunately he turned out to be an adopted brother of Six Fingers, and that night he brought horses and led them to safety.[2]

In March, a trader reported that the Siksikas wanted peace, probably before spring retaliatory raids could begin. At that time, Maskepetoon and other Crees were camped near The Nose, a hill northeast of the present town of Coronation.

"There were many who did not want a truce," said a Cree historian.[3] They wanted revenge for the recent killings. But Maskepetoon insisted and brought together a small peacemaking party of men, women and children to go on the dangerous quest. Among them were Maskepetoon's two sons, a son-in-law and a cousin of Ahenakew, a noted Cree leader.[4] Also included was Rattlesnake Child, a part-Cree and part-Blackfoot man who knew the exact location of the camp and offered to guide them.[5] The Siksikas were located on the upper waters of Berry Creek, east of the Hand Hills and about fifty miles from the Crees.[6] When the Crees came close to the Siksikas, a secret camp was made where the women and children would remain while Maskepetoon and his companions went to make peace.

The camp they were approaching had once been led by The Sun, who was famous for his desire for peace and for his friendship with the traders. However, with his death the leadership had gone to Many Swans (sometimes called Big Swan, or The Swan). He was considered to be the most influential leader at that time, and when the whole tribe gathered together, he took the position of supreme chief.

Many Swans disliked white traders, and the feeling was mutual. A traveller at Fort Edmonton described him as "a man of colossal size and savage disposition, crafty and treacherous."[7] His people followed him with confidence, but unlike chiefs such as Crowfoot, he showed no diplomacy, sympathy or mercy when dealing with an enemy or anyone who opposed him. On one occasion, his youngest wife deserted him and ran off with a Blood Indian. Many Swans' brother complained that this brought shame on the family and asked permission to kill her. Many Swans agreed, so his brother went south to the Blood camps and murdered her. No one tried to stop him, because everyone feared and respected the Siksika head chief.

The members of Maskepetoon's peace party dressed in their finest clothes, cached their horses in a coulee and made for a hill overlooking the Cree camp. There they placed a flag on a staff and sat beneath it with a Bible, pipe and tobacco, waiting for the Siksikas to arrive. This was a common way for a peace party to approach an enemy, rather than boldly walking into the camp and taking them by surprise. Seeing the strangers on the hill, Siksika horsemen galloped to the place and watched them as they calmly and bravely offered the pipe of peace.

As soon as Many Swans saw them, his thoughts were not on peace, but on murder. "I'm going to take away all their guns," he said to his followers.[8] The chief approached the Crees on horseback, holding his two hands in front of him, clasped together with the right hand on top. This was the universal sign for peace. Then the Siksika chief said that if there was to be a truce, no one should be armed; he himself carried no weapons. Maskepetoon agreed, and in a few moments, Many Swans had collected all their weapons. He then turned and rode away, shouting to his warriors, "Go ahead! Shoot and kill them!" The Siksikas dashed among the defenceless peacemakers, and in a few minutes all of them were dead. A young warrior named Running Calf was given credit for having killed Maskepetoon.[9]

The men were stripped of their fine clothes and scalped. According to McDougall, "Not satisfied with this, the Blackfeet dismembered and severed the old hero's body, limb from limb, and dragged these at their horses' tails into their camp."[10] Singing their victory songs and giving their war whoops, the procession was welcomed by the camp. Women with knives and hatchets further desecrated the bodies, children carried their heads around between two poles, and parts of their bodies were thrown to the dogs.

The Blackfoot saw no disgrace in killing an unarmed peace party. To them, they were simply enemy Crees. "Many Swans performed his greatest deed of all," said Crooked Meat Strings, a Siksika patriarch. "He was the only one who ever got a whole batch, more than ten guns at one time. It was a 'good' fight [meaning the Blackfoot had no casualties]; there was none of our blood in it."[11] Many Swans gave all the guns to his relatives and kept none for himself.

The murders had been witnessed at a distance by Rattlesnake Child. "He went back and told Sussewisk what he had seen," said Pearl Crier, "that her husband had been killed. At first, Sussewisk would not believe that he was killed. And her sons. Finally she accepted the news that she had lost her husband, along with her sons."[12] Sadly, she turned away from the secret camp and made her lonely way home. Maskepetoon had been sixty-two.

Meanwhile, Rattlesnake Child had stolen a horse from the Siksikas, and after giving the sad news to Sussewisk, he hurried back to his Cree camp. "In the morning," said Joe Samson, "he arrived from where Maskipiton had departed from. This man,

Rattlesnake Child, told of everything that happened, the killing of Maskipiton and the others who had went with him to make peace with the Blackfoot. When the Crees heard that their leader had been killed, along with two of his sons and his son-in-law, all of the men, all the women and children, cried in grief throughout the day. Everyone cried and cried well into the night. Even the dogs made sounds of grief. There was crying all night."[13]

Late in April, the traders at Fort Edmonton, learning about the murder, reported that, "Two young fellows arrived from the Blackfoot camp & report Old Maskupeeton killed by the Blackfeet, his two sons & grandson also about the same time. The old man was off to make peace & was killed by the Swan in sight of the Camp."[14]

George and John McDougall were told of the killing about the same time, and the elder McDougall reported the tragedy to his fellow Methodists. He stated:

> We received yesterday from the Plains the most painful intelligence. Our noble old chief, Mas-ke-pe-toon, and most of his family, have been killed by the Blackfeet. The old Chief, who has ever been a peace-maker, started about two weeks ago for the Blackfeet camp, hoping to arrange for a peace among the tribes. He was approaching the camp, bearing a white flag with one hand, and carrying his Bible in the other, when a blood-thirsty Blackfoot, called the Swan, rushed upon the old man and shot him, and then the work of death began; seven of our own Crees were literally cut to pieces.
>
> The death of our old Chief is regarded by both Whites and Indians as a national loss. He was a staunch Protestant, a friend of the white man, and exerted more influence than any other Chief east of the Mountains. In two weeks from this date I had arranged to meet him and his people at camp-meeting. Many of our people from White Fish

Lake, Woodville, and Victoria, have already started for the appointed place; but he who would have sat Chief in our Councils is gone. I cannot tell you how deeply my own mind is afflicted. The poor Crees are paralysed. May the blessed God overrule this great calamity for His own glory and the good of a suffering people.[15]

When the chief's former mentor, Thomas Woolsey, learned of the loss, he wrote:

> I can assure you that the mournful intelligence we have received, respecting my old friend, the Cree Chief (Maskepetoon) and his family, has been perused with feeling of unutterable grief. I had the honor of being most intimately acquainted with the aged chieftain during my lengthened sojourn in the Saskatchewan Valley. We have frequently traversed those plains together, amidst vicissitudes too strange for ordinary language to portray. Occasionally, being somewhat acquainted with the vernacular of the Blackfoot nation, he has acted as my interpreter to that people, and I believe that my predecessor, the Rev. R.T. Rundle, was occasionally greatly indebted to him for like service rendered from 1841 to 1848, though Mr. R. had at times another interpreter.[16]

Even the Hudson's Bay Company paid tribute to the chief. Said former chief factor W.J. Christie, "It was through the instrumentality of the Rev. Mr. Rundle that the Cree chief 'Mas-kipi-toon' (Broken Arm) was converted, and became a faithful friend of the missionaries to the day of his death. His end was a sad one. He was treacherously assassinated when on a mission of peace to the Black foot camp."[17]

When the Siksika realized what Many Swans had done, they knew there would be violent repercussions, so many bands moved south. According to Samson, "All of the Blackfoot ran far away to the Old Man River and then further still. They knew that they had killed our Chief. It would not be long before the Crees would send large retaliatory raids against them."[18] True enough, George McDougall estimated that over the spring and summer no less than a hundred Blackfoot were killed by angry Crees. In June, a trader at Edmonton commented that "The Blackfeet & Crees have had several skirmishes. Crees Victorious."[19]

The story of war and peace on the open plains did not end that summer. There was bitterness in the hearts of the Crees, not only those from Maskepetoon's camp, but all across the plains. A punishment was needed that surpassed anything that had happened in the past. Pipes were sent around to the various bands, all the way to the Qu'Appelle Valley. But any thought of revenge was abandoned when a virulent smallpox epidemic swept the area. From the autumn of 1869 and through the next spring, hundreds of bodies littered the plains, and whole camps were abandoned in the face of the disease. Even Bob Tail lost two of his children as he sought sanctuary at St. Paul des Cris.[20] The Blackfoot, with more than two thousand dead, suffered even more severely than the Crees and were humbled by the onslaught of the disease. When the epidemic passed, the people were too busy picking up the pieces of their lives to concentrate on warfare. Bands needed to reorganize and take care of orphans and widows, and the buffalo had to be pursued, in spite of fewer hunters.

In May 1871, traders encouraged Many Swans to take his furs and robes to Fort Edmonton, the Crees being too disorganized by the epidemic to bother him. He agreed, and in August his band went to the fort, where they were well treated. Most of the Blackfoot now shunned the fort and went to Whoop-Up or one of the many whisky forts on the lower plains. While at Edmonton, the chief was given a peace offering of tobacco sent by the Crees. Many Swans' wife, Many Buffalo Stones Woman, convinced her husband that it should be smoked and peace should be made. To emphasize her point, she went to the Cree camp herself with a peace offering. It was accepted, and arrangements were made for the two tribes to meet. By this time, peace and the ability to hunt were more important than revenge.

The two groups came together at The Nose, where they feasted and celebrated their renewed friendship. After two days, they moved to the Rosebud River, where they all camped together. When the time came for presenting gifts, Many Swans loaded a white horse with blankets, robes and other presents. The chief used the side of his horse as a canvas to depict his war exploits in red paint. The horse was led to the middle of a circle, where the gifts were removed and distributed. Then an old Siksika warrior began explaining the meaning of the pictograph paintings. He pointed to one panel and said that Many Swans "is the one who fooled *Manikapi'na*."[21]

The Crees knew that he had spoken the Blackfoot name of their great chief Maskepetoon. In detail, the Siksika went on to describe how Many Swans had tricked the peace party into giving up their guns under a white flag, how he told his men to slaughter the unarmed Crees. The peace delegation was appalled; they had not known that Maskepetoon had been tricked into allowing himself to be disarmed.

The visitors were angry but quiet for the rest of the day and left the following morning. Along the way north, they talked about revenge, but none was willing to break the pact of peace. Then one of the chiefs commented that during the ceremonies, Many Swans had fallen from his horse and had been badly bruised; perhaps his weakness left him vulnerable. When they reached their own camps on the Battle River, the chiefs agreed to send for the most powerful shaman in the tribe. The Cree belief in the supernatural and the powers of shamans was very strong. They believed that by using songs, incantations and secrets known only to himself, a shaman could place a curse on Many Swans; he could send a spirit messenger that would hurl missiles into the man's body, filling it with pain, and after he had suffered for his treachery, he would die.

The shaman's attack was said to have struck Many Swans in his joints. First, it was his arms, then his legs, and finally the pain coursed throughout his whole body. The Blackfoot recognized the signs of "Cree medicine," a power that was often greater than anything their own medicine men could combat. The chief's wife sought out the three best medicine men in the tribe, and one by one they tried to counteract the power of the Cree shaman, but failed. Many Swans could not be cured; his body was filled with ghost missiles of the Cree spirit messenger.

In the autumn of 1871, after weeks of agony, Many Swans died. Some people said the fall from the horse had killed him. The fur traders claimed he had tuberculosis. But his followers believed that the Crees had got their revenge for the killing of Maskepetoon.

This account, with its dramatic stories of spirits and revenge, is the Blackfoot version of the great peace treaty of 1871. The Cree version is much less dramatic. Louis Bull, chief of the Louis Bull Reserve, recalled in about 1900 that it was the Crees, not the Blackfoot, who sued for peace. Sometime following the death of Maskepetoon, they sent four of their tribe with tobacco and gifts to the Siksika camp, which was about fourteen miles south of where the city of Red Deer is located. Bull said:

> After a council meeting, the Blackfeet accepted the tobacco and gifts. Runners were dispatched to the Crees who came over to the Blackfoot camp where a peace pact was made, the Pipe of Peace was smoked, a sacred pledge of amity and peace. The occasion was one of great rejoicing by Crees dancing & beating of drums, lasted several days. Since that time Cree and Blackfoot have been friends and all warfare between the two nations has ended.[22]

Joe Samson had a similar story:

> Those that were within treaty six at every summer they would never be able to sleep in peace. They would try to kill each other and steal each other's horses. It was mostly at night when they stole horses from each other. So that was why the horses were closely guarded at night. That was why both sides hated each other. There were too many young people who would rather continue this. Eventually the Cree did not like this to continue happening so from all their humanity, or collectively as people, they made an agreement to cease hostilities. They sent word to the Blackfoot that "five Cree from all the tribes had made an agreement so that from now on we will be in a friendship. For if we are in friendship we can eat buffalo meat in peace wherever we may be. All of the men and women and children and the young men can sleep in the calm."[23]

Whatever story is true, the 1871 peace treaty held firm. A few small skirmishes took place over the next few years, but the days of pitched battles and the destruction of entire villages were virtually over. In the end, Maskepetoon's ill-fated quest for peace may have been the catalyst that finally caused it to happen.

EPILOGUE

Maskepetoon's leadership took place during a time of rapid change. In a few brief years, his people went from being woodland trappers to buffalo hunters dwelling on the prairies. The buffalo herds were being destroyed, and an old way of life was disappearing forever. Through Maskepetoon's strength, wisdom and courage, he was successfully guiding his people through this unsettled period when his life was suddenly cut short. Over the years, the chief had always held the admiration and support of his people. They saw him as a great leader and a buffer between them and the white man's civilization that was descending upon them. He also won the respect of fur traders by his fairness, friendship and his desire for peace. He was admired by the missionaries for demonstrating those qualities that compared favourably with Christianity, even though they were drawn from his own religion and from his innate sense of honour and justice. By the 1860s, he was known far and wide among friends and enemies alike as the great peacemaker of the Crees. He was called Young Man Chief by the Blackfoot, a man whose word could be trusted.

Maskepetoon had been able to adjust to the times. He had been a good trapper, like his father before him, but when conditions called upon him to venture onto the plains, he did so without fear. He adapted to the role of being a chief on the plains, opening his camp to scores of people from other bands who admired his type of leadership. He could be merciless when conditions demanded it, but preferred peace, both within his own camp and with his enemies. When the followers of Louis Piche broke away under Bob Tail, Maskepetoon respected their decision. When they supported the Oblate missionaries, he made it possible for them to coexist with non-Catholics in their large summer camps. Under missionary influences, religion could be a divisive factor, yet there is no indication that Maskepetoon ever let it cause conflict within his camp.

Like that of some other leaders, Maskepetoon's family life was one of sadness and loss. None of his sons survived the buffalo years, and informants weren't sure about his daughters. Maskepetoon had hoped that his son Joseph would succeed him as chief, but Joseph died, perhaps killed at the same time as his father in the Blackfoot attack. Instead, it ultimately fell to the chief's younger brother, Samson, to carry on the work that Maskepetoon had started. There were a number of known descendents of Maskepetoon, including Eve and Betsy, daughters of Joseph. Betsy later married Louis Natuasis, a chief and nephew of Bob Tail and Ermineskin, and they had at least twelve children.[1]

With the death of Maskepetoon, the band at first fell under the leadership of Sayakimat, or Frightens Them, an elderly man who was well meaning but not assertive, and who lacked the leadership qualities of his predecessor.[2] According to McDougall, Sayakimat "for years always had quite a following, but was now since Maskepetoon's death looked upon as head chief."[3] He was a supporter of the Methodists, and under his leadership the division between Methodist and Catholic became wider. On one occasion during the winter of 1869–70, Father Constantine Scollen suggested to Sayakimat that he move with his band to Sweet Grass' camp on the banks of the Battle River, where there were said to be plenty of buffalo.[4] However, Sayakimat refused to go to the Catholic-led camp and took his followers in another direction. Meanwhile, the priest, with about nine lodges from Sayakimat's camp, presumably with Bob Tail and Ermineskin, went to join Sweet Grass.[5]

In 1871, a delegation of the leading Cree chiefs representing "the Plain Crees from this [Edmonton House] to Carlton" went to Edmonton after hearing about the transfer of Hudson's Bay Company lands to the Dominion of Canada. These chiefs were Sweet Grass, Kehiwin, Little Hunter and Bob Tail. Sayakimat was not present. Sweet Grass, who was the main spokesman, said, "We heard our Lands were sold and we did not like it, we don't want to sell our Lands, it is our property, and no one has a right to sell them."[6] Factor William Christie assured the delegation that the land was still theirs, and if there was a need for the Queen to take it, there would be meetings and a treaty.[7]

The next two years were ones of famine, hardship and death. As George McDougall stated in 1872, "The past year has been one of great anxiety. The transfer of the country has unsettled the native mind, and then there has been unparalleled physical suffering."[8] By the spring of 1873, some of Maskepetoon's followers had forsaken the plains and were back in the old territory. As George McDougall mentioned, "May the 1st, at the foot of the Bear's Hill, we fell in with a party of Victoria Crees, most of them our own people."[9] Starvation was forcing them back home, where they came under the leadership of Samson.

The North West Mounted Police came west in 1874 and were stationed at Fort Saskatchewan. In preparation for a treaty, estimates were made of the populations. These included Sayakimat, with 20 lodges with 160 people; Bob Tail, with 15 lodges with 120 people; Buffalo Lake stragglers, 35 lodges with 280 people; and Samson, with 9 lodges with 72 people.[10]

When the time came to negotiate Treaty Six in 1876, officials assumed that Samson, Sayakimat, Bob Tail and other Crees from the Edmonton area would come to the treaty grounds at Fort Pitt. However, they were far out on the plains on their fall hunt or trapping in the foothills. After the treaty had been signed by Sweet Grass and others, the commissioner sent a message to Sayakimat and Bob Tail, in which he said, in part, "Next year, a Queen's Interpreter will be sent to pay the Indians their annuities at time & place of which notice will be given & you are invited to meet him and take his hand & join the Treaty and so get the benefit of all the goods the Queen deigns to provide for her Indian children. I am sorry you did not hear my words, but I send you my best wishes and my friendship."[11]

Before the end of 1876, Sayakimat had died, and Samson became the leader of the Rocky Mountain Crees. By this time, the northern plains were virtually devoid of large buffalo herds, although smaller bands could be found east and north of Buffalo Lake.[12] But even with these few buffalo, by the spring of 1877, many Crees were starving.[13] The people had three choices: they could follow the last herds into buffalo country, eke out an existence in the Pigeon Lake–Buffalo Lake area, or split off into small family groups and scatter to anywhere they thought food might be found. Inter-tribal warfare had ended, so some Crees decided to go into the heart of Blackfoot country, seeking the herds. In 1877, when Treaty Seven was being negotiated with the Blackfoot, the commissioners were surprised when Bob Tail appeared at Blackfoot Crossing with a few of his followers and asked to sign. After some discussion, he signed an adhesion to Treaty Six.

Samson still had not signed the treaty, but the opportunity came a year later. Many Crees from the Pigeon Lake and Edmonton area had congregated at Tail Creek at the south end of Buffalo Lake. They were starving, and their horses were in such poor condition that they could not travel to Edmonton. The government clerk came to them, and among those paid were Samson and Ermineskin.

In 1879, the Indian Department officially recognized both Ermineskin and Samson as chiefs with their own separate bands.[14] With Bob Tail already a chief from his earlier signing, the old Rocky Mountain Cree group was now effectively split into three, each receiving its own reserve.

With the buffalo gone, with freedom gone and with their old way of life gone, Maskepetoon's people began a new life governed by the Indian agent and the plough, rather than by the chief and the buffalo. It had been a difficult path to follow, and one might speculate if it would have been any different had Maskepetoon not been struck down by a Blackfoot bullet. Certainly he would have been at the Fort Pitt treaty, and he was wise enough to seek a good deal for his followers. But not even Maskepetoon could stem the surging tide of European civilization sweeping over them, nor could he save the buffalo and his old way of life. Would he have adapted?

 Probably.

NOTES

CHAPTER ONE
The Rocky Mountain Crees

1. Interview with Henry Nepoose by Joseph Deschamps, c. 2005, translated by Brian Lightning from a tape in the Samson Band Archives. Conversations used in this book were not created by the author. They are part of the Cree storytelling process whereby conversations and descriptions are part of the narrative.
2. Ibid.
3. Ibid.
4. His Cree name is pronounced *masskippi-tun*, with the accent on *kipp*. Perhaps the most accurate rendition of this would be Maskipiton, but the use of Maskepetoon has been so well established in fur-trade and missionary journals and contemporary sources that it will be used here. Missionary writers stretched their imaginations to explain how Broken Arm received his name. In *Indian Life in the Great North-West* (Toronto: Musson Book Co., 1900), 116, Egerton Young said the name was given "from the fact that one of his arms had been so hacked and wounded in his hand-to-hand conflicts with his most terrible neighbours, the Blackfeet Indians, that, in healing, the muscles had contracted and stiffened, and the arm remained crooked." All such stories ignore the fact that the Woodland Crees usually received a name at birth which they retained for the rest of their lives, unlike some Plains Indians who took new names at various times based upon their war experiences.
5. Gerald M. Hutchinson and Hugh A. Dempsey, eds., *The Rundle Journals, 1840–1848* (Calgary: Historical Society of Alberta, 1977), 388. Hereinafter cited as *Rundle Journals*.
6. *London Daily Free Press*, September 7, 1886.
7. The Blackfoot or Sakoyitapix (Prairie People), consist of three tribes: the Siksika, who were in the northern part of their hunting grounds and were often in contact with the Crees; the Kainai, or Bloods; and the Pikuni, or Peigans, who ranged south to the Missouri River. The latter was divided into two subgroups, the South Peigans and the North Peigans. The North Peigans hunted along the foothills and also met frequently with the Crees. A fourth tribe, the Sarcee, or Tsuu T'ina, were allies of the Blackfoot, but as their hunting area was in close proximity to the Rocky Mountain Crees, they often were at peace with them.
8. Report of trader William Thomison, Manchester House, August 24, 1787. Cited in John S. Milloy, *The Plains Cree: Trade, Diplomacy and War, 1790 to 1870* (Winnipeg: University of Manitoba Press, 1988), 31.
9. Ibid., 30.
10. Ibid., 30–31.
11. Arthur S. Morton, *The Journal of Duncan M'Gillivray of the North West Company at Fort George on the Saskatchewan, 1794–5* (Toronto: The Macmillan Company, 1929), 77.
12. Interview with Ambrose and Catherine Gravelle by Claude E. Schaeffer, October 23, 1965, Schaeffer Papers, Glenbow Archives.
13. Interview with Ambrose Gravelle by Claude E. Schaeffer, June 24, 1969, Schaeffer Papers, Glenbow Archives.
14. Unpublished manuscript 4-5, Schaeffer Papers, Glenbow Archives.
15. Cited in A.M. Johnson, ed., *Saskatchewan Journals and Correspondence* (London: The Hudson's Bay Record Society, 1967), 112.
16. Ibid.

17. "Joe Samson's Manuscript," 1941. Translated from syllabics by Stan Cuthand and Bruce Cutknife, Maskwachees Library, Hobbema.

CHAPTER TWO
Maskepetoon's Early Years

1. John McDougall, *Saddle, Sled and Snowshoe: Pioneering on the Saskatchewan in the Sixties* (Toronto: William Briggs, 1896), 196.
2. During the Maskepetoon years there were two branches of the Assiniboines, those on the Saskatchewan plains and those who dwelt in the Alberta foothills. They were variously called Assiniboines, Stoneys and Stone Indians, but were the same nation. To avoid confusion, we will use Assiniboines to describe those on the plains and Stoneys for those near the Rocky Mountains.
3. Fort Edmonton journals, entry for October 2, 1818. Hudson's Bay Company Archives, B.60/a/17, Provincial Archives of Manitoba. Hereinafter cited as Fort Edmonton journals, HBC Archives.
4. Fort Edmonton journals, entry for August 25, 1806, HBC Archives, B.60/a/6.
5. Letter, James Bird to John McNab, Fort Edmonton journals, entry for December 23, 1806, HBC Archives, B.60/a/6.
6. Fort Edmonton journals, entry for September 22, 1806, HBC Archives, B.60/a/6.
7. Ibid.
8. Fort Edmonton journals, entry for April 7, 1807, HBC Archives, B.60/a/6.
9. Ibid.
10. Letter, James Bird to John McNab, August 13, 1807, Fort Edmonton journals, HBC Archives, B.60/a/6.
11. Fort Edmonton journals, entry for October 11, 1807, HBC Archives, B.60/a/6.
12. Ibid., entry for January 11, 1811, HBC Archives, B.60/a/9.
13. Ibid., entry for October 3, 1813, HBC Archives, B.60/a/12.
14. Ibid., entry for March 5, 1815, HBC Archives, B.60/a/13.
15. Interview with Brian Lightning by the author, Hobbema, October 19, 2007.
16. Interview with Wayne Roan by the author, Joseph Deschamps, interpreter, Ermineskin Reserve, Hobbema, October 19, 2007.
17. Fine Day, *My Cree People* (Invermere, BC: Good Medicine Books, 1973), 40.
18. Interview with Wayne Roan, Hobbema, October 19, 2007.
19. Interview with Peter Shirt Sr. in *O-sak-do* (Saddle Lake newspaper), July 1976, 9.
20. Elliott Coues, ed., *New Light on the Early History of the Greater Northwest: The Manuscript Journals of Alexander Henry, Fur Trader of the Northwest Company, and of David Thompson, Official Geographer of the same Company, 1799–1814* (New York: Francis P. Harper, 1897), 638.
21. Ibid., 596.
22. Ibid.
23. Fort Edmonton journals, entry for March 16, 1812, HBC Archives, B.60/a/10.
24. Ibid., entry for May 3, 1812, HBC Archives, B.60/a/10.
25. Fort Edmonton journals, entry for October 27, 1814, HBC Archives, B.60/a/14.
26. Ibid., entry for January 26, 1823, HBC Archives, B.60/a/23.
27. Ibid.
28. Ibid., entry for March 13, 1823, HBC Archives, B.60/a/21.
29. Ibid., entry for November 2, 1823, HBC Archives, B.60/a/22.
30. Ibid., entry for February 22, 1824, HBC Archives, B.60/a/22.
31. Carlton House journals, entry for October 17, 1824, HBC Archives, B.27/a/14.
32. Ibid., entry for October 25, 1824, HBC Archives, B.27/a/14.
33. Ibid., entry for February 1, 1825, HBC archives, B.27/a/14.
34. Ibid., entry for May 2, 1825. HBC Archives, B.27/a/14.
35. Fort Edmonton journals, entry for September 19, 1825, HBC Archives, B.60/a/23.
36. Ibid., entry for October 9, 1825, HBC Archives, B.60/a/23.

37. Letter, John Rowand to John Peter Pruden, October 12, 1826, Malcolm McLeod Journals and Correspondence, MS-1249, A/B/40/M22K, British Columbia Archives.
38. Ibid.

CHAPTER THREE
Leadership

1. Coues, *New Light*, 609.
2. Ibid.
3. Baptêmes et Mariages faits dans les Missions des Fort des prairies, Oblate Archives, Accn. 71.220/5213, Provincial Archives of Alberta.
4. Scrip application for Louis Piche, Scrip applications, Glenbow Archives.
5. Carlton House journals, entry for March 30, 1825, HBC Archives, B.27/a/14.
6. Sir George Simpson, *An Overland Journey Round the World, During the Years 1841 and 1842* (Philadelphia: Lea & Blanchard, 1847), 95.
7. Fort Edmonton journals, entry for September 25, 1826, HBC Archives, B.60/a/24.
8. Ibid., entry for October 22, 1823, HBC Archives, B.60/a/22.
9. Ibid., entry for May 3, 1826, HBC Archives, B.60/a/23.
10. Ibid., entries for September 25 and 27, 1826, HBC Archives, B.60/a/24.
11. Ibid., entry for December 18, 1826, HBC Archives, B.60/a/24.
12. Ibid., entry for October 5, 1826, HBC Archives, B.60/a/24.
13. Ibid., entry for October 13, 1826, HBC Archives, B.60/a/24.
14. Ibid., entry for November 28, 1826, HBC Archives, B.60/a/24.
15. Ibid., entry for March 25, 1827, HBC Archives, B.60/a/24.
16. Ibid.
17. Carlton House journals, entries for July 14 and 22, 1827, HBC Archives, B.27/a/16.
18. Rocky Mountain House journals, entry for October 18, 1829, HBC Archives, B.184/a/1.
19. Joseph F. Dion, *My Tribe the Crees* (Calgary: Glenbow Museum, 1979), 23.
20. Ibid.
21. Morton, *Journal of Duncan M'Gillivray*, 43.
22. Rocky Mountain House journals, entries for January 11 and 14 and February 27, 1830, HBC Archives, B.184/a/1.
23. Ibid., entry for October 5, 1830, HBC Archives, B.184/a/1.
24. Ibid., entry for October 8, 1830, HBC Archives, B.184/a/1.
25. Ibid., entry for April 1, 1831, HBC Archives, B.184/a/1.
26. Report by George Simpson, August 26, 1830, HBC Archives, D.4/97.
27. Fort Edmonton journals, entry for April 18, 1834, HBC Archives, B.60/a/28.
28. Rundle met Piche's father-in-law near Fort Carlton on August 14, 1845. *Rundle Journals*, 144.
29. Scrip application for Bob Tail, Scrip applications, Glenbow Archives.
30. Fort Edmonton journals, entry for March 25, 1827, HBC Archives, B.60/a/24.

CHAPTER FOUR
Edging onto the Plains

1. *Manitoba Free Press*, August 5, 1886. I am indebted to Dr. Donald B. Smith, University of Calgary historian, for this and other references from Samson's 1886 tour of eastern Canada.
2. Letter, George McDougall, January 9, 1870, *Wesleyan Missionary Notices*, May 1, 1870, 102.
3. McDougall, *Saddle, Sled and Snowshoe*, 196.
4. Interview with Wayne Roan by the author, Joseph Deschamps, interpreter, Ermineskin Reserve, Hobbema, October 19, 2007.
5. Ibid.
6. McDougall, *Saddle, Sled and Snowshoe*, 197.
7. Ibid., 198.
8. Interview with Wayne Roan by the author, Joseph Deschamps, interpreter, Ermineskin Reserve, Hobbema, October 19, 2007; interview with Pearl Crier by the author, Beverly Crier, interpreter, Hobbema, October 30, 2007; Paul Kane, *Wanderings of an Artist*

Among the Indians of North America (Toronto: The Radisson Society of Canada Ltd., 1925), 275.

9. Rundle baptismal records, *Rundle Journals*. The names were translated by Joseph Deschamps.

10. Fine Day, in David G. Mandelbaum, *The Plains Cree: An Ethnological, Historical, and Comparative Study* (Regina, SK: Canadian Plains Research Center, 1979), 147.

11. Hugh A. Dempsey, ed., *Heaven is Near the Rocky Mountains: The Journals and Letters of Thomas Woolsey, 1855–1868* (Calgary: Glenbow Museum, 1989), entry for October 16, 1860, 102.

12. Fort Edmonton journals, entries for October 2, 12 and 13, 1808, HBC Archives, B.60/a/8.

13. John C. Ewers, *The Blackfeet: Raiders on the Northwestern Plains* (Norman: University of Oklahoma Press, 1958), 55.

14. Ibid., 58.

15. Fort Edmonton journals, entry for June 5, 1832, HBC Archives, B.60/a/27.

16. Ibid., entry for September 2, 1832, HBC Archives, B.60/a/27.

17. Ibid., entry for July 17, 1832, HBC Archives, B.60/a/27.

18. Ibid., entry for May 10, 1833, HBC Archives, B.60/a/27.

19. Ibid., entry for July 4, 1833, HBC Archives, B.60/a/27.

20. Ibid., entry for July 11, 1833, HBC Archives, B.60/a/27; Fort Carlton journals, entry for July 19, 1833, HBC Archives, B.27/a/20.

21. Fort Edmonton journals, entry for July 29, 1833, HBC Archives, B.60/a/27.

22. Ibid., entry for September 20, 1833, HBC Archives, B.60/a/28.

23. Ibid., entry for November 30, 1833, HBC Archives, B.60/a/28.

24. Carlton House journals, entry for August 25, 1834, HBC Archives, B.27/a/21.

25. Diamond Jenness, *The Sarcee Indians of Alberta* (Ottawa: National Museum of Canada, 1938), 3–4.

26. Ibid.

27. Carlton House journals, entries for June 21, 1836, and April 15, 1837, HBC Archives, B.27/a/22.

28. Letter, John Rowand to George Simpson, December 25, 1837, HBC Archives, microfilm 3M58.

29. Ibid.

30. Alexander Culbertson claimed that the steamboat had been the *Trapper*, not the *St. Peters*.

31. Hiram M. Chittenden, *The American Fur Trade of the Far West* (Stanford: Academic Reprints, 1954), II: 621–22.

32. Chittenden, *The American Fur Trade*, 625.

33. Jack Holterman, *King of the High Missouri: The Saga of the Culbertsons* (Helena: Falcon Press, 1987), 50.

34. James H. Bradley, "Characteristics, Habits and Customs of the Blackfeet Indians," *Contributions to the Historical Society of Montana* 9 (1923): 278.

35. Hugh A. Dempsey, *A Blackfoot Winter Count* (Calgary: Glenbow Foundation, 1965), 15.

36. Hugh A. Dempsey, ed., "Simpson's Essay on the Blackfoot, 1841," *Alberta History* 38, no. 1 (Winter 1990): 4.

37. Arthur J. Ray, *Indians in the Fur Trade* (Toronto: University of Toronto Press, 1974), 190.

38. Carlton House journals, entry for August 5, 1838, HBC Archives, B.27/a/23.

39. *Edmonton Journal*, August 17, 1929.

40. Ibid.

41. Winter count of Joe Little Chief in Dagmar Siebelt, *Die Winter Counts der Blackfoot* (Münster: Lit Verlag Münster, 2005), 388.

CHAPTER 5

The Other Maskepetoon

1. Letter, Joshua Pilcher to General William Clark, September 15, 1838, Letters Received by the Office of Indian Affairs, 1836–51, microfilm 234, roll 884, 369, National Archives and Records Administration (hereinafter NARA).

2. George Catlin, *North American Indians, Being Letters and Notes on their Manners, Customs, and Conditions* (Philadelphia: Leary, Stuart & Co., 1913), 66.

3. John C. Ewers, "When the Light Shone in Washington," *Montana: The Magazine of Western History* 6, no. 4 (Autumn 1956): 6. Most information relative to Maskepetoon's trip to Washington is from this source.

4. Ibid., 8.
5. Cited in Ewers, "When the Light Shone," 9.
6. David Thomas and Karin Ronnefeldt, eds., *People of the First Man: Life Among the Plains Indians in their Final Days of Glory: The Firsthand Account of Prince Maximilian's Expedition Up the Missouri River, 1833–34* (New York: Promontory Press, 1983), 57.
7. Ibid., 60.
8. Edwin Thomas Denig, *Five Indian Tribes of the Upper Missouri: Sioux, Arikaras, Assiniboines, Crees, Crows*, ed. John C. Ewers. (Norman: University of Oklahoma Press, 1961), 87.
9. Charles Larpenteur, *The Original Journal of Charles Larpenteur: My Travels to the Rocky Mountains between 1833 and 1872*, ed. Michael M. Casler (Chadron, NE: The Museum Association of the American Frontier, 2007), 29.
10. Report of Sub-Agent William N. Fulkenson, October 1, 1837, Letters Received by the Office of Indian Affairs, 1836–51, microfilm 234, roll 884, 181, NARA.
11. Report by Joshua Pilcher, Indian Agent, September 12, 1838, Letters Received by the Office of Indian Affairs, 1836–51, microfilm 234, roll 885, 357, NARA.
12. Report of Sub-Agent William N. Fulkerson, October 1, 1837, Letters Received by the Office of Indian Affairs, 1836–51, microfilm 234, roll 884, 191, NARA.
13. Denig, *Five Indian Tribes*, 161, 114.
14. Charles Larpenteur, *Forty Years a Fur Trader on the Upper Missouri* (Chicago: The Lakeside Press, 1933), 155.
15. Ibid., 161–62.
16. Ibid., 163
17. Ewers, "When the Light Shone," 10.
18. Ibid.
19. I am indebted to Nicholas Vrooman of the Helena Indian Alliance, Montana, for these details. Much of his information came from Francis Cree, or Eagle Heart, a noted ceremonialist, musician and historian, who served as chief of the reservation in the 1960s.
20. Interview with Sylvia Morin, or Black Bear Woman, by the author, Belcourt, North Dakota, May 1, 2009.
21. Interview with Bill Morin, or Sitting Chief, by the author, Dunseith, North Dakota, April 29, 2009.
22. Information from the local history *Prairie Past and Mountain Memories: A History of Dunseith, N. Dakota, 1882–1982* (Dunseith: Dunseith Steering Committee, 1982).
23. Broken Arm is not an unusual name, appearing as it does among the Osage, Nez Perce, Oto, Winnebago, Sioux and other tribes.
24. Hugh A. Dempsey, "Maskepetoon," *Dictionary of Canadian Biography*, vol. 9 (1976), 537–38. Also at www.biographi.ca.
25. Allen Ronaghan, "The Problem of Maskipiton," *Alberta History* 24, no. 2 (Spring 1976): 14–18.

CHAPTER SIX
The Methodists

1. E.H. Oliver, *The Canadian North-West, Its Early Development and Legislative Records*, vol. 2 (Ottawa: Government Printing Bureau, 1915), 811.
2. Ibid., 829.
3. *Rundle Journals*, 59.
4. Ibid., entry for November, 2, 1840.
5. Ibid., entry for January 16, 1841.
6. Ibid., entry for February 26, 1841.
7. Ibid., baptism record for March 14, 1841, 344–45.
8. Ibid., entry for March 19, 1841.
9. Ibid., entry for March 24, 1841.
10. Letter, Rowand to Simpson, January 9, 1841, HBC Archives, D5/6.
11. *Rundle Journals*, entry for February 25, 1841.
12. Ibid., entry for April 1, 1841.
13. Ibid., entry for April 4, 1841.
14. Ibid., entry for April 11, 1841.
15. Ibid., baptism entry for April 12, 1841, 350.
16. Ibid., letter, Rundle to Wesleyan Missionary Society, May 31, 1841, 73.
17. *Notice sur les Missions du Diocèse de Québec qui sont secourues par l'Association de la Propagation de la Foi*, no. 4 (January 1842): 2–3 (Québec: Frechette & Cie.); E.O. Drouin, *Ongoing Mission of Central Alberta* (Hobbema: privately printed, 1968), 6–7.
18. *Rundle Journals*, entry for July 3, 1841.

CHAPTER SEVEN
The Wanderers

1. Simpson's Journals, microfilm D.3/2, 138, Provincial Archives of Manitoba.
2. Ibid., 57.
3. Ibid.
4. Ibid., 64.
5. Ibid.
6. Ibid., 65.
7. Ibid.
8. Ibid., 66.
9. Simpson, *An Overland Journey*, 63.
10. Ibid., 70.
11. Ibid., 72.
12. Ibid., 73.
13. Ibid.
14. Ibid., 74.
15. Ibid., 75–76.
16. Ibid., 76.
17. Aphrodite Karamitsanis, *Place Names of Alberta, Volume 1: Mountains, Mountain Parks and Foothills* (Calgary: University of Calgary Press, 1991), 166, 190.
18. Simpson's Journals, D.3/2, 138, Provincial Archives of Manitoba.
19. Simpson, *An Overland Journey*, 78.
20. Simpson's Journals, D.3/2, 160, Provincial Archives of Manitoba.
21. Ibid., 81.
22. Ibid., 84.
23. Simpson, *An Overland Journey*, 94.
24. Ibid., 94.
25. Letter, McDonald to Harriott, August 21, 1841, Archibald McDonald Papers, A/B/20/C72 M.1, British Columbia Archives.
26. Simpson states in *An Overland Journey* (95) that Piche later went to Vancouver, but the timelines show that this could not have occurred on this journey, and no record has been found of him making the trip at a later date. Simpson implies that he himself was there at the time, so he may have confused Piche with his fellow chief Maskepetoon.
27. Simpson, cited in D. Geneva Lent, *West of the Mountains: James Sinclair and the Hudson's Bay Company* (Seattle: University of Washington Press, 1963), 126.
28. These were the families of Henry Buxton, H.O. Caldron, A. Spence, John Spence, John Tate, James and Alexander Berston, William, James, John and David Flett, John Coningham, Joseph Cline, Baptiste and Pierre La Roque, Charles McKay, Pierre St. Germain, M. Berney, Francis Jaques, Joseph Geneau, Joseph Yell and Anoine Le Blanc.
29. These were William Boldro, John Johnson and John Hudson.
30. Simpson claimed there were 121 people in the party, but John Flett, one of the participants, said there were 80.
31. John Flett, *Tacoma Daily Ledger*, February 18, 1885.
32. Ibid.
33. Ibid.
34. Ibid. Simpson claimed Bird "treacherously deserted" the Sinclair party, but this was obviously untrue. It reflects the animosity that the governor held for Bird because of his earlier desertion.
35. Ibid. Actually, the pass was too far north to provide drainage to the Missouri River system.
36. Simpson, *An Overland Journey*, 83.
37. *Tacoma Daily Ledger*, February 18, 1885.
38. Letter, Archibald McDonald to John McLaughlin, September 19, 1841, Fort Colvile Correspondence, A/B/20/C72 M.1, British Columbia Archives.
39. Letter, Archibald McDonald to James Douglas, January 18, 1842, Fort Colvile Correspondence.
40. *Tacoma Daily Ledger*, February 18, 1885.
41. *Rundle Journals*, 113.
42. *Tacoma Daily Ledger*, February 18, 1885.
43. Ibid.
44. Ibid.
45. Sir George Simpson, *Narrative of a Journey Round the World during the Years 1841 and 1842* (London: Henry Colburn, 1847), 241–42.
46. Letter, Archibald McDonald to George Simpson, January 7, 1842, Fort Colvile Correspondence.
47. Letter, Archibald McDonald to James Douglas, January 18, 1842, Fort Colvile Correspondence.
48. Ibid.
49. Letter, Archibald McDonald to Patrick McKensie, January 8, 1842, Fort Colvile Correspondence.

CHAPTER EIGHT
Battle for Souls

1. Letter, J.E. Harriott to James Evans, January 7, 1842, Donald Ross Papers, MS-0635, British Columbia Archives.
2. *Notice sur les Missions du Diocèse de Québec qui sont secourues par l'Association de la Propagation de la Foi*, no. 1 (Québec: Frechette et Cie, January 1839), 1–2, hereinafter cited as *Missions du Diocèse de Québec*. I wish to thank Dr. Juliette Champagne for this and other translations from the French text.
3. Lettre de M. Thibault à Mgr. l'évêque de Québec, June 18, 1843, *Missions du Diocèse de Québec*, 74.
4. Ibid.
5. *Rundle Journals*, 116.
6. Lettre de M. Thibault à Mgr. l'évêque de Québec, June 18, 1843, *Missions du Diocèse de Québec*, 77–78.
7. Ibid., 78.
8. Extrait d'une lettre de Mgr. l'évêque de Juliopolis à Mgr. l'évêque de Québec, January 2, 1843, *Missions du Diocese de Quebec*, 21.
9. Ibid.
10. Kane, *Wanderings of an Artist*, 277–78.
11. Hiram Martin Chittenden and Alfred Talbot Richardson, eds., *Life, Letters and Travels of Father Pierre-Jean De Smet, S.J., 1801–1873* (New York: Francis P. Harper, 1905), 522.
12. Ibid.
13. *Rundle Journals*, 128.
14. Letter, John Rowand to James Hargrave, June 20, 1843, G.P. de T. Glazebrook, ed., *The Hargrave Correspondence, 1821–1843* (Toronto: The Champlain Society, 1938), 441.
15. *Rundle Journals*, 126.
16. Bruce Peel, "When the Bible Came to the Cree," *Alberta Historical Review* 6, no. 2 (Spring 1958): 15.
17. Ibid., 136. Maskepetoon's name is written in syllabics, phonetically Ma-s-ki-pi-to-n.
18. *Rundle Journals*, 136. The Cayen brothers are identified by name by Father Thibault in a letter of December 26, 1843, *Missions du Diocèse de Québec*, 97.
19. Interview with Wayne Roan by the author, Joseph Deschamps, interpreter, Ermineskin Reserve, Hobbema, October 19, 2007.
20. Rundle Papers, Glenbow Archives. The letter is illustrated and translated in Hugh A. Dempsey, *Treasures of the Glenbow Museum* (Calgary: Glenbow Museum, 1991), 170. This is the only Maskepetoon letter known to exist.
21. *Rundle Journals*, entry for May 19, 1847, 260.
22. Ibid., entry for January 28, 1848, 292.
23. *Rundle Journals*, entry for January 6, 1844, 148.
24. E.O. Drouin, *Lac Ste. Anne Sakahigan* (Edmonton: Editions de l'Ermitage, 1973), 12.
25. Letter, J.E. Harriott to Sir George Simpson, May 12, 1846, cited by Gerald Hutchinson in *Rundle Journals*, 1977, xlviii.

CHAPTER NINE
Visitors

1. Sir Henry James Warre, "Mss. of Oregon Journey, June–December, 1845." National Archives of Canada, MG-24, f. 17, vol. 27, 2183. Hereinafter cited as Warre MSS.
2. Also called Wig Wam, Indian Dwelling House or Souris River by Warre.
3. Ibid., 2186–87.
4. Ibid., 2686.
5. Ibid., 2687.
6. Ibid., 2688.
7. Ibid., 2370. Warre wrote at least three versions of this incident, which he did not learn about until a year later, when he was on his way back to Red River. In one version he said, "I do not know how many escaped but the few that reached Edmonton whither they fled for safety, gave such an alarming account, that serious apprehensions were entertained for our safety." In another, "Many Cree men were tomahawked in their Camp. Women and Children were taken prisoner & treated as Slaves. Of the few that escaped to tell the tale, some found their way to Edmonton." A third version reports, "The Blackfeet attacked these Indians, killed several of the Men & took the Women & Children prisoners, leaving but a few to tell their tale."
8. *Rundle Journals*, 189–90.

NOTES ◆ 239

9. Ibid., 191
10. Warre MSS, 2190.
11. Ibid., 2191–92.
12. Ibid., 2192.
13. Ibid., 2193.
14. Ibid., 2195.
15. Ibid., 2196.
16. Ibid., 2200.
17. Ibid., 2201–2.

CHAPTER TEN
The Life of a Chief

1. Interview with Pearl Crier by the author, Beverly Crier, interpreter, Hobbema, October 30, 2007.
2. J.P. Berry, *Maskepetoon: Alberta's First Martyr to Peace* (Toronto: United Church of Canada, 1945), n.p.
3. Information provided by Marvin Littlechild, November 26, 2008.
4. Fort Edmonton journals, entries for October 4 and 6, 1859, HBC Archives, B.60/a/30.
5. Dion, *My Tribe the Crees*, 4; interview with Peter Shirt Sr. in *O-sak-do* (Saddle Lake newspaper), July 1976, 3.
6. John Palliser, *The Journals, Detailed Reports, and Observations Relative to the Expedition, by Captain John Palliser... During the Years 1857, 1858, 1859, and 1860* (London: Queen's Printers, 1863), 201.
7. Ibid., 217.
8. Frederick Ulric Graham, *Notes of a Sporting Expedition in the Far West of Canada, 1847,* (London: privately printed, 1898), 58–59.
9. Ibid., 68–69.
10. Ibid., 71.
11. Milloy, *The Plains Cree*, 98.
12. James H. Bradley, "Affairs at Fort Benton from 1831 to 1869," *Contributions to the Historical Society of Montana* 3 (1900): 257.
13. The name was listed in the register as Sampson.
14. *Rundle Journals*, entries for March 18 and April 4, 1845.
15. Chittenden and Richardson, eds., *Life, Letters and Travels*, 519.
16. *Rundle Journals*, entry for October 26, 1845.
17. Ibid., entry for October 27, 1845.
18. Ibid., entry for May 24, 1847.
19. Ibid, memo, February 7, 1848, 261.
20. Ibid., entries for May 31 and June 1, 1847.
21. Ibid., entry for May 28, 1847.
22. Ibid., entry for June 9, 1847.
23. Ibid., entries for July 21 and 24, 1847.
24. Dion, *My Tribe the Crees*, 55.
25. Ibid., 15.
26. Shirt, *O-sak-do*, 7.
27. Ibid., 1976, 8.
28. "Joe Samson's Manuscript," 1941. These stories have been slightly edited for punctuation, grammar, etc.
29. Ibid.
30. Ibid.
31. Ibid.

CHAPTER ELEVEN
Out to the Plains

1. The Piches seemed to be as comfortable with Rundle as they were with their own priest. In late 1847, Piche's sons helped open a road from Edmonton to the Woodville mission, and the following spring, Rundle married Alexis Piche and Jane Tanazebechagge, a Stoney woman, and the two lived in the area.
2. Allen Ronaghan, "Where Did Paul Kane Meet Maskipiton?" *Alberta History* 39, no. 3 (Summer 1991): 6–8.
3. *Rundle Journals*, entries for January 11 and February 19, 1848.
4. Kane, *Wanderings of an Artist*, 276.
5. Ibid., 275.
6. Ibid., 275–76.
7. Lent, *West of the Mountains*, 222.
8. Letter, Sinclair to Simpson, November 1, 1853. Cited in Lent, *West of the Mountains*, 232.
9. Letter, Simpson to Sinclair, December 11, 1853. Cited in Lent, *West of the Mountains*, 232.
10. Lent, *West of the Mountains*, 243.
11. John V. Campbell, "The Sinclair Party—An Emigration Overland Along the Old Hudson Bay Route from Manitoba

to the Spokane Country in 1854," *The Washington Historical Quarterly* 7, no. 3 (July 1916): 189.
12. Campbell, cited in Lent, *West of the Mountains*, 246.
13. Donald Whitford Papers, microfilm M-256, Glenbow Archives.
14. Letter, James Sinclair to Dr. William Cowan, October 24, 1854, Cowan Papers, E/B/Si6, British Columbia Archives.
15. Ibid.
16. Whitford Papers.
17. Campbell, "The Sinclair Party," 191.
18. Ibid.
19. Lent, *West of the Mountains*, 254–57.
20. Ibid.
21. Dempsey, *Heaven is Near the Rocky Mountains*. Woolsey entry for December 4, 1855, 27.
22. Ibid., 51.
23. Ibid.
24. Ibid., 96.
25. Ibid., 180–81.
26. Ibid., 26.
27. Ibid., 30–31.
28. Fort Edmonton journals, entries for September 29 and October 25, 1855, HBC Archives, B.60/a/29a.
29. Ibid., entry for September 30, 1855, HBC Archives, B.60/a/29a.
30. Ibid., entry for October 4, 1855. HBC Archives, B.60/a/29a.
31. The minutes record that Commissioner Isaac Stevens said, "the Cree here present, who came up with the 'Little Dog' is with him, a witness to the friendly spirit manifested by the Assiniboines and Crees, and their sending by me some tobacco as a token of their friendship and desire for peace, and I will now distribute it." To "come up" to the meeting would refer to Broken Arm coming up the Missouri River. Albert J. Partoll, ed., "The Blackfoot Indian Peace Council," *Frontier and Midland* 17, no. 3 (Spring 1937).
32. Fort Edmonton journals, entry for November 26, 1855, HBC Archives, B.60/a/29a.
33. Ibid., entry for January 18, 1856, HBC Archives, B.60/a/29a.
34. Ibid., entry for March 18, 1856, HBC Archives, B.60/a/29a.
35. Dempsey, *Heaven is Near the Rocky Mountains*, entry for June 3, 1856, 35.
36. Ibid., entry for June 4, 1856, 35.
37. Ibid., entry for August 11, 1856, 41.
38. Fort Edmonton journals, entry for September 26, 1856, HBC Archives, B.60/a/29a.
39. Ibid., entry for October 6, 1856, HBC Archives, B.60/a/29a. As chief of the Beaver Hills Crees, Lapotac's hunting grounds were adjacent to Fort Edmonton, and as a result he was better known to the traders than Maskepetoon. In addition, Lapotac was the elder of the two and highly respected for the fact that he did not drink.
40. Ibid., entry for December 7, 1856, HBC Archives, B.60/a/29a.

CHAPTER TWELVE
The Buffalo

1. E.H. Oliver, *The Canadian North-West, Its Early Development and Legislative Records*, vol. 1 (Ottawa: Government Printing Bureau, 1914), 654.
2. Letter, Letitia Hargrave to Mrs. Dugald MacTavish, March 29, 1849, MacLeod, Margaret Arnett, ed., *The Letters of Letitia Hargrave* (Toronto: Champlain Society, 1947), 241.
3. Ray, *Indians in the Fur Trade*, 223.
4. Sweet Grass had a second name of Little Chief, but was not identified by fur traders under that title.
5. Fort Edmonton journals, entry for April 30, 1857, HBC Archives, B.60/a/29b.
6. Milloy, *The Plains Cree*, 110.
7. Letter from Henry Bird Steinhauer, *Wesleyan Missionary Notices*, November 1857, 322.
8. Fort Edmonton journals, entry for September 7, 1857, HBC Archives, B.60/a/29b.
9. Cited in Milloy, *The Plains Cree*, 111.
10. Fort Edmonton journals, entry for September 27, 1857, HBC Archives, B.60/a/29b.
11. Ibid., entry for March 11, 1858, HBC Archives, B.60/a/29b.
12. Earle Pliny Goddard, "Notes on the Sun Dance of the Cree of Alberta,"

American Museum of Natural History 16 (1919): 304.

13. Peter Erasmus, *Buffalo Days and Nights*, as told to Henry Thompson, ed. Irene M. Spry (Calgary: Glenbow-Alberta Institute, 1976), 50.
14. In his book, Peter Erasmus claimed the Crees went back to the plains and that Woolsey accompanied them as far as the Iron Stone. Woolsey, in his diary, however, indicated he was at Rocky Mountain House and Fort Edmonton for the winter. Dempsey, *Heaven is Near the Rocky Mountains*, 62–68.
15. Dempsey, *Heaven is Near the Rocky Mountains*, 68.
16. Fort Edmonton journals, entry for March 25, 1858, HBC Archives, B.60/a/29b; Dempsey, *Heaven is Near the Rocky Mountains*, 69.
17. Fort Edmonton journals, entry for April 27, 1859, HBC Archives, B.60/a/29b.
18. Correspondence of William Roland Mitchell, 1857–60. Irene M. Spry Papers, MG 30, Accn. C249, vol. 56, Library and Archives Canada.
19. Fort Edmonton journals, entry for October 27, 1858, HBC Archives, B.60/a/29b.
20. Ibid., entry for March 7, 1859, HBC Archives, B.60/a/29b.
21. Dempsey, *Heaven is Near the Rocky Mountains*, 86.
22. Fort Edmonton journals, entries for March 22 and April 2, 1859, HBC Archives, B.60/a/30.
23. Ibid., entry for August 4, 1859, HBC Archives, B.60/a/30.
24. Ibid., entry for September 3–5, 1859, HBC Archives, B.60/a/30.
25. Dwight L. Smith, *Survival on a Westward Trek, 1858–59: The John Jones Overlanders* (Athens: Ohio University Press, 1989), 69.
26. William F. Butler, *The Great Lone Land: A Narrative of Travel and Adventure in the North-West of America* (London: Sampson Low, Marston, Low, & Searle, 1874), 286–87.
27. Fort Edmonton journals, entry for October 19, 1859, HBC Archives, B.60/a/30.
28. *Rundle Journals*, entry for March 18, 1845, 172.
29. Fort Edmonton journals, entry for April 17, 1860, HBC Archives, B.60/a/30.
30. Ibid., entry for April 18, 1860, HBC Archives, B.60/a/30.
31. Dempsey, *Heaven is Near the Rocky Mountains*, entry for August 21, 1860, 94.
32. Ibid., entry for August 24, 1860, 94.
33. Ibid., entry for August 22, 1860, 94.
34. Ibid., entry for August 27, 1860, 95.
35. "Joe Samson's Manuscript," 1941.
36. Ibid.

CHAPTER THIRTEEN
War Again

1. Dempsey, *Heaven is Near the Rocky Mountains*, entry for September 12, 1860, 97–98.
2. Ibid., entry for September 15, 1860, 98.
3. Joe Little Chief papers, M4394, Glenbow Archives.
4. Dempsey, *Heaven is Near the Rocky Mountains*, entry for September 29, 1860, 98–99.
5. Henry John Moberly, *When Fur Was King* (New York: E.P. Dutton, 1929), 188.
6. Dempsey, *Heaven is Near the Rocky Mountains*, entry for September 29, 1860, 99.
7. Fort Edmonton journals, entry for October 18, 1860, HBC Archives, B.60/a/31.
8. Ibid., entries for December 15 and 18, 1860, HBC Archives, B.60/a/31.
9. Ibid., entry for December 29, 1860, HBC Archives, B.60/a/31.
10. Ibid., entry for February 9, 1861, HBC Archives, B.60/a/31.
11. Ibid., entry for March 28, 1861, HBC Archives, B.60/a/31.
12. Ibid., entries for April 14–May 10, 1861, HBC Archives, B.60/a/31.
13. Ibid., entry for June 9, 1861, HBC Archives, B.60/a/31.
14. Ibid., entry for September 8, 1861, HBC Archives, B.60/a/32.
15. Ibid., entry for September 12, 1861, HBC Archives, B.60/a/32.
16. *The Nor'Wester*, Red River Settlement, March 5, 1862.
17. Jenness, *The Sarcee Indians*, 4.
18. Siebelt, *Die Winter Counts*, 390.

19. Jenness, *The Sarcee Indians*, 4–6.
20. Fort Edmonton journals, entry for September 10, 1861, HBC Archives, B.60/a/32.
21. Ibid., entries for January 26 & March 6, 1862, HBC Archives, B.60/a/32.
22. Ibid., entries for March 5 & September 24, 1862, HBC Archives, B.60/a/33.
23. Ibid., entry for December 2, 1861, HBC Archives, B.60/a/32.
24. *The Nor'Wester*, April 13, 1863.
25. Fort Edmonton journals, entries for December 7–10, 1861, HBC Archives, B.60/a/31.
26. George Flett, letter, May 10, 1863, in *The Nor'Wester*, June 30, 1863.
27. Erasmus, *Buffalo Days and Nights*, 131.
28. Ibid.

CHAPTER FOURTEEN
The McDougalls

1. *The Nor'Wester*, June 30, 1863.
2. John McDougall, *Forest, Lake and Prairie* (Toronto: William Briggs, 1910), 190.
3. Woolsey, letter to the *Christian Guardian*, September 8, 1862, cited in Dempsey, *Heaven is Near the Rocky Mountains*, 137–38.
4. Ibid., 138.
5. Fort Edmonton journals, entry for October 23, 1863, HBC Archives, B.60/a/33.
6. Viscount Milton and W.B. Cheadle, *The North-West Passage by Land, Being the Narrative of an Expedition from the Atlantic to the Pacific* (London: Cassell, Petter, and Gilpin, 1865), 174.
7. Ibid., 175.
8. McDougall, *Saddle, Sled and Snowshoe*, 193–94.
9. *Regina Leader*, December 10, 1885.
10. *The Nor'Wester*, June 30, 1863.
11. McDougall, *Saddle, Sled and Snowshoe*, 85.
12. Ibid., 83–85.
13. Ibid., 200–1.
14. Edward Ahenakew, *Voices of the Plains Cree* (Toronto: McClelland & Stewart Ltd., 1973), 54–55.
15. Fort Edmonton journals, entry for August 16, 1863, HBC Archives, B.60/a/33.
16. Ibid., entry for January 29,1864, HBC Archives, B.60/a/33.
17. McDougall, *Saddle, Sled and Snowshoe*, 129–30.
18. Fort Edmonton journals, entries for April 5, 6 and 10 and June 24, 1864; Katherine Hughes, *Father Lacombe, The Black-Robed Voyageur* (Toronto: William Briggs, 1911), 99–102.
19. George Flett in *Manitoba Free Press*, 1884, reprinted as "'Broken Arm' as a Peace Maker" in *Manitoba Pageant* 7, no. 1 (September 1961). A much embellished version of Flett's account is carried in McDougall, *Saddle, Sled and Snowshoe*, 237–44.
20. George Mann papers, M809, Glenbow Archives. The dates likely are wrong. The incident probably took place in 1864, as it is known that the main peace treaty ("seven years later") was made in 1871.
21. Fort Edmonton journals, entry for September 19, 1864, HBC Archives, B.60/a/34.
22. Ibid., entry for November 10, 1864, HBC Archives, B.60/a/34.
23. Ibid., entry for November 20, 1864, HBC Archives, B.60/a/34.
24. John McDougall, *Pathfinding on Plain and Prairie* (Toronto: William Briggs, 1898), 59–62.
25. Fort Edmonton journals, entry for January 23, 1865, HBC Archives, B.60/a/34.
26. Ibid., entry for March 27, 1865, HBC Archives, B.60/a/34.
27. McDougall, *Saddle, Sled and Snowshoe*, 40.

CHAPTER FIFTEEN
A Christian Leader

1. Baptismal records, McDougall Papers, Glenbow Archives.
2. "Joe Samson's Manuscript," 1941.
3. John Maclean, *The Hero of the Saskatchewan* (Barrie, ON: Barrie Examiner Printing & Publishing House, 1891), 18.

4. McDougall, *Saddle, Sled and Snowshoe*, 70.
5. Hughes, *Father Lacombe*, 105.
6. Fort Edmonton journals, entry for January 25, 1866, HBC Archives, B.60/a/35.
7. Ibid., entry for May 29, 1865, HBC Archives, B.60/a/34.
8. Cited in Hugh A. Dempsey, *Red Crow: Warrior Chief* (Saskatoon: Prairie Books, 1980), 59.
9. Erasmus, *Buffalo Days and Nights*, 131.
10. Ahenakew, *Voices of the Plains Cree*, 37–39.
11. The British priests translating Father Lacombe's account mistakenly wrote "Creeks" instead of "Crees."
12. Society for the Propagation of the Faith. *Annals of the Propagation of the Faith* (London, 1860–69), vol. 3, 252.
13. Ahenakew, *Voices of the Plains Cree*, 37–39.
14. Ibid.
15. Erasmus, *Buffalo Days and Nights*, 131.
16. Fort Edmonton journals, entries for January 6, 19 and 25, February 10 and March 6, 1866, 35. HBC Archives, B.60/a/35.
17. McDougall, *Pathfinding on Plain and Prairie*, 191–92.
18. Ibid., 194.
19. Fort Edmonton journals, entry for March 23, 1866, HBC Archives, B.60/a/35.
20. *Annals of the Propagation of the Faith* (London, 1860–69), vol. 3, 259. Two weeks later, a party of Blackfoot met some Crees at Edmonton, and they too made peace. Fort Edmonton journals, entry for April 16, 1866, HBC Archives, B.60/a/35.
21. John McDougall, *George Millard McDougall, Pioneer, Patriot and Missionary* (Toronto: William Briggs, 1902), 146–47.
22. Letter, Constantine Scollen to his father, April 16, 1868, Scollen Papers, M8873/5, Glenbow Archives.
23. Journal de la Mission de St. Paul des Cris, entry for September 26, 1867, Oblate Archives, 71.220/2238/M.15, Provincial Archives of Alberta. The entry reads, "Arriveé de plusieurs sauvages de la prairie—Kiskayu."
24. Ibid., entry for July 22, 1869. It reads, "Kiskayu et sa bande sont arriver..."
25. Ibid.
26. Hugh A. Dempsey, *Firewater: The Impact of the Whisky Trade on the Blackfoot Nation* (Calgary: Fifth House Publishers, 2002), 18–21.
27. Circular letter, Fort Edmonton, January 2, 1867, HBC Archives, B.60/a/36.
28. Fort Edmonton journals, September 1, 1866, HBC Archives, B.60/a/36.
29. Fort Edmonton journals, October 31, 1866, HBC Archives, B.60/a/36.
30. Letter, William Christie to Richard Hardisty, November 2, 1866, HBC Archives, B.60/b/2, fo.616.
31. Fort Edmonton journals, December 4, 1866, HBC Archives, B.60/a/36.
32. Letter, J.E. Brazeau to W.B. Cheadle, April 20, 1867, W.B. Cheadle Papers, Department of Rare Books & Special Collections, McGill University.
33. Fort Edmonton journals, entry for May 3, 1867, HBC Archives, B.60/a/36.
34. W.A. Griesbach, ed., "The Narrative of James Gibbons." *Alberta Historical Review* 6, no. 3 (Summer 1958): 5; also see Hughes, *Father Lacombe*, 142 and 151.
35. McDougall, *Pathfinding on Plain and Prairie*, 207–8.
36. Ibid., 219.
37. Hughes, *Father Lacombe*, 161.

CHAPTER SIXTEEN
Death on the Plains

1. Interview with Henry Nepoose, by Joseph Deschamps, c. 2005, Brian Lightning, translator, tape-recorded copy in Samson Archives, Hobbema.
2. Ibid.
3. Ahenakew, *Voices of the Plains Cree*, 55.
4. Depending on who is telling the story, the makeup of the peace party varies. Versions include the chief, his son and grandson; or four men, which included a son; or the chief and two sons; or the chief and one son.
5. "Joe Samson's Manuscript," 1941.
6. Allen Ronaghan, "A Short Note on Maskipiton," *Alberta History* 50, no. 2 (Spring 2002): 25.
7. Hugh A. Dempsey, *The Amazing Death of Calf Shirt and Other Blackfoot Stories* (Calgary: Fifth House Publishers, 1994), 68.

8. Interview with Crooked Meat Strings, Siksika Indian, by Lucien Hanks, July 28, 1939, Hanks Papers, Glenbow Archives.
9. Ahenakew, *Voices of the Plains Cree*, 55.
10. John McDougall, *In the Days of the Red River Rebellion* (Toronto: William Briggs, 1903), 50–51.
11. Interview with Crooked Meat Strings, Siksika Indian, by Lucien Hanks, July 28, 1939, Hanks Papers, Glenbow Archives.
12. Interview with Pearl Crier by the author, Beverly Crier, interpreter, Hobbema, October 30, 2007.
13. "Joe Samson's Manuscript."
14. Fort Edmonton journals, entry for April 23, 1869, HBC Archives, B.60/2/36.
15. George McDougall, *Wesleyan Missionary Notices*, May 1, 1869, 59.
16. Thomas Woolsey, July 23, 1869, cited in Dempsey, *Heaven is Near the Rocky Mountains*, 180–81.
17. *Wesleyan Missionary Notices*, 3rd series, no. 8, June 1875.
18. "Joe Samson's Manuscript."
19. Eagle Shoe Chief, Fort Edmonton journals, entry for June 29, 1869, HBC Archives, B.60/a/36.
20. Scrip applications for Angéle and Catherine Piché, Crown Documents SC-039 and SC-045, Glenbow Archives.
21. Cited in Dempsey, *The Amazing Death of Calf Shirt and Other Blackfoot Stories*, 77.
22. George Mann papers, M809, Glenbow Archives.
23. "Joe Samson's Manuscript."

EPILOGUE

1. I wish to thank Roy Louis and artist George Littlechild for this information.
2. Dempsey, *The Amazing Death of Calf Shirt and Other Blackfoot Stories*, 79–80.
3. McDougall, *In the Days of the Red River Rebellion*, 79.
4. Ibid., 33.
5. Ibid.
6. Ibid.
7. Ibid.
8. Letter, George McDougall, April 25, 1873, *Wesleyan Missionary Notices*, New Series, no. 20, August 1873, 310–11.
9. Letter, George McDougall, May 28, 1873, *Wesleyan Missionary Notices*, New Series, no. 20, August 1873, 311.
10. Ibid.
11. Letter, David Laird to "Big Bear (mis tuki-mis qua), Short Tail (kis ka yu), Sa kee mat, chiefs of the Crees," September 11, 1876, Alexander Morris Papers (Ketcheson Collection), MG-12, BK-2, item 88, Provincial Archives of Manitoba.
12. Maurice F.V. Doll, Robert S. Kidd and John P. Day, *The Buffalo Lake Metis Site: A Late Nineteenth Century Settlement in the Parkland of Central Alberta* (Edmonton: Provincial Museum of Alberta, 1988), 61.
13. Ibid.
14. Treaty paysheets for 1879, Bobtail, Ermineskin, and Samson bands, microfilm, Glenbow Archives.

BIBLIOGRAPHY

BOOKS AND ARTICLES

Ahenakew, Edward. *Voices of the Plains Cree.* Toronto: McClelland & Stewart Ltd., 1973.

Arnett, Margaret, ed. *The Letters of Letitia Hargrave.* Toronto: Champlain Society, 1947.

Berry, J.P. *Maskepetoon: Alberta's First Martyr to Peace.* Toronto: United Church of Canada, 1945.

Bradley, James H. "Characteristics, Habits and Customs of the Blackfeet Indians." *Contributions to the Historical Society of Montana* 9 (1923): 256–87.

———. "Affairs at Fort Benton from 1831 to 1869." *Contributions to the Historical Society of Montana* 3 (1900): 201–87.

Butler, William F. *The Great Lone Land: A Narrative of Travel and Adventure in the North-West of America.* London: Sampson Low, Marston, Low, & Searle, 1874.

Campbell, John V. "The Sinclair Party—An Emigration Overland Along the Old Hudson Bay Route from Manitoba to the Spokane Country in 1854." *The Washington Historical Quarterly* 7, no. 3 (July 1916): 187–201.

Catlin, George. *North American Indians, Being Letters and Notes on their Manners, Customs, and Conditions.* Philadelphia: Leary, Stuart & Co., 1913.

Chittenden, Hiram M. *The American Fur Trade of the Far West.* Stanford: Academic Reprints, 1954.

———, and Alfred Talbot Richardson, eds. *Life, Letters and Travels of Father Pierre-Jean De Smet, S.J., 1801–1873.* New York: Francis P. Harper, 1905.

Coues, Elliott, ed. *New Light on the Early History of the Greater Northwest: The Manuscript Journals of Alexander Henry, Fur Trader of the Northwest Company, and of David Thompson, Official Geographer of the same Company, 1799–1814.* New York: Francis P. Harper, 1897.

Dempsey, Hugh A. *The Amazing Death of Calf Shirt and Other Blackfoot Stories.* Calgary: Fifth House Publishers, 1994.

———. *A Blackfoot Winter Count.* Calgary: Glenbow Foundation, 1965.

———. *Firewater: The Impact of the Whisky Trade on the Blackfoot Nation.* Calgary: Fifth House Publishers, 2002.

———. "Maskepetoon." *Dictionary of Canadian Biography,* vol. 9 (1976), 537–38. Also at www.biographi.ca.

———. *Red Crow: Warrior Chief.* Saskatoon: Prairie Books, 1980.

———. *Treasures of the Glenbow Museum.* Calgary: Glenbow Museum, 1991.

———, ed. *Heaven is Near the Rocky Mountains: The Journals and Letters of Thomas Woolsey, 1855–1868.* Calgary: Glenbow Museum, 1989.

———, ed. "Simpson's Essay on the Blackfoot, 1841." *Alberta History* 38, no. 1 (Winter 1990): 2–14.

Denig, Edwin Thomas. *Five Indian Tribes of the Upper Missouri: Sioux, Arikaras, Assiniboines, Crees, Crows.* Edited by John C. Ewers. Norman: University of Oklahoma Press, 1961.

Dion, Joseph F. *My Tribe the Crees.* Calgary: Glenbow Museum, 1979.

Doll, Maurice F.V., Robert S. Kidd, and John P. Day. *The Buffalo Lake Metis Site: A Late Nineteenth Century Settlement in the Parkland of Central Alberta.* Edmonton: Provincial Museum of Alberta, 1988.

Drouin, E.O. *Lac Ste. Anne Sakahigan.* Edmonton: Editions de l'Ermitage, 1973.

———. *Ongoing Mission of Central Alberta.* Hobbema: privately printed, 1968.

Dunseith Steering Committee. *Prairie Past and Mountain Memories: A History of Dunseith, N. Dakota, 1882–1982.* Dunseith: Dunseith Steering Committee, 1982.

Edmonton Journal, August 17, 1929.

Erasmus, Peter. *Buffalo Days and Nights*. As told to Henry Thompson. Edited by Irene M. Spry. Calgary: Glenbow-Alberta Institute, 1976.

Ewers, John C. "When the Light Shone in Washington." *Montana: The Magazine of Western History* 6, no. 4 (Autumn 1956): 2–6.

———. *The Blackfeet: Raiders on the Northwestern Plains*. Norman: University of Oklahoma Press, 1958.

Fine Day, *My Cree People*. Invermere, BC: Good Medicine Books, 1973.

Flett, George. "'Broken Arm' as a Peace Maker." *Manitoba Pageant* 7, no. 1 (September 1961).

Glazebrook, G.P. de T., ed., *The Hargrave Correspondence, 1821–1843*. Toronto: The Champlain Society, 1938.

Goddard, Earle Pliny. "Notes on the Sun Dance of the Cree of Alberta." *American Museum of Natural History* 16 (1919): 295–310.

Graham, Frederick Ulric. *Notes of a Sporting Expedition in the Far West of Canada, 1847*. London: privately printed, 1898.

Griesbach, W.A., ed. "The Narrative of James Gibbons." *Alberta Historical Review* 6, no. 3 (Summer 1958): 1–6.

Holterman, Jack. *King of the High Missouri: The Saga of the Culbertsons*. Helena: Falcon Press, 1987.

Hughes, Katherine. *Father Lacombe, The Black-Robed Voyageur*. Toronto: William Briggs, 1911.

Hutchinson, Gerald M., and Hugh A. Dempsey, eds., *The Rundle Journals, 1840–1848*. Calgary: Historical Society of Alberta, 1977.

Jenness, Diamond. *The Sarcee Indians of Alberta*. Ottawa: National Museum of Canada, 1938.

Johnson, A.M., ed., *Saskatchewan Journals and Correspondence*. London: The Hudson's Bay Record Society, 1967.

Kane, Paul. *Wanderings of an Artist Among the Indians of North America*. Toronto: The Radisson Society of Canada Ltd., 1925.

Karamitsanis, Aphrodite. *Place Names of Alberta, Volume 1: Mountains, Mountain Parks and Foothills*. Calgary: University of Calgary Press, 1991.

Larpenteur, Charles. *Forty Years a Fur Trader on the Upper Missouri*. Chicago: The Lakeside Press, 1933.

———. *The Original Journal of Charles Larpenteur: My Travels to the Rocky Mountains between 1833 and 1872*. Edited by Michael M. Casler. Chadron, NE: The Museum Association of the American Frontier, 2007.

Lent, D. Geneva. *West of the Mountains: James Sinclair and the Hudson's Bay Company*. Seattle: University of Washington Press, 1963.

London Daily Free Press, September 7, 1886.

Maclean, John. *The Hero of the Saskatchewan*. Barrie, ON: Barrie Examiner Printing & Publishing House, 1891.

Mandelbaum, David G. *The Plains Cree: An Ethnological, Historical, and Comparative Study*. Regina, SK: Canadian Plains Research Center, 1979.

Manitoba Free Press, August 5, 1886.

McDougall, John. *George Millard McDougall, Pioneer, Patriot and Missionary*. Toronto: William Briggs, 1902.

———. *Forest, Lake and Prairie*. Toronto: William Briggs, 1910.

———. *In the Days of the Red River Rebellion*. Toronto: William Briggs, 1903.

———. *Pathfinding on Plain and Prairie*. Toronto: William Briggs, 1898.

———. *Saddle, Sled and Snowshoe: Pioneering on the Saskatchewan in the Sixties*. Toronto: William Briggs, 1896.

Milloy, John S. *The Plains Cree: Trade, Diplomacy and War, 1790 to 1870*. Winnipeg: University of Manitoba Press, 1988.

Milton, Viscount, and W.B. Cheadle. *The North-West Passage by Land, Being the Narrative of an Expedition from the Atlantic to the Pacific*. London: Cassell, Petter, and Gilpin, 1865.

Moberly, Henry John. *When Fur Was King*. New York: E.P. Dutton, 1929.

Morton, Arthur S. *The Journal of Duncan M'Gillivray of the North West Company at Fort George on the Saskatchewan, 1794–5*. Toronto: The Macmillan Company, 1929.

Notice sur les Missions du Diocèse de Québec qui sont secourues par l'Association de la Propagation de la Foi, no. 1 (January 1839), no. 4 (January 1842). Québec: Frechette & Cie.

Oliver, E.H. *The Canadian North-West, Its Early Development and Legislative Records*. Vols. 1 and 2. Ottawa: Government Printing Bureau, 1914–15.

Palliser, John. *The Journals, Detailed Reports, and Observations Relative to the Expedition, by Captain John Palliser... During the Years 1857, 1858, 1859, and 1860*. London: Queen's Printers, 1863.

Partoll, Albert J., ed. "The Blackfoot Indian Peace Council." *Frontier and Midland* 17, no. 3 (Spring 1937): 3–1.

Peel, Bruce. "When the Bible Came to the Cree." *Alberta Historical Review* 6, no. 2 (Spring 1958): 15–18.

Ray, Arthur J. *Indians in the Fur Trade*. Toronto: University of Toronto Press, 1974.

Regina Leader, December 10, 1885.

Ronaghan, Allen. "The Problem of Maskipiton." *Alberta History* 24, no. 2 (Spring 1976): 14–18.

———. "A Short Note on Maskipiton." *Alberta History* 50, no. 2 (Spring 2002): 25.

———. "Where Did Paul Kane Meet Maskipiton?" *Alberta History* 39, no. 3 (Summer 1991): 6–8.

Shirt, Peter Sr. Interview in *O-sak-do* (Saddle Lake newspaper), July 1976, 1–18.

Siebelt, Dagmar. *Die Winter Counts der Blackfoot*. Münster: Lit Verlag Münster, 2005.

Simpson, Sir George. *An Overland Journey Round the World, During the Years 1841 and 1842*. Philadelphia: Lea & Blanchard, 1847.

———. *Narrative of a Journey Round the World during the Years 1841 and 1842*. London: Henry Colburn, 1847.

Smith, Dwight L. *Survival on a Westward Trek, 1858–59: The John Jones Overlanders*. Athens: Ohio University Press, 1989.

Society for the Propagation of the Faith. *Annals of the Propagation of the Faith*. Vol. 3. London, 1860–69.

Tacoma Daily Ledger, February 18, 1885.

The Nor'Wester (Red River Settlement), March 5, 1862; April 13, 1863; June 30, 1863.

Thomas, David, and Karin Ronnefeldt, eds. *People of the First Man: Life Among the Plains Indians in their Final Days of Glory: The Firsthand Account of Prince Maximilian's Expedition Up the Missouri River, 1833–34*. New York: Promontory Press, 1983.

Young, Egerton. *Indian Life in the Great North-West*. Toronto: Musson Book Co., 1900.

MANUSCRIPTS AND DOCUMENTS

Baptismal records. McDougall Papers. Glenbow Archives, Calgary.

Carlton House journals, HBC Archives, Provincial Archives of Manitoba, Winnipeg.

Cheadle, W.B. Papers. Department of Rare Books & Special Collections. McGill University, Montreal.

Cowan, Dr. William. Papers. E/B/Si6, British Columbia Archives.

Fort Colvile Correspondence, A/B/20/ C72 M.1, British Columbia Archives, Victoria.

Fort Edmonton journals, HBC Archives, Provincial Archives of Manitoba, Winnipeg.

Hanks, Lucien. Papers. Glenbow Archives, Calgary.

Hudson's Bay Company Archives, Provincial Archives of Manitoba, Winnipeg.

Letters Received by the Office of Indian Affairs, 1836–51. Microfilm 234, rolls 884 and 885, National Archives and Records Administration, Washington, DC.

Little Chief, Joe. Papers. M4394, Glenbow Archives, Calgary.

Mann, George. Papers. M809, Glenbow Archives, Calgary.

McDonald, Archibald. Papers. British Columbia Archives, Victoria.

McLeod, Malcolm. Journals and Correspondence. MS-149, A/B/40/ M22K, British Columbia Archives, Victoria.

Morris, Alexander. Papers (Ketcheson Collection). MG-12, BK-2, Provincial Archives of Manitoba, Winnipeg.

Oblate Archives, Provincial Archives of Alberta, Edmonton.

Rocky Mountain House journals. HBC Archives. Provincial Archives of Manitoba, Winnipeg.

Ross, Donald. Papers. MS-0635, British Columbia Archives, Victoria.

Samson, Joe. "Joe Samson's Manuscript," 1941. Translated from syllabics by Stan Cuthand and Bruce Cutknife. Maskwachees Library, Hobbema.

Schaeffer, Claude E. Papers. Glenbow Archives, Calgary.

Scollen, Constantine. Papers. M8873/5, Glenbow Archives.

Scrip applications. Glenbow Archives, Calgary.

Scrip applications for Angéle and Catherine Piché, Crown Documents SC-039 and SC-045, Glenbow Archives, Calgary.

Simpson's Journals, Provincial Archives of Manitoba, Winnipeg.

Sir Henry James Warre, "Mss. of Oregon Journey, June–December, 1845." MG-24, f. 17, vol. 27, National Archives of Canada, Ottawa.

Treaty paysheets for 1879, Bobtail, Ermineskin, and Samson bands. Microfilm. Glenbow Archives.

Wesleyan Missionary Notices I (1854–59); New Series, II (1868–74); III (1875–78). Glenbow Archives, Calgary.

Whitford, Donald. Papers. Microfilm M-256, Glenbow Archives, Calgary.

INDEX

Acton House, 16, 20
adoption, adult, 181
Ahenakew (Cree Indian), 219
American Fur Company, 49
Assiniboine, Fort, 105
Assiniboine Indians, 234n2; moved southward, 58; peace with, 39-40; warfare, 19, 32-33, 35, 55, 189, 190-92
Augustus, Fort: established, 13

Banff, AB, 81, 85
Bashaw, AB, 128
Battle River, 33, 58, 78, 109, 137, 157, 175, 183, 185, 190, 214, 218-19, 225
Bear Hills, 137
beaver, 20; value of, 13
Beaver (steamboat), 91-92; image of, 199
Beaver Hills Crees, 26, 32, 34, 37, 39, 43, 53, 54, 76. *See also* Cree Indians
Benton, Fort, 117-18, 212-13
Berland, Edward, 81, 83
Berry Creek, 219
Big Lake (Peigan Indian), 52
Big Swan. *See* Many Swans
Big Thunder (Cree Indian), 37
Birch Creek, 209
Bird, James, 21
Bird, Jimmy Jock, 85-87, 122, 123
Blackfoot Indians, 21, 26; attacked Cree, 124; friends with Crees, 12; masters of plains, 20; moved south, 58; religion, 123; warfare, 12, 32, 34, 38, 68, 75-76, 86, 102, 108-9, 116-17, 149, 153, 161-63, 167, 169, 182, 189, 214-15. *See also* Siksika Indians
Blind Man River, 26, 78, 137
Blood Indians, 50, 77, 137-38, 153, 166, 189, 214; peace with, 21; warfare, 12, 137, 182-83
Bob Tail (Cree Indian), 44, 104, 151-52, 188, 189, 190, 218, 224, 230-31; divided from Maskepetoon, 211, 228

Bourassa, Joseph, 106
Bow River, 58, 77, 80, 110-11, 121, 124, 137, 139
Bow River Traverse, 75, 81, 85, 87
brandy. *See* liquor
Bras Casse. *See* Maskepetoon
Bras Croche. *See* Maskepetoon
Brazeau, Joseph, 169-70
Breban (Metis), 35
Brenow, Baptiste, 71, 115
Broken Arm, 237n23. *See also* Maskepetoon
Broken Wing (Cree Indian), 189
Buckingham House, 13
buffalo: availability of, 12, 17, 21, 23-24, 32, 43, 39, 41-42, 111, 116, 128, 136, 143-44, 148-49, 153, 154-55, 157-58, 176, 214, 216; mythology about, 58, 126-27; population of, 146
Buffalo Child (Cree Indian), 57-8
Buffalo Lake, 31, 51, 128, 230, 231
Bull, Louis (Cree Indian), 184-85, 226
Bull Back Fat (Blood Indian), 39-40
Bull Head (Sarcee Indian), 168
Bull Straight Hair (Blackfoot Indian), 167-68
Bull's Head (Peigan Indian), 122
Burlow, Edward, 71
Butler, William F., 156

Cadien, Pierre, 71
Campbell, John, 135-36, 138
Canal Flats, 88, 112, 139
Carlton, Fort, 26, 31-32, 37, 40, 52, 53, 55, 57, 68, 85, 169
Cascade Falls, 80
Cascade Mountain, 111
Cascades, 89
Catholics, 70, 72, 84, 90, 96, 99, 101, 104, 106, 119, 188, 211-12, 213, 229. *See also* Christianity
Catlin, George, 60

250

Cayen, Paul, 103
Cayuse Indians, 89
Charlo, 83
Cheadle, W.B., 177-78
Chiniki (Stoney Indian), 123
Christianity, 5-6, 47, 66, 70, 99-101, 105-6, 119, 133, 159, 173, 174-75, 180, 187-88, 211-12, 228
Christie, W.J., 223, 230
Cline, Joseph, 88, 91
Cochrane, AB, 121
Columbia River, 88-89, 112, 138
Colvile, Fort, 81, 82, 83, 88, 93-94, 112, 134, 139
Coronation, AB, 51, 219
Cree Indians: fight with Sarcees, 167; peace at The Nose, 225; troublesome, 167-68; "ungrateful dogs," 53; warfare, 20, 31, 33-34, 52, 68, 75-76, 86, 102, 108-9, 116-17, 121, 137, 149, 153, 161, 163, 165-69, 182, 189-90, 215, 219. *See also* Beaver Hills Crees; Rocky Mountain Crees
Cree medicine, 226
Cree, Sylvia (Cree Indian), 63
Crier, Pearl (Cree Indian), 221
Crooked Meat Strings (Siksika Indian), 221
Cross River, 87
Crowfoot (Siksika Indian), 192
Crow Shoes (Cree Indian), 38-39, 41, 42, 43; killed, 75
Crying Eyes. *See* Maton-now-a-cap
Cut Nose (Sarcee Indian), 40

Dalles, The, 90, 93
De Smet, Jean, 85, 100, 119
Dog Pound Creek, 98, 121, 137
Dog Rump Creek, 31
Douglas, James, 91, 94
Drunken Lake, 115
Dumont, Gabriel, 97
Durand, Paul, 98

Eagle Hill, 32, 121
Eagle Leggings (Siksika Indian), 162, 164
Eagle Man (Cree Indian), 109, 119
Eamowishk (Cree Indian), 37
Edmonton, Fort, 20-21, 23, 26, 31, 34, 37, 41, 50, 52-53, 66, 76, 86, 106, 136-37, 141, 144, 148, 167, 168-69, 209, 214, 217, 222, 224; defences, 108; described, 76-77;

drinking at, 155-56; established, 13; liquor prohibited, 166; painting of, 194; raided, 34-36, 162; threatened, 162, 164; visited by priest, 97, 98
education, 120, 180
Elbow River, 124
Entering Bear (Cree Indian), 38
Erasmus, Peter, 152, 173, 190, 209
Ermine Skin (Cree Indian), 44, 104, 151-52, 190
Evans, James, 66, 96, 101-2
Ewers, John, 49, 60
Eyes on Both Sides (Cree Indian). *See* Maskepetoon: American Maskepetoon

Fairmont Hot Springs, BC, 82
farming, 153, 180, 215, 216
Feather, The (Siksika Indian), 20-21, 27-28, 40
Fidler, Peter, 15
Fierce Woman. *See* Susihiskayo
fires, 23, 24, 32, 143, 163, 209
Fish Creek, 122
Flatbow Indians, 82
Flett, George, 174, 183
Flett, John, 86-89
Four Ponds, Battle of, 190-92
Frightens Them. *See* Sayakimat
Frog Creek, 106

games, children's, 25
gardening. *See* farming
George, Fort, 13
Ghost River, 87
Gibbons, James, 216
gold miners, 212, 215
Good Hunter. *See* Onahtah-me-nahoose
Gowler (prospector), 179
Graham, Frederick, 117
Grande Queue (Kootenai Indian), 83
Grease Creek, 79
Green Lake, 38
Green Leaves (Cree Indian), 120
Gull Lake, 51, 73, 78, 80, 97, 102, 110, 119

Hand Hills, 219
Harriott, John, 67-68, 69-70, 83, 95, 96, 102, 106, 119, 196

Healy Creek, 81
Henry, Alexander, 27, 37
He Who Has Eyes Behind Him. *See*
Maskepetoon: American Maskepetoon
Hopkins, Edward, 77
Horn Hill, 121
Horse (Cree Indian), 121
horse racing, 9, 75-76
Hudson's Bay Company, 49-50, 66, 75, 84-85, 90-91, 93, 96, 107, 146, 166

impoundments. *See* pounds
Indian Sweatlodge River, 108
Innisfail, AB, 121
Iron Mouth (Cree Indian), 52
Iron Stone, 158, 159, 161

Kananaskis River, 138
Kanatakasu. *See* Samson
Kane, Paul, 34, 99, 113, 133-35, 194, 196
Kehiwin (Cree Indian), 188, 212, 214, 217
Kinnewitts (Cree Indian), 185
Kiskayu. *See* Bob Tail
Kline, Joseph. *See* Cline, Joseph
Koominikoos (Cree Indian), 162
Kootenai Indians, 14-16, 39, 52, 82, 123, 180
Kootenay Plains, 20
Kootenay River, 87-88, 112, 135, 139
Kootonais Pelly (Kootenai Indian), 83

Lac La Biche, 140, 149, 163
Lac la Pluie, 66
Lacombe, Albert, 139-40, 183, 188, 190-91, 193, 210, 215; wounded, 192
Lac Ste. Anne, 106, 139-40, 188
La Graisse, Baptiste, 135-36, 139
LaGrise (courier), 93-95
Lake Wabamum, 38
Lake Where the Sarcees Were Killed, 121
Lambert, Augustin, 68
Lapotac (Cree Indian), 68, 73, 76, 99, 144-46, 149, 155, 157-58, 162, 163; described, 164
Laughlin, J.E., 202, 206
Lee, Daniel, 90, 92, 141
Lent, D. Geneva, 134, 135
liquor, 163, 166; described, 155-57; prohibited, 166; use in trade, 114-15, 118;

Little Assiniboine (Stoney Indian), 36
Little Chief (Cree Indian), 43, 149, 150, 154, 163, 164, 165, 177
Little Dog (Peigan Indian), 143
Little Hunter (Cree Indian), 131, 132, 133, 149, 158, 174, 180, 188, 212, 230
Little Pine (Cree Indian), 182
Little Sarcee Chief (Sarcee Indian), 165
Lone Pine, 137
Lougheed, AB, 158
Lucier, Francois, 24

Makokis, George, 105
Manchester House, 12
Manikapina. *See* Maskepetoon
Mann, George, 184
Many Buffalo Stones Woman (Siksika Indian), 224
Many Swans (Siksika Indian): described 220, 224; killed Maskepetoon, 220, 222; makes peace, 225
marriage, inter-tribal, 47-48
Maskepetoon (Broken Arm, Manikapina, Young Man Chief), 76, 98, 103-4, 118, 120, 123-24, 140, 141, 142, 154-55, 158-60, 161, 164, 165, 175, 177, 179, 181, 183, 185, 188, 209, 212, 216, 217; aloof from priest, 99; American Maskepetoon, 59-65, 143, 201; as Blackfoot interpreter, 120; as a child, 28-29; as Methodist symbol, 174; as peacemaker, 149-51, 162, 170-71; as warrior, 45; attempted conversion by priest, 90; baptized, 187; child's grave, 121; described, 178; described as Sinclair's "own Indian," 89; duties, 33; early talent, 24; 1862 treaty, 171-72, 177; engaged by Sinclair, 134; epidemic at his camp, 186; faced Crees, 184; family, 45, 180; fondness for liquor, 115, 145; foundling, 10; given New Testament, 90; horses stolen, 214; hunted on plains, 143; Joseph and father killed, 180; Lapotac, with, 144-45; leadership, 113-14; married, 47; met McDougalls, 175; met Rundle, 69; missionary story about, 46; moved onto plains, 131; name in Blackfoot, 120; name in syllabics, 102; named, 11, 233n4; quotes by, 92, 99, 104, 133, 172, 176, 179, 180-81, 210; remained on the plains, 157, 163, 169, 182; revenge for, 225; rode on steamboat, 91-92; syllabic letter, 200; third trip with Sinclair, 135-39; travels, 74; trip over Rockies, 84-95; visiting Peigans, 121-23; Warre and Vavasour, with, 107-12; went to make peace, killed, 219-21; wife killed, 124

252 ◆ INDEX

Maskepetoon, Abraham Wood, baptized, 187. *See also* Maskepetoon
Maskepetoon, Benjamin (son), 104-5, 180
Maskepetoon, Betsy (granddaughter), 229
Maskepetoon, Eve (granddaughter), 229
Maskepetoon, John (son), 103, 104
Maskepetoon, Joseph (son), 71, 104, 113, 180, 229
Maskepetoon, Joshua (son), 104, 123, 180
Maskepetoon, Peter (son), 71, 104
Maskepetoon, Sarah, baptized, 187. *See also* Sussewisk
Mason, William, 66
Maton-now-a-cap (wife), 47, 71, 124
McDonald, Archibald, 83, 88-89, 93-94
McDonald (Fort Pitt trader), 214
McDougall, George, 45, 69, 174-76, 187, 211, 215, 222, 224, 230; image of, 205
McDougall, John, 45, 174-75, 178-79, 180, 182, 185, 186, 209, 215, 216-17, 222; image of, 207, 221, 229
McGillivray, Duncan, 13
McIntyre (member of Simpson party), 77
McKensie, Patrick, 94
McKenzie, Fort, 50, 56
McKenzie, Kenneth, 50
McLoughlin, John, 91, 93
measles, 186-87
Medicine Lodge River, 110
meteorite. *See* Iron Stone
Methodists, 6, 47, 66-67, 70, 73, 90, 96, 98-99, 118, 133, 139-41, 173, 174, 188, 212, 216, 222, 229. *See also* Christianity
Metis, 98, 35, 44, 68, 69, 71, 84-85, 97, 99, 101, 106, 140, 160, 161, 188, 214, 216
Mikisinew (Cree Indian), 109
Miller, Alfred Jacob, 49
Milloy, John, 148
Minnewanka, Lake, 20, 80, 87
Missouri Fur Company, 49
Moar, John, 137
Moberly, Henry, 162
Monkman (interpreter), 174
Moose Hills, 39, 43
Moose Mountain, 122
Morin, Bill (Cree Indian), 64
Muddy River Indians. *See* Peigan Indians
Mutakayk (Cree Indian), 124

Natos (Siksika Indian), 190
Natuasis, Louis (Cree Indian), 229
North West Mounted Police, 230
Norway House, 66, 96
Nose, The, 51, 75, 219, 225

O-ka-mai-ka-na-wa-sis (Cree Indian), 191
Ogden, Peter Skene, 91, 107-8
Ojibwa Indians, 190
Okaine (Cree Indian), 185
Oldman River, 126
Olds, AB, 137
Old Squirrel (Cree Indian), 52
Onahtah-me-nahoose (wife), 47
O-pe-pon-oik (Cree Indian), 192
Oregon Territory, 84, 107

Paddling River, 88
Palliser, John, 116
Papas (Cree Indian), 11
Park, John, 27
peace, 165, 170, 185, 220; between Blackfoot and Cree, 20-21, 39-40, 52, 55, 68, 75, 141-42, 165, 166, 184, 210; between Blackfoot and United States government, 46, 122, 142, 165, 189; between Crees and Kootenais, 14; described, 142, 170-71; great 1857 treaty, the, 150-51, 161-62; proposed, 149-50; treaty in 1871, 224-27
Peace Hills, 184-85
Peace Maker (Cree Indian), 119, 120
Peagan Post, 50, 121
Peechee, Mount, 80
Peigan Indians, 49-50, 77, 166; visited by Maskepetoon, 121-23; warfare, 19, 26, 34, 52, 117, 142-43
Pend d'Oreille, Lake, 88
Pepin (Metis), 35
Piche, Alexis, 240n1
Piche, Catherine, 68-69, 106
Piche, Cecile, 106
Piche, Leleet, 69
Piche, Louis, 37-44, 68-69, 70-71, 72-73, 97, 106, 118, 228, 240n1; biography 37; meets Thibault, 98; murdered, 103-4; proselytizing, 96; remains Catholic, 101; travels, 74, 76-84
Piche, Margaret, 69
Piche, Marie, 69

INDEX ❖ 253

Piche family, 119, 132
Piet Eagle, Stephen. *See* Stephen
Pigeon Lake, 30, 108, 120, 128, 131, 140, 145, 158, 173, 180, 185, 216, 231
Pigeon Lake Crees. *See* Rocky Mountain Crees
Pion, William, 83
Pipestone Creek, 26
Pitt, Fort, 52, 55, 68, 73, 75, 105, 106, 117, 132, 135, 156, 162-63, 169, 177-78, 188-89; attacked, 213; established, 43; few buffalo, 154
Ponoka, AB, 167
pounds, 33, 41-42, 51, 68, 123, 167, 216
Prince's River, 110
Provencher, Joseph-Norbert, 72, 96, 97
Pumois, Baptiste, 35

Radium Hot Springs, BC, 82, 88, 112
Raft Lake, 132
Rainy Chief (Blood Indian), 183
Rattlesnake Child (Cree Indian), 219, 221-22
Ray, Arthur, 57
Red Deer Hills, 39
Red Deer Lake, 122, 167
Red Deer River, 20, 43, 70, 78, 98, 110, 121, 137
Red Rock, 82, 88, 139
Remington, Frederic, 193
Rocky Mountain Crees, 37, 111, 173, 216; avoided smallpox, 57; described, 116; divided in three groups, 145; hunting area, 37; hunting and trapping methods, 22; Maskepetoon, the leader, 104; met Rundle, 67-68; met Simpson, 78; met Thibault, 98; met Warre and Vavasour, 109; migration, 12; moved eastward, 51, 58; native religion, 124, 187-88; on the plains, 152; Piche, their chief, 74; remained neutral, 52-53; routine, 114; separated from Beaver Hills Crees, 43; singing hymns, 101; together, 158; trading pattern 16-17; warfare, 26, 39, 54, 190-92, 209. *See also* Cree Indians
Rocky Mountain Fur Company, 49
Rocky Mountain House, 23, 30-31, 41, 42, 43, 67-69, 73, 95, 100, 118-19, 142, 186, 209; abandoned, 24, 50, 164; established, 16; painting of, 197
Rocky Mountains: crossing, 80-83; described, 79-80, 110, 137

Roman Catholics. *See* Catholics; Christianity
Ronaghan, Allen, 64
Rosebud River, 225
Round Timber, 189
Rowand, John, 35-36, 50, 55, 57, 70, 72, 74-75, 77, 84, 95, 97, 101, 135
Rowland, William, 105
rum. *See* liquor
Rundle, Mount, 111
Rundle, Robert, 66-73, 78, 85, 96, 105, 109, 118-20, 132, 140, 178, 187, 223; competition with priest, 97; Cree perceptions of, 70; image of, 195; learned syllabics, 102; leaves country, 133; witnessed Piche murders, 103
Running Calf (Siksika Indian): killed Maskepetoon, 221

St. Albert, 183, 188
St. Paul des Cris, 188, 210, 211, 217, 224
Sakahikanihk Lake, 129
Salt Lake, 146
Samson (brother), 11, 45, 118, 216, 229, 230, 231; adventures of, 126-30, 132; image of, 208
Samson, Joseph: recollections of, 18, 126-30, 221, 223
Sarcee Indians, 24, 31, 40, 51, 53-55, 77, 79, 144, 155, 161-62, 165, 167, 218; almost destroyed, 168-69
Sarcee Land. *See* Sussewisk
Sayakimat (Cree Indian), 146, 229, 230-31
scarlet fever, 186
Schaeffer, Claude, 15
Scollen, Constantine, 210-12, 229
Seenum, James, 35
Sekacheen (Cree Indian), 11
Siksika Indians, 77, 118, 153, 162, 166, 182-83, 185, 190, 218-19; peace with, 21, 165
Simpson, George, 55, 56, 66, 84-85, 87, 91, 92, 93, 101, 106, 135; trip over Rockies, 72-73, 74-83
Simpson, James, 132
Simpson Pass, 81
Simpson River, 82
Sinclair, Benjamin, 140
Sinclair, James, 107, 112; second trip, 134-35; third trip, 135-39; westward trip, 84-95
Sinclair, John, 143
Sinclair Canyon, 88

Sistianwi (Kootenai Indian), 14
Six Fingers (Cree Indian), 218-19
Slave Indians. *See* Blackfoot Indians
Sleeps on Top (Blackfoot Indian), 168
Small, Patrick, 52
smallpox, 55-57, 61, 224
Snare Indians, 26-27
Sounding Lake, 152
Spokane WA, 88
Spray River, 87
St. Albert, 183, 188
Stanley, John Mix, 198
starvation, 24, 31, 102, 131, 143-44, 148-49, 155, 157, 209-10, 217, 230, 231
Steinhauer, Henry, 149-50, 153
Stephen (Cree Indian), 132, 140, 141, 143-44, 145, 153, 158-59, 173, 188, 216
Stoney Indians, 20, 69, 100, 104, 111, 118, 119, 122, 124, 138-39, 166, 177, 185-86, 214, 234n2
St. Paul des Cris, 188, 210, 211, 217, 224
Strong Current River, 139
Sun, The (Siksika Indian), 153-54, 190-91, 214, 220
Susihiskayo (wife), 47
Sussewisk (wife), 47-48, 71, 105, 114, 115, 118, 120, 132, 221
Sutherland, Robert, 137
Swan, The. *See* Many Swans
Sweet Grass (Cree Indian), 149, 164, 169-70, 177, 185, 186, 188, 211, 216, 217, 230
Sweet Grass Hills, 51
syllabics, 101-2, 120, 132, 140, 159; example of, 200
Sylvan Lake, 78

Tail Creek, 231
Tanazebechage (Stoney Indian), 240n1
Thibault, Jean-Baptiste, 72-73, 97-99, 101, 106, 133, 139
Three Bulls (Cree Indian), 32
Three Hills, 119
Thunder Bird (Cree Indian), 120
Thunderchild (Cree Indian), 190, 191-92
Tobacco Plains, 94
Tombstone Mountain, 80
Treaty Seven, 231
Treaty Six, 230

tuberculosis, 226
Turnip (Cree Indian), 76
Turtle Mountain, ND, 59, 143
Two Hills, 131

Vancouver, Fort, 90, 93, 108, 139, 198
Vavasour, Mervin, 107-12
Vegreville, AB, 216
Vermilion Creek, 32
Vermilion River, AB, 168
Vermilion River, BC, 82
Victoria mission, 173, 175, 178-79, 182, 186, 188, 209-10, 211, 212, 216, 223
Vrooman, Nicholas, 237n19

Wabamun Creek, 27, 30
Walking Bear (Cree Indian), 121
Walking Crow (Blood Indian), 117
Walking Wolf (Cree Indian), 52
Walla Walla, 89, 139
Wanakew (Cree Indian), 37
warfare, various kinds, 29-30
war parties, various types, 53
Warre, Henry, 107-12
Washington, DC, 59
Wetaskiwin, AB, 184, 185
Whidbey Island, WA, 91
whisky. *See* liquor
Whitefish Lake, 39, 43, 131, 163, 222
White Man's Pass, 87, 111, 134, 139
White Mud Creek, 38, 115, 118
Whitford, Donald, 137
Whitford, John, 216
Whoop-Up, Fort, 224
Windermere, Lake, 81, 82, 88, 112
woman, as warrior, 80
women, massacred, 189
Woodville, 223
Woolsey, Thomas, 140-41, 143, 145, 153, 154, 158, 159, 161-62, 174, 178, 180, 187, 223; image of, 203
writing, 93. *See also* syllabics
Writing Coulee, 121

Young Man (Cree Indian), 63
Young Man Chief. *See* Maskepetoon

ABOUT THE AUTHOR

Hugh A. Dempsey is an author, historian and researcher. He is the former associate director of the Glenbow Museum, Calgary, and is currently its chief curator emeritus. He also is editor of the quarterly *Alberta History*.

Dempsey holds a number of honours, including the Order of Canada, an honorary doctorate from the University of Calgary, an honorary chieftainship of the Blood tribe, the Sir Frederick Haultain Award for Excellence, an Alberta Booksellers Award, an Alberta Non-Fiction Award and a life membership in the Calgary Exhibition and Stampede.

Dempsey is the author of nineteen books on western Canadian history and has edited another seventeen. He has written nine monographs and more than two hundred articles for periodicals, books and newspapers. He is a well-known lecturer and specialist on the history of the Native peoples of western Canada and the early history of Alberta.

Among the books he has written are *Crowfoot: Chief of the Blackfeet*; *The Golden Age of the Canadian Cowboy*; *Calgary: Spirit of the West*; *Charcoal's World*; *Big Bear: The End of Freedom*; *Treasures of the Glenbow Museum*; *Firewater: The Impact of the Whisky Trade on the Blackfoot Nation*; *Christmas in the West*; and *The Vengeful Wife and Other Blackfoot Stories*.

Hugh is married to Pauline (née Gladstone) of the Blood tribe, and they have five children, eleven grandchildren and two great-grandchildren. Pauline and Hugh celebrated their 57th wedding anniversary this year.